쉽게 배우는

영문법

Words and Sentences | Verbs | Tense | Auxiliary Verbs
Subjunctive Mood | The Passive | Review | Infinitives and Gerunds
Participles | Relatives | Comparatives | Conjunctions | Review

성 은 경

EASY-TO-LEARN ENGLISH GRAMMAR

한국외국어대학교 출판부

Preface

영문법은 간단히 말해서, '어떻게 영어 문장을 만드는가'에 관한 것입니다. 영문법을 익힘으로써, 우리는 생각과 감정을 영어로 어떻게 표현하는지 그 틀을 배우게 됩니다. 흔히들 영어가 어렵다고 하면서, 그저 단편적인 어휘 구사력 향상이나 패턴 익히기에 치중할 뿐, 기본이 되는 문법을 등한시하는 경향이 있습니다. 그러나 영문법을 소홀히 하는 것은 공부의 효율성 측면에서 절대 바람직하지 않습니다. 영문법은 독해는 물론, 말하고 듣기와 쓰기의 기본이 되기 때문입니다. 특히, 영어라는 외국어 습득을 위하여 많은 시간을 투입하기 어려운 우리 입장에서 언어 학습의 효과를 높이기 위해서는, 기본에 좀 더 충실할 필요가 있습니다.

이 책은 2007년에 출간된 '쉽게 배우는 영문법'의 개정판입니다. 영문법의 기초 원리와 필수 구문을 좀 더 쉽게 익힐 수 있도록 Check-up 부분을 수정하고 예문을 보강하였습니다. Review test도 새로 넣었습니다. 필자의 또 다른 책인 '에센스 영문법'(한국외국어대학교 출판부)보다 영문법에 좀 더 쉽게 접근할 수 있도록 하는데 주안을 두었습니다. 부록의 mp3 CD에는 이 책에 나오는 모든 예문이 원어민의 음성으로 담겨 있습니다. Listening과 발음 연습에도 많은 도움이 될 거라고 기대합니다.

이 책은 13개의 chapter로 구성되어 있는데, 각 chapter는 Check-up, Focus 1, 2 & 3, Review test, Final tip 등으로 꾸며져 있습니다. Check-up에서는 드라마 대본과 같은 Ben & Olivia's everyday 이야기를 통해서 일상적으로 쓰는 표현을 익히고, 기본적인 문법 실력을 점검해 볼 수 있습니다. Focus 1, 2, 3에서는 핵심적인 문법 사항을 공부하게 됩니다. 예문들은 가능한 한 실생활에서 자주 쓰는 문장을 골랐습니다. 각 주차의 마지막에 있는 Review test를 통해서 배운 내용을 복습할 수 있습니다. 이 외에도 영어 만화로 꾸며진 Rest area와 영어권 문화를 소개한 Culture corner를 통해서 영어의 또 다른 재미를 느껴 보시기 바랍니다.

모쪼록 이 책이 영어의 기본 골격을 가장 효과적이고 쉽게 익히는데 도움이 되기를 바랍니다. 끝으로 이 책이 나오기까지 많은 도움을 준 William Hart, Robert Leis, Kyong Min Lee, 교정을 맡아 수고해 준 김수민 조교, 그리고 한국외국어대학교 출판부 여러분에게 감사를 드립니다.

All things are difficult before they are easy.
(처음부터 쉬운 일은 없다.)

2010년 3월
성은경

Table of Contents

Chapter 13 Review (Chapter 8–12) 237

부록 해답 편 251

ocus1-Focus3

Chapter 1

Words and Sentences

Introduction

Lesson objectives

1. Components of English sentences 영어 문장의 구성 요소

- word, phrase, and clause (단어, 구, 절)
- main clause and subordinate clause (주절과 종속절)
- turning phrases into clauses (구에서 절로 전환)

2. Parts of speech 품사

- noun, pronoun, verb, adjective, adverb, article, and preposition, conjunction (명사, 대명사, 동사, 형용사, 부사, 관사, 전치사, 접속사)
- words in sentences (문장 속에서의 단어)

3. Sentence roles 문장 안에서의 역할

- subject and predicate (주부와 술부)
- subject, verb, object, complement, and adverbial (주어, 동사, 목적어, 보어, 부사적 어구)

Check-up

Ben & Olivia's everyday

Olivia : Mom is ________ (coming, come) to stay with us on Friday. So make sure you mow the lawn and clean the garage.

Ben : What? Your mother is so ________ (annoy, annoying).

Olivia : What is your problem ________ (to, with) Mom? She is always nice to you.

Ben : All that woman does is talk. I can never hear myself when she is around. She makes it impossible to watch TV.

Olivia : Try to be a bit more ________ (generous, generously). It is not like your parents are fun to spend time with.

Ben : Anyway, how ________ (long, longer) will she be here for?

Olivia : One or two weeks. Maybe even a bit longer.

Ben : My Gosh!

Check-up

Answers

Olivia : Mom is (coming) to stay with us on Friday. So make sure you mow the lawn and clean the garage.

Ben : What? Your mother is so (annoying).

Olivia : What is your problem (with) Mom? She is always nice to you.

Ben : All that woman does is talk. I can never hear myself when she is around. She makes it impossible to watch TV.

Olivia : Try to be a bit more (generous). It is not like your parents are fun to spend time with.

Ben : Anyway, how (long) will she be here for?

Olivia : One or two weeks. Maybe even a bit longer.

Ben : My Gosh!

Translation

Olivia : 엄마가 금요일에 우리랑 함께 지내러 오실 거야. 그러니까 잔디 깎아놓고 차고 청소도 해.

Ben : 뭐? 너희 어머니 너무 귀찮게 하신다.

Olivia : 엄마가 왜? 너한테 항상 잘해주시잖아.

Ben : 너희 어머니는 말씀이 너무 많으셔. 너희 어머니가 곁에 계시면 난 말 한 마디 못 한다고. TV보는 것도 불가능해.

Olivia : 좀 더 관대해지도록 노력해 봐. 너희 부모님도 함께 지내기 좋은 분은 아니야.

Ben : 아무튼 얼마나 오래 계실 거래?

Olivia : 일주일이나 이주일. 더 오래 계실 수도 있고.

Ben : 이런!

1 Focus

Components of English Sentences
영어 문장의 구성 요소

1 Word (단어)

단어란 말이나 글의 최소 단위로 단어가 여러 개 모여 구(phrase)나 절(clause)을 형성하게 된다. 단어는 그 쓰임새에 따라 명사(Nouns), 동사(Verbs), 형용사(Adjectives), 부사(Adverbs), 대명사(Pronouns), 관사(Articles), 전치사(Prepositions), 접속사(Conjunctions) 등으로 분류한다.

A	small	bomb	killed	several	people	at	the	airport	yesterday.
Art	Adj	N	V	Adj	N	Prep	Art	N	Adv

2 Phrases (구)

몇 개의 단어가 모여서 명사, 형용사, 부사 등 하나의 품사의 역할을 하는 어구이다. '주어 + 동사' 형태는 들어있지 않다.

(1) Noun Phrases(명사구)

주어, 목적어, 보어 등 명사의 기능을 대신하는 구이다.

Repairing the machine is not easy.
(그 기계를 수리하는 것은 쉽지 않습니다.)

He bought a small red car.
(그는 작은 빨간색 자동차를 구입했습니다.)

Her dream is to be an interpreter.
(그녀의 꿈은 통역가가 되는 것입니다.)

(2) Adjective Phrases(형용사구)

명사를 수식하거나 설명하는 형용사의 기능을 대신하는 구이다. 전치사구가 형용사구의 역할을 하기도 한다.

The girl with brown hair is my classmate.
(갈색 머리 소녀는 나의 반 친구입니다.)

He has finished the novel written in English.
(그는 영어로 쓰여진 소설을 다 읽었습니다.)

This vending machine is out of order.
(이 자동판매기는 고장입니다.)

(3) Adverb Phrases(부사구)

형용사나 동사를 수식하는 부사의 기능을 대신하며, 장소, 시간, 목적, 원인 등을 나타내는 구이다. 전치사구가 부사구의 역할을 하기도 한다.

She saw the advertisement in the newspaper.
(그녀는 신문에서 그 광고를 보았습니다.)

It'll be done by this Friday's meeting.
(그것은 이번 금요일 회의 때까지는 마무리 될 것입니다.)

They left to meet her at the airport.
(그들은 공항에서 그녀를 마중하기 위해 출발했습니다.)

Not knowing what to say, he kept silent.
(무슨 말을 해야 할지 몰라, 그는 침묵을 지켰습니다.)

3 Clauses (절)

'주어와 동사'의 형태를 갖고 있으나 완전한 문장을 이루지는 못한다. 명사, 형용사, 부사 등의 기능을 대신하는 역할을 한다.

(1) Noun Clauses(명사절)

'접속사+ 주어+동사'의 형태를 갖추고, 주어, 목적어, 보어 등 명사의 기능을 대신한다.

What you say doesn't make any sense to us.
(우린 당신이 무슨 말을 하는지 도통 모르겠습니다.)

It is certain that John smokes.
(John이 담배를 피우는 것이 분명합니다.)

He asked whether she had been to Europe.
(그는 그녀가 유럽에 가 본 적이 있는지 물었습니다.)

The truth is (that) money isn't everything.
(진실은 돈이 전부가 아니라는 것입니다.)

(2) Adjective Clauses(형용사절)

명사를 수식하는 형용사의 기능을 한다.

This is the bar where Bob drank last night.
(여기가 Bob이 어젯밤 술 마셨던 바입니다.)

Here is the file you have been looking for.
(당신이 그 동안 찾았던 파일이 여기 있습니다.)

(3) Adverb Clauses(부사절)

부사의 기능을 대신하며, 대개 문장 전체를 수식한다. 시간, 장소, 이유, 조건, 목적, 양보 등을 나타낸다.

When he saw her, he ran away.
(그는 그녀를 보자 달아났습니다.)

You can live wherever you want to.
(당신이 원하는 곳 어디에서든 살 수 있습니다.)

Our flight has been canceled because the pilots are on strike.
(조종사들이 파업 중이기 때문에 비행기편이 취소됐습니다.)

If you don't understand it, you should ask your teacher.
(그게 이해되지 않으면 선생님께 물어보아야 합니다.)

She works hard so that she can support her family.
(그녀는 가족을 부양하기 위해 열심히 일합니다.)

Although he is bright, we don't like him.
(비록 그가 똑똑하지만, 우린 그를 좋아하지 않습니다.)

4 Main clauses and Subordinate clauses (주절과 종속절)

주절은 독립절(Independent clause)이라고도 하며, 그 자체로 완전한 뜻을 나타낸다. 종속절은 주절이 있어야만 그 뜻이 완전해지기 때문에 의존절(Dependent clause)이라고도 한다.

While they were watching TV, somebody knocked at the door.
(Subordinate) (Main)
(그들이 TV를 보는 동안 누군가 문을 두드렸습니다.)

He is wearing the red cap that she bought at the shop.
(Main) (Subordinate)
(그는 그녀가 상점에서 산 빨간 모자를 쓰고 있습니다.)

5 Turning phrases into clauses(구에서 절로 전환)

같은 의미를 구 또는 절로 나타낼 수 있다.

I don't know how to explain the situation briefly.
→ I don't know how I can explain the situation briefly.
(상황을 어떻게 간단히 설명해야 할지 모르겠습니다.)

The last person to leave the office must turn off the switch.

→ The last person who leaves the office must turn off the switch.

(사무실을 마지막으로 나가는 사람이 스위치를 꺼야 합니다.)

Turning right, you will see the store sign.

→ If you turn right, you will see the store sign.

(우회전하면 상점 간판이 보일 겁니다.)

Task 1

A. Underline the noun phrases in the following sentences. Each sentence has one or more noun phrase.

1. Hot tea is great on a cold morning.
2. Some customers complained about the service.
3. The apartment on the top floor has a fantastic view.

B. Underline the noun clauses in the following sentences.

1. What I want to know is the name of the man.
2. She doesn't care how long it will take.
3. He said that Susan couldn't come to the meeting.

Task 2

Underline the subordinate clauses(dependent clauses) in the following sentences.

1. Before he came to Seoul, David had taught English in Busan.
2. The lion roared when the hunter appeared.
3. My cat doesn't eat food that comes from a can.
4. I wonder whether the car was sold.
5. As the plane was landing, a bird flew into one of the jet engines.

2 Focus

Parts of Speech
품사

전통적인 문법에서는 명사, 동사, 형용사, 부사를 지칭하는 주요 4품사와 대명사, 전치사, 접속사, 감탄사를 합해서 8품사로 지칭하고 있다. 여기서는 대명사를 명사와 분리하여 설명하고, 감탄사 대신에 문법의 개념을 이해하는데 더 중요한 관사를 포함시키도록 한다.

1 Nouns(명사)

사람, 동물, 장소, 물건의 이름이나 추상적인 개념을 나타낸다.
형태가 있는 것: cat, woman, flower, stone, house, etc.
형태가 없는 것: absence, fact, idea, beauty, sensitivity, etc.

Ann left.
(Ann은 떠났습니다.)

The coffee tastes awful.
(그 커피 맛이 형편없습니다.)

What does age have to do with love?
(사랑에 나이가 무슨 상관입니까?)

2 Pronouns(대명사)

명사를 대신하여 쓰이는 말이다.

(1) Personal pronoun(**인칭대명사**): 사람을 일컬을 때 쓴다.

I, you, him, themselves, etc.

(2) Demonstrative pronoun(**지시대명사**): 사람이나 사물을 가리킨다.

this, that, those, such, etc.

(3) Indefinite pronoun(**부정대명사**): 정해져 있지 않은 것을 가리킨다.

any, one, each, something, both, neither, etc.

(4) Interrogative pronoun(**의문대명사**): 의문사와 대명사의 역할을 한다.

who, what, which, etc.

(5) Relative pronoun(**관계대명사**): 접속사와 대명사의 역할을 한다.

who, that, which, etc.

3 Verbs(동사)

상황이나 행동을 나타내는 말로, 문장 구성에 핵심적인 역할을 한다.

(1) **주동사**(main verb): 조동사와 구별되며, 모든 문장에서 핵심적인 역할을 한다.

work, succeed, play, etc.

(2) **조동사**(auxiliary verb): 주동사와 함께 쓰이며, 도와주는 역할을 한다.

have, do, will, should, etc.

이들 동사 중, be, have, do는 주동사와 조동사로 모두 쓰일 수 있다.

Main verb	Auxiliary verb
Jane is a violinist. (Jane은 바이올리니스트입니다.)	Jane is working at the hospital. (Jane은 병원에서 근무 중입니다.)
Max has a bad cold. (Max는 독감에 걸렸습니다.)	Max has been feeling dizzy all morning. (Max는 아침 내내 현기증이 났습니다.)
The maid does the dishes. (그 가정부가 접시를 닦습니다.)	The maid does not clean the floor. (그 가정부는 바닥을 청소하지 않습니다.)

4 Adjectives(형용사)

성질, 수량, 상태 등을 나타내는 말로 명사를 수식하거나 설명해 주는 역할을 한다.

(1) **한정 형용사**(attributive adjective): 명사 앞에 와서 명사를 수식한다.

(2) **서술 형용사**(predicative adjective): 대개 'be' 동사 등의 뒤에 와서 명사를 서술적으로 설명한다.

The old lady raced to her favorite store.
(노부인은 좋아하는 상점으로 달려갔습니다.)

A waiter should be attentive, cordial, and careful.
(웨이터는 친절하고, 성의 있어야 하고, 세심해야 합니다.)

5 Adverbs(부사)

동사, 형용사, 다른 부사, 문장 전체 등을 수식한다.

Rachel often travels to Paris.
(Rachel은 종종 파리로 여행갑니다.)

The man talked slowly when he was with his grandmother.
(그 남자는 할머니와 있을 때는 천천히 이야기 했습니다.)

The stewardess was very kind.
(그 스튜어디스는 매우 친절했습니다.)

Her son learned English amazingly quickly.
(그녀의 아들은 영어를 매우 빨리 배웠습니다.)

Tomorrow I'll book the flight.
(내일 난 비행기를 예약할 겁니다.)

6 Articles (관사)

형용사 중에서 가장 자주 쓰이는 것이 바로 a, an, the이고, 이것을 관사라고 지칭한다. A와 an을 부정관사라고 하는데, 한 그룹에서 어떤 것이든 하나를 가리킨다(any member of a general group). 그에 반해 the는 정관사라고 하는데, 특정 사람이나 사물을 가리킨다(someone or something in particular).

(1) Indefinite article(부정관사): a, an

(2) Definite article(정관사): the

They've been walking around this block for half an hour.
(그들은 30분 동안 이 구역을 돌아다니고 있습니다.)

The antique doll was dressed in a sailor hat and a blue suit.
(그 오래된 인형은 수병모자를 쓰고 푸른 신사복을 입고 있었습니다.)

7 Prepositions(전치사)

명사 또는 대명사 앞에 쓰여서 다른 낱말과의 관계를 나타낸다.

After class, Alex had a cup of tea in a restaurant.
(방과 후, Alex는 레스토랑에서 차를 마셨습니다.)

An ape is like a monkey with no tail.
(유인원은 꼬리 없는 원숭이와 비슷합니다.)

8 Conjunctions(접속사)

낱말과 낱말, 구와 구, 절과 절을 연결한다.

(1) Coordinate conjunctions (**등위접속사**): and, but, or, so, etc.

(2) Subordinate conjunctions (**종속접속사**): if, because, when, that, etc.

Mary and Jim are not at home, so please come back tomorrow.
(Mary 와Jim은 집에 없으니, 내일 다시 오세요.)

Before Julie bought a new car, she only had a bicycle.
(Julie는 새 자동차를 구입하기 전엔 자전거만 가지고 있었습니다.)

9 Words in sentences(문장 속에서의 단어)

품사는 하나로 고정되어 있는 것이 아니라, 문장 속 단어의 쓰임새에 따라 다른 품사로 바뀌기도 한다.

Shall we go for a walk? / Shall we walk to the subway station?
(산책하러 갈까요?) (지하철역까지 걸어갈까요?)

The room is not clean. / Did he clean the windows?
(그 방은 깨끗하지 않습니다.) / (그가 창문을 닦았습니까?)

He has a bad cough. / Please try not to cough or sneeze.
(그는 기침이 심합니다.) / (기침과 재채기를 자제해 주십시오.)

Don't drink too many soft drinks.
(음료수를 너무 많이 마시지 마세요.)

A large record company records several types of records.
(대형 음반 회사는 여러 종류의 음반을 발매하였다.)

Dark objects cannot be seen in the dark.
(어두운 색의 물체는 어둠 속에선 보이지 않습니다.)

Task 3

Indicate the class of the underlined words using the following.

N(=noun), V(=verb), Adj(=adjective), Adv(=adverb), Pro(=pronoun), Aux(=auxiliary verb), Prep(=preposition), Art(=article). Conj(=conjunction)

1. Alex needed a new pencil so he bought one at the supermarket.
2. The insects have attacked every tree on my block.
3. Female lions will defend their cubs from males.
4. Gracefully, the ballerina leaped across the stage.
5. Ants and spiders represent different species.

REST AREA

Translation

Max	이 큰 양말로 넌 모든 것을 다 할 수 있어.
Max	응. 내가 나의 각각의 귀에 걸고 또 나의 코에 이렇게 걸면…..
Alex	그래. 코끼리다! 나도 해보게 양말 좀 줘!
Father	버스 놓치면 엄청 화를 낼거야 !!

3 Focus

Parts of a sentence
문장 구성성분

① Subjects and Predicates(주부와 술부)

절이나 문장의 기본 구조는 주부와 술부로 되어있다. 주부는 문장의 주체가 되는 부분으로 행위를 하는 사람이나 사물을 지칭한다. 술부는 주부의 동작이나 상태를 설명하는 부분이다.

Subject	Predicate
Mr. Anderson	flew to London.
(Anderson 씨는 런던으로 갔습니다.)	
Some people	looked bored.
(몇몇 사람들은 따분해 보였습니다.)	
What he said	made me angry.
(그가 한 말에 나는 화가 났습니다.)	
To be in love	is a wonderful feeling.
(사랑한다는 것은 굉장히 멋진 느낌입니다.)	

② Subjects, Verbs, Objects, Complements, Adverbial phrases (주어, 동사, 목적어, 보어, 부사적 어구)

문장 안에서의 각 단어나 어구의 역할은 주어, 동사, 목적어, 보어, 부사적 어구 등으로 다시 나누어 볼 수 있다.

Subjects	Verbs	Objects	Complements	Adverbial phrases
Mary	drinks	milk		in the morning.
(Mary는 아침에 우유를 마십니다.)				
The weather	will be		cloudy	tomorrow.
(내일 날씨는 흐릴 것입니다.)				

(1) Subjecst(주어)

주어는 문장의 주체이다. 주어 자리에 올 수 있는 것은 명사, 대명사, 명사구, 명사절 등이 있다.

The cat catches a mouse every morning.
(고양이는 매일 아침 쥐를 잡습니다.)

The shop on the corner is selling plants.
(코너에 있는 가게에서 식물을 팔고 있습니다.)

The new bridge that connects the two islands has improved business opportunities.
(두 섬을 연결하는 새 다리가 사업 기회를 개선시켰습니다.)

(2) Verbs(동사)

동사는 주어를 서술해준다. 모든 영어 문장에는 동사가 있어야 한다.

Go!
(가!)

The train left the station two minutes ago.
(기차가 2분전에 역을 떠났습니다.)

The ministers are suggesting changes in policy.
(장관들이 정책 변경을 제안하고 있습니다.)

(3) Objects(목적어)

동작을 받는 역할을 한다. 주어와 마찬가지로 명사, 대명사, 명사구, 명사절 등이 목적어 자리에 온다.

Roger pulled the car out of the mud.
(Roger는 차를 진흙에서 빼냈습니다.)

I met a friend of yours.
(나는 당신의 친구 한 명을 만났습니다.)

They know that she is honest.
(그들은 그녀가 정직하다는 것을 압니다.)

(4) Complements(보어)

주어나 목적어를 보충해준다.

Albert Schweitzer was a doctor in Africa.
(Albert Schweitzer는 아프리카에서 의사였습니다.)

The price of the painting is incredibly high.
(그림의 가격은 놀라울 정도로 비쌉니다.)

She always makes me happy.
(그녀는 나를 항상 기쁘게 만듭니다.)

(5) Adverbial phrases(부사적 어구)

부사적 어구는 행위나 상태의 시간, 장소, 방법, 이유, 정도 등을 나타낸다. 여러 종류의 절이나 구가 올 수 있다.

She went to bed very early.
(그녀는 매우 일찍 잠자리에 들었습니다.)

There will be another train in twenty minutes.
(20분 후에 다른 기차가 올 겁니다.)

The man left the country because he wanted a job in Italy.
(남자는 이탈리아에서 일하는 것을 원했기 때문에 그 나라를 떠났습니다.)

Task 4

Underline the subjects in the following sentences.

1. The man who lives next door works for the government.
2. Most of the students learn a foreign language
3. On the grass sat an enormous toad.
4. In fall, the leaves on the trees fall to the ground.
5. Helping other people makes me feel alive.
6. The policy of the United States government in regard to nuclear weapons is uncertain at present.

Task 5

Indicate the sentence roles of the underlined parts in the following sentences.

S(=subject), V(=verb), O(=object), SC(=subject complement),

OC(=object complement), Adv(=adverbial)

1. The hurricane destroyed the city in a few hours.
2. Phillip is depressed because of the bad news.
3. This sandwich tastes good.
4. We invited a lot of people to the party.
5. She wants him to walk the dog.

Culture Corner

Real McCoy

틀림없는 본인, 진짜라는 뜻으로 the real McCoy 또는 the McCoy라는 표현이 쓰인다. 이 표현의 유래에 관해서는 여러 가지 이야기가 있다. 그 중 하나는 1898-1900년 사이에 welterweight champion을 지낸 Charles 'Kid' McCoy라는 권투선수로부터 나왔다. McCoy가 하루는 선술집에 갔다가 어떤 남자와 시비가 붙었는데, 그 남자에게 자기가 권투 선수인 McCoy라고 했으나 믿지 않고 계속 덤벼들었다. 화가 난 McCoy가 한방에 그 남자를 날려보냈다. 잠시 후 정신을 차린 그 남자는 옆 사람들에게 'He's the real McCoy' 라고 말했다고 한다.

또 다른 설도 있다. 원래는the real McKay라는 표현이었는데, 이는 Scotland에서 품질 좋은 whiskey를 만들어내던 Mackay사에서 나온 것이다. 이 회사에서는 술 이름에다가 'The Real McKay'라는 상표를 붙여 판매를 했는데 미국인들이 이 술을 가리켜 'McCoy'로 발음했다는 것이다.

또, 미국 최초의 흑인 발명가인 Elijah McCoy(1843-1929)로부터 the real McCoy라는 표현이 유래했다는 설도 있다. 그는 증기 기관을 멈추지 않고 돌아가는 상태에서 계속 기계에 기름을 공급할 수 있는 윤활장치를 만들어 냈는데 이것이 아주 큰 인기를 얻게 되었다. 그러자 다른 사람들이 이 윤활장치를 모방하여 비슷하게 만들었지만, 그 성능이 McCoy가 만든 것에는 미치지 못하였다. 사람들은 당연히 McCoy Lubricator(윤활장치)를 찾게 되었고, 그의 발명품이 진짜이고 최고라는 뜻에서 the real McCoy라고 부르게 되었다고 한다. 어느 설이 맞는 지는 아무도 모른다.

He's the real Mc Coy.
(= He's the real deal.)

Wrap-up

1. Components of English sentences: words, phrases, clauses
   - He bought a small red car.
   - What you say doesn't make any sense to us.
2. Parts of speech
   - noun, pronoun, verb, adjective, adverb, determiner, preposition, conjunction
   - Don't drink too many soft drinks.
3. Parts of a sentence
   - subject, verb, object, complement, adverbial phrases
   - The cat catches a mouse every morning.
   - The weather will be cloudy tomorrow.

Final Tips

Subjects, Verbs, Objects & Complements

(1) They would like to study at university.
S V

(2) How he managed to pass the class is a mystery.
S V C

(3) One of my cousins has visited Ghana.
S V O

영어 문장의 주요 성분은 주어와 동사, 목적어, 보어 등으로 이루어집니다.

Translation

그들은 대학에서 공부하고 싶어합니다.
그가 그 수업을 어떻게 용케 통과했는지 이해가 안됩니다.
내 조카 중의 한 명이 가나를 방문했습니다.

Review Test

1. 다음 문장에서 명사구(noun phrase)를 고르시오.

All children under 16 and their mothers can leave the city.

(1) All children under
(2) the city
(3) leave the
(4) can leave

2. 다음 문장에서 종속절(subordinate clause)을 고르시오.

Although she is in her thirties, she looks much younger than I expected.

(1) in her thirties
(2) younger than I expected
(3) although she is in her thirties
(4) she looks much younger

3. 다음 밑줄 친 부분이 부사구(adverb phrase)가 <u>아닌</u> 것을 고르시오.

(1) She saw the advertisement <u>in the newspaper</u>.
(2) This project will be done <u>by this coming Saturday</u>.
(3) He went to the airport <u>to see her off</u>.
(4) The girl <u>dancing on the stage</u> is my classmate.

4. 다음문장에서 주어(subject)를 고르시오.

The most interesting and important way to customize a site is to create a page of stories based on your unique interests.

(1) a page of stories
(2) your unique interests
(3) the most interesting and important way to customize a site
(4) to create a page of stories based on your unique interests.

5. 다음 문장에서 밑줄 친 부분이 명사절(noun clause)이 아닌 것을 고르세요.

(1) <u>Since the music was so loud</u>, we couldn't talk.
(2) I don't know <u>if I can attend the meeting</u>.
(3) <u>What you say</u> doesn't make any sense to me.
(4) Liberal democracy means <u>that everyone is treated the same</u>.

ocus1-Focus2

Chapter 2

Verbs

Introduction

Lesson objectives

1. Kinds of verbs and their usages 동사의 종류와 용법

- ❖ 자동사와 타동사
- ❖ 상태나 감각을 나타내는 동사
- ❖ 목적어가 필요 없는 타동사
- ❖ 수여동사
- ❖ 수여동사로 착각하기 쉬운 타동사
- ❖ 목적보어로 to부정사를 취하는 동사
- ❖ 사역동사
- ❖ 지각동사

2. Subject and verb agreement 주어와 동사의 일치

Check-up

Ben & Olivia's everyday

Olivia : Dinner is ready. I have made your favorite: meatloaf. Come inside before it _________ (get, gets) cold.

Ben : I will _________ (be, is, are) there in a minute. I just have to finish this.

Olivia : What are you doing anyway?

Ben : I am putting a new engine in the Chevy.

Olivia : A new engine? You didn't tell me that you were going to buy anything for your car. How much did that __________ (spend, cost)?

Ben : Don't worry about the price…

Olivia : Ben, tell __________ (me, to me) how much you spent.

Ben : Well, it was cheaper than getting a new car. Which I would have had to do if I didn't purchase a new engine…

Olivia : Ben, for the last time, how much __________ (were, was) it?!

Ben : Like I said, I got a good deal. I got it for $4000.

Olivia : You spent that much on your stupid car? Where did you get the money?

Ben : I have been saving a bit.

Olivia : You have been secretly saving money? You know how much I have been wanting to go on a vacation. Give the engine back ____________ (the store, to the store) and get the money.

Ben : But I made a deal...

Olivia : Just do it.

Ben : All right. Now let's _________ (eat, to eat) some meatloaf.

Olivia : You are dreaming if you think you are eating any of my meatloaf. Stay out here with your stupid car.

Ben : But honey!

Check-up

Answers

Olivia : Dinner is ready. I have made your favorite: meatloaf. Come inside before it (**gets**) cold.

Ben : I will (**be**) there in a minute. I just have to finish this.

Olivia : What are you doing anyway?

Ben : I am putting a new engine in the Chevy.

Olivia : A new engine? You didn't tell me that you were going to buy anything for your car. How much did that (**cost**)?

Ben : Don't worry about the price…

Olivia : Ben, tell (**me**) how much you spent.

Ben : Well, it was cheaper than getting a new car. Which I would have had to do if I didn't purchase a new engine…

Olivia : Ben, for the last time, how much (**was**) it?!

Ben : Like I said, I got a good deal. I got it for $4000.

Olivia : You spent that much on your stupid car? Where did you get the money?

Ben : I have been saving a bit.

Olivia : You have been secretly saving money? You know how much I have been wanting to go on a vacation. Give the engine back (**to the store**) and get the money.

Ben : But I made a deal...

Olivia : Just do it.

Ben : All right. Now let's (**eat**) some meatloaf.

Olivia : You are dreaming if you think you are eating any of my meatloaf. Stay out here with your stupid car.

Ben : But honey!

Check-up

Translation

Olivia : 저녁 준비 다 됐어. 당신이 제일 좋아하는 미트 로프 만들어 놨어. 식기 전에 얼른 와.

Ben : 바로 갈게. 이것만 끝내고.

Olivia : 그런데 뭐하고 있는 거야?

Ben : Chevy에 새 엔진 설치하고 있어.

Olivia : 새 엔진? 자동차 부품 살 거라는 얘기 한 적 없잖아. 얼마 주고 샀어?

Ben : 가격에 대해선 걱정 하지마.

Olivia : Ben, 얼마 썼는지 말해.

Ben : 차 새로 사는 것보다 더 싸. 새 엔진 안 샀으면 차를 샀어야 했을 걸.

Olivia : Ben, 마지막으로 말하는데 얼마였어?

Ben : 내가 말했듯이 싸게 샀다니까. 4000 달러 주고 샀어.

Olivia : 당신 똥차에 그 많은 돈을 썼다고! 돈은 어디서 났어?

Ben : 조금씩 저금한 거 있어.

Olivia : 몰래 저금해 왔어? 내가 얼마나 휴가 가고 싶어하는지 알잖아. 그 가게에 엔진 갖다 주고 돈 받아와.

Ben : 하지만 이미 거래한 건데.

Olivia : 당장 바꿔.

Ben : 알았어. 이제 미트 로프 먹자.

Olivia : 미트 로프 조금이라도 먹을 꿈도 꾸지 마. 당신 그 똥차랑 밖에 계속 서 있어.

Ben : 하지만 여보!

1
Focus

Kinds of verbs and their usages
동사의 종류와 용법

동사는 주로 주어의 행동이나 상태를 설명한다. 또한 주어의 행동이나 상태의 시점을 나타내기도 한다.

The woman looks very excited. - 현재 상태
(그 여인은 아주 흥분한 것 같아 보입니다.)

My doctor recommended yoga to me. - 과거 행동
(의사는 내게 요가를 권했습니다.)

1 자동사와 타동사(Intransitive verbs and transitive verbs)

동사는 목적어 유무에 따라 자동사와 타동사로 분류한다.

a. 자동사(intransitive verbs): 목적어(object)가 필요 없다.
b. 타동사(transitive verbs): 목적어가 필요하다.

The class begins at 8:30 every morning.
(수업은 매일 아침 8:30에 시작합니다.)

We should help the handicapped.
(우리는 장애인들을 도와야 합니다.)

많은 동사들은 자동사와 타동사로 모두 쓰인다.

Intransitive verbs	Transitive verbs
Linda writes daily. (Linda는 매일 글을 씁니다.)	Linda writes poetry. (Linda는 시를 씁니다.)
Billy studies hard. (Billy는 열심히 공부합니다.)	Billy studies Chinese after school. (Billy는 방과 후에 중국어를 공부합니다.)
The store doesn't open on Sunday. (그 가게는 일요일에 문을 닫습니다.)	Could you open the window? (그 창문을 열어주시겠어요?)

2 상태나 감각을 나타내는 동사 (Linking verbs)

상태(be, seem, appear, remain, keep), 상태의 변화(come, grow, go, turn, become), 감각(feel, look, taste, sound, smell) 등을 나타내는 동사 뒤에는 주어를 설명하는 주격보어로 명사 상당어구 또는 형용사가 온다.

My father is a taxi driver.
(내 아버지는 택시기사입니다.)

John looks funny in his gorilla costume.
(고릴라 의상을 입고 있는 John이 우스워 보입니다.)

Leaves turned red and yellow in the fall.
(가을엔 잎들이 빨갛고 노랗게 변합니다.)

3 전치사가 필요 없는 타동사

reach(~에 도달하다), attend(~에 참석하다), greet(~에게 인사하다), discuss(~에 대해 논의하다), mention(~에 대해 언급하다), obey(~에게 순종하다), resemble(~와 닮다), marry(~와 결혼하다, get married to), answer(~에 답하다), approach(~에 접근하다) 등은 타동사로 전치사와 함께 쓸 수 없다.

Don't mention my little problem when we're in public.
(여러 사람들 앞에서 나의 사소한 문제를 언급하지 마세요.)

cf Don't mention about my little problem when we're in public. (X)

I don't want to attend the meeting.
(나는 회의에 참석하고 싶지 않습니다.)

cf 전치사를 필요로 하는 동사
graduate from(~을 졸업하다), apologize to (~에게 사과하다), object to(~에 반대하다), wait for(~를 기다리다), account for(~을 설명하다)

4 수여동사 (Verb + two objects)

간접 목적어(~에게)와 직접 목적어(~을) 두 개의 목적어를 필요로 하는 동사이다.
S + V + IO(indirect object) + DO(direct object)의 형태로 쓰인다.

John gave Mary the flowers.
(John은 Mary에게 꽃을 주었습니다.)

Please pass me the ball.
(공을 좀 건네주세요.)

I asked him a question.
(나는 그에게 질문했습니다.)

간접 목적어를 전치사구로 바꾸어 직접 목적어 뒤로 보내기도 한다.

Henry gave Rachel a CD player. → Henry gave a CD player to Rachel.
(Henry는 Rachel에게 CD 플레이어를 주었습니다.)

They found me a ticket. → They found a ticket for me.
(그들은 나에게 그 표를 구해주었습니다.)

cf 전치사 to를 쓰는 동사: give, hand, lend, offer pass, pay, sell, send, post, show, teach, tell write, read, owe

cf 전치사 for를 쓰는 동사: buy, choose, find, get, make, order, cook, pick, save

전치사 for나 to 다음에 나오는 간접목적어에 주의를 기울일 때, 또는 간접 목적어가 직접목적어보다 훨씬 길 때 이러한 구문을 쓴다.

She taught art to many children at the school.
(그녀는 그 학교에서 많은 어린이들에게 미술을 가르쳤습니다.)

직접목적어가 대명사인 경우도 이 구문을 쓴다.

We bought it for them.
(우리는 그들에게 주려고 그것을 샀습니다.)

5 수여동사로 착각하기 쉬운 타동사

Explain, introduce, suggest, propose, mention, say, announce, describe 등은 수여동사가 아니므로, 사람 앞에 전치사 to를 써야 한다.

He suggested the plan to us.
(그는 우리에게 그 계획을 제안했습니다.)

cf He suggested us the plan. (X)

Let me introduce you to my sister.
(당신을 내 여동생에게 소개하겠습니다.)

6 목적보어로 to부정사를 취하는 동사

요청, 바램, 설득, 허용 등을 나타내는 ask, beg, request, require, want, expect, encourage, persuade, force, urge, tell, order, allow, advice, promise 등의 동사 뒤에는 목적어 다음에 to 부정사가 목적보어로 온다.

They want him to leave soon.
(그들은 그가 곧 떠나길 바랍니다.)

Drug companies have encouraged doctors to prescribe more and more drugs in recent years.
(제약회사들은 최근 의사들이 더 많은 약을 처방하도록 부추겼습니다.)

7 사역동사

make, have, let, help 등의 사역동사 뒤에는 목적어 다음에 목적보어로 동사원형(능동)이나 -ed형(수동)이 온다.

Let me treat you this time.
(이번엔 내가 당신을 대접하겠습니다.)

Could you help me (to) carry these bags?
(이 가방들을 옮기는 걸 도와주시겠습니까?)

I've just had my car serviced.
(제 차는 방금 서비스를 받았습니다.)

8 지각동사

see, watch, look at, feel, hear, notice 등의 지각동사 뒤에는 목적어 다음에 목적보어로 동사원형(능동)이나 ~ing형(능동 진행)이 온다.

They heard someone slam the door.
(그들은 누군가 문을 쾅 닫는 것을 들었습니다.)

I saw him entering that building.
(나는 그가 저 건물로 들어가는 것을 봤습니다.)

Task 1

Choose the right expressions.

1. She grew (impatient, impatiently) with his constant excuses for not doing his duties.
2. His illness forced him (cancel, to cancel) his visit.
3. The whole-wheat bread smelled (delicious, deliciously).
4. He sent (me, to me) an email last week.
5. Ann (resembles, resembles with) her father.

Task 2

Indicate the ungrammatical parts and correct them.

1. The government did not address about the criticism that it had done nothing about the homeless.
   (A: address about / B: that / C: had done / D: nothing)

   → ________

2. Why is Bill Gates so successfully?
   (A: Why / B: is / C: so / D: successfully)

   → ________

3. Although his mother is in her seventies, she looks like much younger.
   (A: Although / B: in / C: looks like / D: much)

   → ________

4. I wanted to watch the film but my parents made me to go to bed.
   (A: to watch / B: made / C: me / D: to go)

   → ________

5. If anything happens, you can reach at me by email any time.
   (A: anything / B: happens / C: reach at / D: by email)

   → ________

6. The man explained me how to operate the machine.
   (A: The man / B: me / C: how / D: to operate)

   → ________

REST AREA

Translation

Max	선생님이 무엇을 주셨어?
Wendy	선생님이 우리의 성적표를 주셨어.
Max	우리의 성적표?
Wendy	응, 알잖아. 우리 점수 말이야.
Max	뭐라구? 그러니까 우리가 점수를 받는단 말이야?
Wendy	물론이지, 바보야! 넌 어떻게 생각했는데?
Max	우리가 처음에 단지 몇 학기도 연습을 할 수 없다는 거야?

2 Focus

Subject and verb agreement
주어와 동사의 일치

1 현재 시제 (Present tense)

현재 시제인 경우에, 주어가 3인칭 단수(he, she, it etc.)면 동사에 -s가 붙는다. be동사의 경우에도 형태가 변한다.

He works at the factory.
(그는 공장에서 일합니다.)

They work at the factory.
(그들은 공장에서 일합니다.)

Nancy looks tired.
(Nancy 는 피곤해 보입니다.)

Nancy and Linda look tired.
(Nancy와 Linda는 피곤해 보입니다.)

The boy is tall.
(그 소년은 키가 큽니다.)

The boys are tall.
(그 소년들을 키가 큽니다.)

2 주어가 둘 이상인 경우

(1) 원칙적으로 복수형 동사를 쓴다.

Jane and Annie were walking together.
(Jane과 Annie는 함께 걷고 있었습니다.)

John and I like to go dancing once in a while.
(John과 나는 가끔 춤추러 가길 좋아합니다.)

(2) 두 개의 명사가 동일한 주어를 가리키는 경우에는 단수형 동사를 쓴다.

The artist and author is very famous.
(그 화가이자 작가는 매우 유명합니다.)

cf The artist and the author are very famous.
(그 화가와 작가는 매우 유명합니다.)

(3) 하나의 단위로 취급될 때는 단수 동사를 쓴다.

Spaghetti and meatballs is my favorite food.
(스파게티와 미트볼은 내가 가장 좋아하는 음식입니다.)

Romeo and Juliet was written by William Shakespeare.
(로미오와 줄리엣의 작가는 윌리엄 셰익스피어입니다.)

cf peanut butter and jelly(땅콩버터 젤리), bacon and eggs(베이컨 계란), curry and rice(카레라이스), a watch and chain(줄 달린 시계), gin and tonic(진토닉)

3 There 구문

there, here, where 등의 부사로 시작하는 경우, 동사의 뒤에 오는 명사에 따라 동사의 수가 결정된다.

There is a van near his house.
(그의 집 근처에 밴이 있습니다.)

There are two patients in the waiting room.
(대합실에 환자가 두 명 있습니다.)

Where are the students?
(그 학생들은 어디에 있습니까?)

cf 그러나 구어체에서는 뒤에 오는 명사에 관계없이 동사 단수형이 쓰이기도 한다.

There's been a lot of fires in this area.
(이 지역에서 많은 화재가 났습니다.)

How's your brother and sister these days?
(요즘 네 형과 누이는 어떻게 지내니?)

4 대명사 주어

(1) either, neither, each, everybody, somebody, nobody, someone, anybody 다음에는 주로 동사의 단수형이 온다.

Everybody dies alone in this world.
(이 세상의 모든 이들은 홀로 죽음을 맞이합니다.)

Is there somebody we can contact in an emergency?
(비상 사태에 우리가 연락을 할 수 있는 사람이 있습니까?)

Does anybody know where Sue is?
(Sue가 어디에 있는지 아는 사람 있나요?)

Each of these guidebooks has been written carefully.
(이 각각의 안내책자는 모두 정성껏 쓰여졌습니다.)

cf 그러나 구어체에서는 each 다음에 동사의 복수형을 쓰기도 한다.

(2) some, any, most, none, half 다음에 of 가 뒤따라올 때, of 다음에 오는 명사에 따라 동사의 수가 결정된다.

Some of us want to get the tickets.
(우리 중 몇몇은 티켓을 구하고 싶습니다.)

Some of the cake has been eaten.
(케이크의 일부를 먹었습니다.)

Most of the fire in the mountains was extinguished.
(산불이 거의 진압되었습니다.)

4 주어가 수식을 받을 때

주어가 전치사구나 관계대명사절 등의 수식을 받더라도 동사의 수는 영향을 받지 않는다.

Mary, accompanied by her two sisters, is going to France.
(Mary는 여동생 2명과 프랑스로 갈 것입니다.)

People who want to attend the ceremony need to book in advance.
(그 의식에 참가하기 원하는 사람은 사전에 예약을 해야 합니다.)

Everything I've seen in the cities is interesting.
(그 도시들에서 본 모든 것이 흥미롭습니다.)

5 그 외 단수로 취급되는 주어

(1) 영화나 책의 제목, 학과명, 병명, 게임명, 국가명 등도 단수로 취급된다.

Star Wars was a huge box-office hit.
(스타워즈는 크게 히트 쳤습니다.)

Physics is not easy for her.
(물리학은 그녀에게 어렵습니다.)

Chickenpox is a disease which gives you a high temperature and red spots.
(수두는 고열과 붉은 반점을 수반하는 질병입니다.)

Checkers is still a popular game.
(서양장기는 여전히 인기 있는 게임입니다.)
The Philippines consists of more than 7,000 islands.
(필리핀은 7천 개 이상의 섬으로 구성돼 있습니다.)

(2) 돈, 시간, 거리 등도 하나의 개념으로 생각할 때는 단수로 취급된다.

Five miles is a long way to walk in cold weather.
(추운 날씨에 5마일은 걷기 먼 거리입니다.)

Twenty dollars is a large sum to him.
(20달러는 그에게 큰 액수입니다.)

Task 3

Choose the right words in the parentheses.

1. The bird flu (has, have) spread to the outskirts of Europe.
2. (Were, Was) there many people in the room?
3. Some of the movies these days (contains, contain) too much violence.
4. Neither the passengers nor the pilot (was, were) injured.
5. The powerful people in a company always (gets, get) respect.

Task 4

Correct the error in each sentence. If the sentences have no errors, write "correct".

ex

Where was the teachers when the accident happened?

was → were

1. Half of the work is done by machine.
   _______ → _______
2. Mike, with some help from his classmates, are organizing a book club for the sixth grade.
   _______ → _______
3. The president or his representatives is to attend the press conference.
   _______ → _______

4. Three hours of skiing provides plenty of exercise.
_______ → _______

5. Listening to very loud music at rock concerts have caused hearing loss in some teenagers.
_______ → _______

Task 5

Fill in the blanks with the correct form of the given verbs. Use only the simple present tense.

1. Several paintings by that artist _______ (be) now on exhibit at the mall.
2. Studying a foreign language often _______ (lead) students to learn about the culture of the country where it is spoken.
3. Sensitivity to other people's feelings _______ (make) her an understanding person.
4. Both my father and my mother sometimes _______ (visit) me.
5. Twenty minutes _______ (be) more than enough time to finish the task.

Task 6

Choose all the verbs which are incorrect.

In Sweden, adults and children celebrates (1) St. Lucia's Day. Everyone there know (2) St. Lucia as the Queen of Light. Many people eagerly look (3) forward to the December holiday. Girls especially enjoys (4) the day. By tradition, the oldest girl in the family dresses (5) as St. Lucia. A crown of lit candles are (6) put on her head. Each of the young girls also wear (7) a white robe. Early in the morning, the costumed girls bring (8) breakfast to the adults of the household.

Culture Corner

Lame duck

언론에서 'lame duck'이라는 말을 흔히 보게 된다. 이는 임기 만료를 앞둔 공직자를 '절름발이 오리'에 비유한 말이다. 미국에서 남북전쟁 때부터 사용되었는데, 재선에 실패한 현직 대통령이 남은 임기 동안 마치 절름발이 오리처럼 뒤뚱거리며 정책집행에 일관성이 없다는 데서 생겨났다고 한다. 즉, 일단 선거에서 패배한 정치가는 'I don't care what the voters think."와 같은 태도를 가지고, 책임감 없는 행동을 보이기도 한다. 1933년 이전에는 11월 선거에서 패배한 현직 대통령이 다음해 3월 4일까지 재직하도록 되어 있었다. 그러나 1933년 10월 헌법 수정 조항을 채택하여 대통령과 부통령의 취임 일을 1월 20일로 앞당겨서 대통령이 권력을 이양하는 기간을 한 달 남짓 줄였다.

왜 'chicken'이나 'goose'가 아니라 'duck'이 사용되는지 그 유래에 대해서는 알려진 바가 없다. 그러나 'duck'이 언제나 부정적인 의미로 쓰이는 것은 아니다.

Always behave like a duck.
Keep calm and unruffled on the surface
but paddle like the devil underneath.
(Jacob Braude)
항상 오리처럼 행동하라.
물 위에서는 항상 고요하게 평온을 유지하지만
물 밑에서는 악마처럼 버둥거려라.
He has become a lame duck.

Wrap-up

1. Kinds of verbs and their usages
   - The class begins at 8:30 every morning.
   - John looks funny in his gorilla costume.
   - John gave Mary the flowers.
   - They want him to leave soon.
2. Subject and verb agreement
   - He works at the factory.
   - They work at the factory.

Final Tips

(1) appear

The city appears calm after last night's fighting. (O)

The city appears calmly after last night's fighting. (X)

appear 뒤에는 보어로 형용사가 옵니다.

(2) introduce

He introduced his girlfriend to me. (O)

He introduced me his girlfriend. (X)

introduce 다음에는 '~에게'라는 뜻으로 명사 앞에 to가 필요합니다.

(3) agreement of subjects and verbs

A variety of different factors have contributed to the company's failure. (O)

A variety of different factors has contributed to the company's failure. (X)

a variety of~ 다음에 오는 명사의 수에 따라서 단수 · 복수가 결정됩니다.

Translation

그 도시는 지난밤 싸움이 끝난 이후 평온해 보입니다.
그는 나에게 그의 여자 친구를 소개해 주었습니다.
다양한 다른 요소들로 인해 그 회사는 도산을 했습니다.

Review Test

Choose the correct words.

1. They (rose, raised) the prices of their products.

2. We (discussed, discussed about) the problem, but we didn't (reach, reach to) a final decision.

3. Either the station or the theater (is, are) a good place to meet.

4. Her parents didn't allow her (go, to go) out that night.

5. All the workers are asked to (attend, come) the meeting.

6. The book he gave me looks (easy, easily) to read.

7. The doctor suggested (me, to me) that I should take a break.

8. Everyone we've met here (has, have) been very helpful.

9. You have described it (perfect, perfectly).

10. They saw her (sat, sitting) on a chair.

ocus1-Focus4

Chapter 3

TENSE

Introduction

Lesson objectives

1. **Verb forms** 동사 형태
2. **Simple tense** 단순 시제
3. **Perfect** 완료형
4. **Progressive** 진행형

Check-up

Ben & Olivia's everyday

Olivia : I ________ (picked, pick) up these brochures at a travel agency on the way home from work. Have a ________ (look, looking) through and decide where you want to go.

Ben : All these brochures are for Italy!

Olivia : Yeah, but we have to decide where in Italy we want to go.

Ben : But I don't want to go to Italy. I told you that before we got ________ (married, marry). I don't like Italy. I went there when I was (working, worked in Europe and I hated it. I am not wasting my money on a trip to Italy.

Olivia : I am sure Italy has ________ (changed, change) a lot since then. And I have never been there before. So we are going. So hurry up and start looking through the brochures. How about this resort? It ________ (look, looks) like they have decorated it nicely.

Ben : It looks like they ________ (built, builded) it in a swamp. I'm not staying there.

Olivia : Then how about this island? Look at the swimming pool!

Ben : As long as there are plenty of cocktails I will be happy.

Olivia : Well, it is decided then. I will ________ (talk, talking) to the agent tomorrow. I will have to get a new bikini…

Ben : But you bought a new swimsuit this summer.

Olivia : I am not ________ (wear, wearing) that thing in Italy. I will need some new sunglasses, too. Oh, and a…

Ben : Here we go…

Check-up

Check-up

Answers

Olivia : I (picked) up these brochures at a travel agency on the way home from work. Have a (look) through and decide where you want to go.

Ben : All these brochures are for Italy!

Olivia : Yeah, but we have to decide where in Italy we want to go.

Ben : But I don't want to go to Italy. I told you that before we got (married). I don't like Italy. I went there when I was (working) in Europe and I hated it. I am not wasting my money on a trip to Italy.

Olivia : I am sure Italy has (changed) a lot since then. And I have never been there before. So we are going. So hurry up and start looking through the brochures. How about this resort? It (looks) like they have decorated it nicely.

Ben : It looks like they (built) it in a swamp. I'm not staying there.

Olivia : Then how about this island? Look at the swimming pool!

Ben : As long as there are plenty of cocktails I will be happy.

Olivia : Well, it is decided then. I will (talk) to the agent tomorrow. I will have to get a new bikini…

Ben : But you bought a new swimsuit this summer.

Olivia : I am not (wearing) that thing in Italy. I will need some new sunglasses, too. Oh, and a…

Ben : Here we go…

Check-up

Translation

Olivia : 일 끝나고 집에 오는 길에 여행사에서 이 홍보책자들 좀 가져왔어. 살펴보고 어디 가고 싶은지 결정해.

Ben : 다 이탈리아 홍보책자잖아!

Olivia : 응, 그런데 이탈리아 내에서 어디로 갈지 정해야지.

Ben : 하지만 난 이탈리아에 가고 싶지 않아. 우리 결혼하기 전에 말했잖아. 난 이탈리아 안 좋아해. 유럽에서 일할 때 거기 갔었는데 마음에 안 들었어. 이탈리아 여행하는데 내 돈 낭비하고 싶지 않아.

Olivia : 그 후로 분명히 이탈리아도 많이 변했을 거야. 그리고 난 한 번도 거기 안 가봤단 말이야. 그러니까 가도록 하자. 빨리 홍보책자 봐봐. 이 휴양지 어때? 멋지게 꾸며놓은 것 같은데.

Ben : 늪지대에 지어놓은 것처럼 보이는군. 거기서 머물고 싶지는 않아.

Olivia : 그러면 이 섬은 어때? 수영장 좀 봐!

Ben : 칵테일만 많이 있다면 좋아.

Olivia : 그럼 여기로 결정된 거다. 내일 여행사 직원과 말해봐야겠어. 비키니도 새로 사야겠네.

Ben : 당신 이번 여름에 수영복 새로 샀잖아.

Olivia : 이탈리아에서는 그런 거 안 입지. 새 선글라스도 필요하겠다. 아, 그리고...

Ben : 또 시작이군......

Focus 1

Verb forms
동사 형태

모든 동사는 원형이 있지만, 시제에 따라 다양한 모습으로 활용되어 쓰인다.

She plays tennis. (현재)
(그녀는 테니스를 칩니다.)
She played tennis. (과거)
(그녀는 테니스를 쳤습니다.)
She is playing tennis. (현재진행)
(그녀는 테니스를 치고 있습니다.)
She has played tennis. (현재완료)
(그녀는 테니스를 지금까지 쳐왔습니다.)

1 현재 시제(Present tense)

주어가 3인칭 단수이고 현재 시제이면, 동사의 원형에 -s, -es, -ies를 붙인다.

i) 동사가 -s, -z, -x, -ch, -sh, -o로 끝나면 -es를 붙인다

ex

kisses, buzzes, mixes, fixes, catches, watches, pushes, washes, goes, does

ii) 동사가 자음+y로 끝나면, y를 i로 고치고 -es를 붙이고, 모음+y로 끝나면, -s만 붙인다.

ex

studies, hurries, tries, enjoys, plays, buys

iii) 그 외 경우엔 -s를 붙인다.

ex

walks, eats, hears, opens, dies

② 현재분사형 (Present participle)

진행형을 만들 때는 동사의 현재 분사형을 쓰는 데, 동사의 원형에 -ing를 붙이면 된다.

i) 동사가 -e로 끝나면 -e를 삭제하고 -ing를 붙인다.

ex
creating, making, leaving, causing

ii) 동사가 -ie로 끝나면 -ie를 -y로 바꾸고 -ing를 붙인다.

ex
dying(die), lying(lie)

iii) 동사가 단모음+단자음으로 끝나면 마지막 자음을 한 번 더 쓰고 -ing를 붙인다.

ex
sitting, betting, hopping, dropping

iii) 그 외 동사에는 -ing만 붙이면 된다.

ex
visiting, playing, crying, sleeping, washing

③ 과거형 (Past), 과거분사형 (Past participle)

과거 시제를 표현하기 위해서는 동사의 과거형(past)을 쓰고, 수동태(be+p.p.)나 완료형(have+p.p.)을 나타내기 위해서는 동사의 과거분사형(past participle)을 쓴다. 동사 원형에 -(e)d를 붙여서 과거형과 과거분사형을 만드는 규칙변화가 있고, 불규칙적으로 변하는 것이 있다.

(1) 규칙 변화

i) 동사가 -e로 끝나면 -d만 붙인다.

ex
arrived, baked, used, agreed

ii) 동사가 단모음+단자음으로 끝나거나, 2음절 이상의 단어에서 뒷 부분에 강세가 오면, 마지막 자음을 한 번 더 쓰고, -ed를 붙인다.

ex
begged, stopped, robbed, omitted, preferred, occurred

iii) 동사가 자음+-y로 끝나면, y를 i로 고치고 -ed를 붙이고, 모음+y로 끝나면, -ed만 붙인다.

ex

tried, studied, dried, enjoyed, played, obeyed

iv) 그 외 동사에는 -ed를 붙이면 된다.

ex

worked, visited, entered, ended

(2) 불규칙 변화

원형(root)	과거형(past)	과거분사(past participle)
i) AAA형		
cut	cut	cut
hit	hit	hit
put	put	put
set	set	set
let	let	let
ii) ABB형		
bring	brought	brought
catch	caught	caught
buy	bought	bought
leave	left	left
hear	heard	heard
iii) ABA형		
come	came	come
run	ran	run
iv) ABC형		
break	broke	broken
choose	chose	chosen
wear	wore	worn
begin	began	begun
sing	sang	sung
go	went	gone
eat	ate	eaten
see	saw	seen
do	did	done

Task 1

Fill in the blanks with the correct verb forms.

ex

원형	-ing	과거	과거분사
skate	skating	skated	skated

1. rain	________	________	rained
2. imagine	________	________	imagined
3. run	________	ran	________
4. worry	________	worried	________
5. ________	robbing	robbed	robbed
6. sleep	sleeping	________	________

Task 2

Choose the correct verb forms.

1. We have just (began, begun) our project.
2. Lenny and Gina (drove, driven) across the country.
3. Their team (chose, chosen) another topic for the debate.
4. The wind has (blew, blown) fiercely for three days.
5. He (did, done) the experiment that very afternoon.
6. In last night's ballgame, John (hit, hitted) another home run.

2 Focus

Simple tense
단순 시제

시간은 현재(present), 과거(past), 미래(future)로 나눌 수 있다. 동사의 시제도 기본적으로는 이 세 가지인데, 여기에 진행과 완료를 표현할 수 있도록 더 세분하여 시제를 나타내고 있다.

consistency of tense(시제의 일관성): 같은 시간대에 일어난 일에 대해 말할 때는 같은 시제를 일관성 있게 써야 한다. 불필요하게 시제를 바꾸지 않도록 유의한다.

- ► He went across the road and catches a taxi. (X)
- ► He went across the road and caught a taxi. (O)

1 단순 현재 (Simple present)

(1) 현재의 사실이나 상태

He lives in France.
(그는 프랑스에 삽니다.)

We are proud of you.
(우리는 당신이 자랑스럽습니다.)

(2) 현재의 습관적인 동작이나 상태

She drinks a cup of coffee every morning.
(그녀는 매일 아침 커피 한잔을 마십니다.)

The cafeteria food is usually bad.
(카페테리아의 음식은 대개 형편없습니다.)

(3) 진리

The moon circles the earth every twenty-eight days.
(달은 28일 주기로 지구를 회전합니다.)

All living things are composed of one or more cells.
(모든 생물은 하나 또는 그 이상의 세포로 구성돼 있습니다.)

(4) 미래 대용

왕래발착을 나타내는 동사(come, go, start, leave, arrive, etc.)가 미래를 나타내는 부사구와 함께 쓰일 때는 현재 시제의 형태로 미래를 대신한다. 또한 시간이나 조건을 나타내는 접속사(when, while, till, before, after, if, etc.)와 함께 쓰일 때도 현재 시제 형태로 미래를 대신한다.

We start for Vietnam this weekend.
(우리는 이번 주말에 베트남으로 출발할 것입니다.)

Danny finishes school next summer.
(Danny는 내년 여름에 학교를 마칩니다.)

We'll go hiking if the weather is nice tomorrow.
(내일 날씨가 좋으면 우리는 하이킹을 갈 것입니다.)

2 단순 과거 (Simple past)

(1) 과거의 동작, 상태, 습관

Dan went to the basketball game last night.
(Dan은 어젯밤 농구 경기를 보러 갔습니다.)

She was very sick ten years ago.
(그녀는 10년 전 몹시 아팠습니다.)

They used to walk to the park every Sunday.
(그들은 매주 일요일에 공원으로 산책 가곤 했습니다.)

(2) 과거완료 대용

시간을 나타내는 접속사(when, after, till, before, etc.)와 함께 쓰일 때, 시간의 전후 관계가 명확하므로 과거완료를 쓰지 않아도 된다.

After I finished my homework, I watched TV.
(나는 숙제를 끝낸 후 TV를 봤습니다.)

The boy ran away when he saw the teacher.
(그 소년은 선생님을 보자마자 도망갔습니다.)

3 단순 미래 (Simple future)

미래에 대한 단순한 예측, 기대, 가능

The committee will notify you of its decision.
(위원회에서 그들의 결정을 당신에게 통지할 것입니다.)
I'll hit you if you do that again.
(다시 그런 짓을 하면 당신을 때릴 것입니다.)

I think it is going to rain.
(비가 올 것 같습니다.)

단순한 미래를 나타낼 때는 will과 be going to를 다 쓸 수 있으나, 곧 일어날 일에 대한 확실한 예측이나 계획을 표현할 때는 be going to를 쓴다.

The ice is going to break.
(얼음이 곧 깨지려고 합니다.)

She is going to have a baby.
(그녀는 아이를 낳을 겁니다.)

Task 3

Fill in the blanks with the correct verb forms by using the words in the parentheses.

1. Water ________ (freeze) at 0° Celsius.
2. He was ________ (live) in Saudi Arabia at that time.
3. I ________ (spend) all my childhood in Germany.
4. They needed more money, so they ________ (sell) the house.
5. She'll pay her debt when she ________ (get) a job.

Task 4

Change the underlined parts for consistency of tense.

1. The cat jumped onto the counter and <u>steals</u> the sandwich.
→ ___________
2. Since our school has a computer network, we <u>chatted</u> with students from other schools.
→ ___________
3. Every student <u>had</u> e-mail. E-mail makes it easy to ask questions about assignments.
→ ___________
4. When Dad was a boy in Iowa, he <u>keeps</u> bees.
→ ___________
5. Before I <u>lie</u> down to sleep, I packed everything I would need for the trip.
→ ___________

REST AREA

Translation

Max	아시잖아요. 저 하나도 안 아파요! 그건 뭐죠? 아프게 할 건가요?
Doctor	이건 혀를 누르는 거야. 걱정하지마. 전혀 아프지 않을 테니까.
Max	또 이건 뭐죠? 아파요?
Doctor	전혀 그렇지 않아. 이건 청진기란다.
Max	저건 또 뭐죠? 아픈가요?
Doctor	이건 소몰이 막대란다. 그런데 좀 많이 아플꺼야.
Doctor	유머를 모르는군.

REST AREA

Translation

Max 선생님, 지금 무얼 하시는 거예요? 왜 저의 팔을 솜으로 문지르시는 거죠? 저에게 거머리를 붙이려는 거죠?

Max 피를 뽑으려구요? 제발 저의 팔을 자르지 마세요.!!!

Max 이건 또 뭐야? 바늘인가요? 뭐하시려는.. ···아아아앙! 진짜 아파요!!!

Max 오, 이런. 저 죽을 것 같아요. 저 선생님 고소할 거예요. 엄마 어딨어요?

3 Focus

Perfect
완료형

1 현재완료 (Present perfect)

have/has + past participle(p.p.)
현재 완료는 과거의 일이 현재에까지 영향을 미치고 있음을 나타낼 때 쓰인다.

- ► She bought a new car. (과거에 차를 샀다는 것을 표현)
- ► She has bought a new car. (과거에 차를 사서 지금도 가지고 있음을 표현)

명백한 과거를 나타내는 어구(ago, yesterday, then, last, when 등)와는 함께 쓰이지 않는다.

- ► He has lost the bag yesterday. (X)
- ► He lost the bag yesterday. (O)

(1) 완료

과거의 한 시점에서 시작된 행위가 현재 막 끝난 경우에 쓴다. 주로 just, now, already 등의 부사와 함께 쓰인다.

Karl has just passed the exams.
(Karl은 막 그 시험을 통과했습니다.)

They have already gone out.
(그들은 이미 외출했습니다.)

(2) 경험

과거부터 지금까지 경험을 나타낼 때 쓴다. 부사 ever, never, once, twice, before 등과 같이 쓰인다.

She has been to France twice.
(그녀는 프랑스에 두 번 간 적이 있습니다.)

I have never flown in a helicopter.
(나는 헬리콥터를 타 본 적 없습니다.)

(3) 계속

과거에 시작된 일이 현재까지 계속되고 있음을 나타낸다. for, since등과 같은 전치사/접속사와 함께 쓰이는 경우가 많다.

I've lived in New York for three years.
(나는 3년째 뉴욕에 살고 있습니다.)

He has known her since they were in high school.
(그는 그들이 고등학교 때부터 그녀를 알고 있습니다.)

(4) 결과

과거의 일이 현재에 미치는 결과를 나타낸다.

I've lost my passport. (= I don't have my passport now.)
(나는 여권을 잃어버렸습니다.)

She's recovered from her illness. (= She's well again now.)
(그녀는 병에서 회복되었습니다.)

(5) 미래 완료 대용

when, after, until, if 등이 나오는 시간 또는 조건의 부사절에서는 미래 완료 시제를 대신한다.

Please tell me when you have finished.
(일이 끝나면 나에게 말해 주세요.)

She will go out if she has done her duty.
(그녀는 임무를 다 마치면 외출할 것입니다.)

2 과거완료 (Past perfect)

had + p.p.

(1) 과거 특정 시점까지의 완료, 경험, 계속 등을 나타낸다.

He had just finished his dinner when we visited him.
(우리가 그를 방문했을 때, 그는 막 저녁 식사를 끝냈습니다.)

I recognized her at once since I had seen her a few times before.
(나는 한 눈에 그녀를 알아봤습니다. 예전에 그녀를 몇 번 본 적이 있었으니까요.)

Jane had lived in China for five years before she came to Korea.
(Jane은 한국에 오기 전 5년간 중국에 살았습니다.)

(2) 대과거

과거보다 앞선 시제를 나타낸다.

John had died before his daughter was born.
(John은 자신의 딸이 태어나기 전에 세상을 떠났습니다.)

3 미래완료 (Future perfect)

will/shall + have + p.p.

미래 시점을 기준으로 그 때까지의 완료, 경험, 계속 등을 나타낸다.

Will you have saved enough money by then?
(당신은 그때까지 충분한 돈을 모을 겁니까?)

By next month, he'll have been in the hospital for three years.
(다음 달이 되면 그는 3년째 병원에 있게 됩니다.)

Task 5

Choose the correct answer to complete each of the following sentences.

1. How long ___________ in this room?
   (1) did you be (2) have you been
   (3) you were (4) were you been

2. I _________ to call Daniel last night but I forgot.
   (1) meant (2) have meant
   (3) mean (4) am meaning

3. We _________ a party this weekend. Would you like to come?
   (1) had (3) were having
   (3) will have had (4) are having

4. By 2030, scientists __________ a remedy for the disease.
   (1) will have discovered (2) discover
   (3) have discovered (4) discovering

5. Since I joined the traveling company in 2002, I ___________ all sorts of people from many countries.
   (1) met (2) meet
   (3) have met (4) will meet

Focus 4

Progressive
진행형

1 현재 진행 (Present progressive)

am/is/are + ~ing

(1) 현재 진행 중인 동작

Ben is talking on the phone.
(Ben은 전화 통화 중입니다.)

We're staying at a wonderful place.
(우리는 멋진 곳에 머무르고 있습니다.)

(2) 현재 습관적인 동작

주로 always, constantly, continually 등의 부사와 함께 쓰이면 반복적인 동작이나 습관 등을 나타낸다. 상대방을 비난할 때 자주 쓰인다.

My mother is always losing her keys.
(어머니는 늘 열쇠를 잃어버리십니다.)

You're continually interrupting me!
(당신은 계속해서 날 방해하고 있습니다!)

(3) 미래대용

She is coming home on Friday.
(그녀는 금요일에 집에 올 것입니다.)

What are you doing tomorrow afternoon?
(당신은 내일 오후에 무엇을 하실 겁니까?)

cf know, want, like와 같이 상태를 나타내는 동사들은 진행형으로 잘 쓰지 않는다.
Olivia enjoyed the party, but Ben was wanting to go home. (X)
Olivia enjoyed the party, but Ben wanted to go home. (O)

2 과거 진행 (Past progressive)

was/were + ~ing
과거 진행중인 동작

When we left home, it was snowing.
(우리가 집을 떠났을 때, 눈이 오고 있었습니다.)

I was taking a shower when the phone rang.
(전화벨이 울렸을 때 나는 샤워 중이었습니다.)

3 미래 진행 (Future progressive)

will/shall + be + ~ing
미래 진행중인 동작

He will be teaching an English class in the village school.
(그는 마을 학교에서 영어를 가르치고 있을 겁니다.)

Carol will be waiting for you when your plane lands.
(Carol은 비행기가 착륙할 때 당신을 기다리고 있을 겁니다.)

4 현재 완료 진행 (Present perfect progressive)

have + been + ~ing
현재 완료형과 현재 진행형이 합쳐진 것으로 현재에 미치는 영향이 강조 되어진다.

It has been raining since last night.
(어젯밤부터 비가 내리고 있습니다.)

I've been working for the company for 12 years.
(나는 그 회사에서 12년째 일하고 있습니다.)

Task 6

Identify the incorrect verb form in the following sentences. Then, write the correct form.

ex

In 1928, Amelia Earhart has become the first woman to fly across the Atlantic.

has become → became

1. They were married for three years when they got divorced.

_________ → _________

2. Mary eats breakfast right now.

_________ → _________

3. Edward has handed in the report an hour ago.

_________ → _________

4. We went to Ben's house, but he isn't at home.

_________ → _________

5. By next year, Bob wrote his fourth novel.

_________ → _________

Task 7

Fill in the blanks with the correct verb forms by using the words in the parentheses.

1. Since 1993, the space telescope has _________ (provide) us with important pictures of the universe.
2. Kathy has been _________ (work) here for nine years.
3. I enjoy drinking coffee, although it sometimes _______ (keep) me awake at night.
4. When he arrived, the principal was ________ (introduce) the guest speaker.
5. I _______ (be) very tired, so I lay down on the bed for a while.
6. He's _______ (try) four times to pass his driver's license exam.
7. Yesterday, everyone _______ (rise) when he scored a goal.

Culture Corner

A fifth wheel

영미인들에게 자동차는 필수품이어서, 자동차와 관련된 표현이 많다. 예를 들면 a fifth wheel이라는 말은 '아무데도 쓸모 없는 물건이나 사람을 가리킬 때 쓰인다. 원래 '다섯 번 째 바퀴'는 갑작스런 사고에 대비하여 가지고 다니던 예비용 바퀴를 뜻하는데, 평소에는 무게만 늘릴 뿐 별로 쓸모가 없는 물건이라는 데서 유래한 것이다.

또, '서두르다, 빨리 가다'라는 뜻으로 step on it이라는 것이 있다. 이 표현은 자동차를 타고 가면서 더 속력을 내기 위해 accelerator를 밟으라는 데서 나온 것이다.

한 가지 더 예를 들면, '모든 기능을 제대로 다 발휘하다, 선전하다, 전력 투구하다' 라는 뜻으로 'fire on all cylinders'라는 표현이 있다. 원래 '자동차 엔진의 모든 기통이 동시에 작동하다' 라는 뜻이지만 비유적으로 더 자주 쓰인다. 'fire' 대신에 'hit, function, operate, run' 등의 동사를 쓰기도 한다.

I'm feeling like a fifth wheel. I don't have a partner.
We're late. Step on it.
We're firing on all cylinders.

Wrap-up

1. He lives in France.
2. He went across the road and caught the taxi.
3. The committee will notify you of its decision.
4. Karl has just passed the exam.
5. Jane had lived in China for five years before she came to Korea.
6. Ben is talking on the phone.
7. When we left home, it was snowing.

Final Tips

1. present tense

I will call you after I arrive there. (O)

I will call you after I will arrive there. (X)

시간을 나타내는 부사절에서는 현재 시제로 미래의 뜻을 나타냅니다.

2. past tense

When did he return home? (O)

When has he returned home? (X)

yesterday, last~, ago, 의문사 when 등 분명한 과거를 나타내는 말은 현재완료를 표현하는 동사와 함께 쓰일 수 없습니다.

3. progressive

I know that she is a liar. (O)

I am knowing that she is a liar. (X)

상태를 나타내는 동사는 진행형을 만들 수 없습니다.

Translation

거기 도착하면 전화할게요.
그가 언제 집에 돌아왔습니까?
전 그녀가 거짓말쟁이라는 것을 알고 있습니다.

Review Test

Write the correct forms of the verbs in parentheses to complete the sentences.

1. Andy first __________ (play) on the national team 5 years ago.

2. I'll be happy if he __________ (buy) me the earrings for my birthday.

3. We have been __________ (think) about renovating our kitchen for a long time.

4. Sarah was late for school yesterday. When she __________ (get) to the classroom, the lesson had already started.

5. We have __________ (learn) English for two years from Catherine.

Choose the correct words.

6. Do you know when she (join, will join) us?

7. I have (gone, been) to Europe several times.

8. The teacher told us that the Korean War (ended, had ended) in 1953.

9. Mary and Jane (have been knowing, have known) each other since elementary school.

10. By the time you come back, things (have, will have) changed for the better.

ocus1-Focus3

Chapter 4

AUXILIARY VERBS

Introduction

Lesson objectives

1. Characteristics of auxiliary verbs 조동사의 특징

2. Modal auxiliary verbs 법조동사

Can/could, may/might, will/would, shall, should, must

3. May/could/must/should + have done

May/could/must/should의 완료형

Check-up

Ben & Olivia's everyday

Olivia : Have you seen the car Kathy and Tim are driving? It's a Mercedes Benz! He's a handyman and she's a secretary. They __________ (wouldn't, couldn't) make enough money to afford that car. They __________ (will, must) be drug dealers.

Ben : Oh, Olivia. Mind your own business. They __________ (could have, should have) inherited the money. Or they __________ (may have, will have) won the car in a contest. We don't know.

Olivia : And did you see their recycling container last week? There __________ (should have, must have) been a dozen wine bottles. They __________ (could, should) be alcoholics.

Ben : Oh, Olivia. It __________ (may, shall) be that Kathy and Tim had a party. Or they __________ (may have, should have) invited friends over for dinner. Mind your own business.

Olivia : I'm right. They are up to something suspicious. You ________ (will, may) see.

Check-up

Answers

Olivia : Have you seen the car Kathy and Tim are driving? It's a Mercedes Benz! He's a handyman and she's a secretary. They (**couldn't**) make enough money to afford that car. They (**must**) be drug dealers.

Ben : Oh, Olivia. Mind your own business. They (**could have**) inherited the money. Or they (**may have**) won the car in a contest. We don't know.

Olivia : And did you see their recycling container last week? There (**must have**) been a dozen wine bottles. They (**could**) be alcoholics.

Ben : Oh, Olivia. It (**may**) be that Kathy and Tim had a party. Or they (**may have**) invited friends over for dinner. Mind your own business.

Olivia : I'm right. They are up to something suspicious. You (**will**) see.

Translation

Olivia : Kathy와 Tim의 차 본 적 있어? 메르세데스 벤츠야. Tim은 잡역부이고, Kathy는 비서라서 그런 차를 살 만한 돈이 없을 텐데. 마약 거래자들이 분명해.

Ben : Olivia, 상관 마. 그들이 돈을 상속 받았거나, 우승 상품으로 차를 받았을 수도 있어. 모르는 일이잖아.

Olivia : 지난 주에 그 사람들의 재활용 컨테이너를 봤어? 와인 병이 12병쯤 있었을 거야. 알코올 중독자일 수도 있어.

Ben : Olivia, 그들이 파티를 열었거나, 저녁 식사에 친구들을 초대했을 수도 있잖아. 제발 신경 꺼.

Olivia : 내 말이 맞는다니까. 저 사람들 뭔가 수상해. 두고 보면 알게 되겠지.

Focus 1

Characteristics of Auxiliary Verbs

조동사의 특징

1 조동사는 본동사를 도와서 본동사만으로 나타내기 힘든 문법형식과 의미를 나타낸다.

(1) be, have, do - 의문문, 부정문, 진행형, 완료형, 수동태 등을 만들 때 쓰인다.

(2) can/could, may/might, must, will/would, shall, should, ought to - 가능, 허가, 의무, 개연성, 추측 등을 나타낸다. 특히 화자의 태도와 판단을 나타내는 이러한 조동사를 법조동사(Modal auxiliary verbs)라고 한다.

2 조동사에는 시제 변화가 없고, 3인칭 단수 현재 '–s'도 붙지 않는다. 또한 조동사 다음에는 동사의 원형이 온다.

He might be French.
(그는 프랑스인일 것입니다.)

► He mights be French. (X)

► He might is French. (X)

3 Negation (부정)

조동사 바로 다음에 not이 온다.

She may not come early.
(그녀는 일찍 오지 않을 겁니다.)

► She does not may come early. (X)

► She comes not early. (X)

4 Question and Inversion (의문과 도치)

조동사는 의문문이나 강조문에서 주어 앞으로 나간다.

Can you come to the party?
(파티에 올 수 있습니까?)

Never have I felt happier.
(나는 지금 가장 행복합니다.)

5 조동사 + have + p.p.는 대개 과거시제를 나타낸다.

I was so tired. I could have slept for a week.
(나는 너무 피곤했습니다. 일주일 동안 잠을 잘 수도 있었을 겁니다.)

You should have seen the play. It was great.
(당신은 그 연극을 봤어야 합니다. 정말 좋았습니다.)

Task 1

Choose the right words to complete each sentence.

1. You don't __________ (have to, must) get up early tomorrow morning.
2. Carol will give her first violin recital today. She must __________ (is, be) very nervous.
3. Each passenger can _________ (take, takes) two bags onto the plane.
4. I could __________ (skated, skate) faster when I was a child.
5. I'm not sure where Peter is. He might be __________ (having, have) lunch.

Task 2

Complete the sentences with the words in parentheses.

1. He ________ (be/not/may) late.
2. This sign means you _________ (not/drive/must) over 70 kilometers per hour.
3. My cat's sick. I think he _________ (eaten/may/have) some poison.
4. __________ (tell/you/could) me when the train arrives?

5. I promise I ________ (will/smoking/stop).

6. Sarah ______ (left/have/must) very quietly - nobody noticed her go.

REST AREA

Translation

Mother Max야, 쓰레기통을 비워 줄래?

Max 쓰레기통을 비우라구요? 저는 엄마의 하인이 아니예요. 엄마가 하지 그러세요?

Mother 좋아. 내가 할께. 그러면 지금부터 매일 네 자신의 세탁을 하고, 네 자신의 식사를 만들어 먹어. 그리고 네가 먹은 것은 네가 설거지해. 그리고 네가 어지른 것은 스스로 치우렴!

Max 몇몇 여자들은 엄마라고 할 수가 없다니까.

2 Focus

Modal Auxiliary Verbs
법조동사

① can/could

(1) 능력(ability), 가능성(possibility), 허락(permission), 요청(request) 등을 나타낸다.

Bob can drive, but he doesn't have a car.
(Bob는 운전은 할 수 있지만 차가 없습니다.)

Swimming after eating can be dangerous.
(음식을 먹은 직후 수영하는 것은 위험할 수 있습니다.)

You can come if you wish.
(원하면 와도 좋습니다.)

Can/Could you lend me 10 dollars?
(10달러만 빌려줄 수 있으세요?)

(2) can't, couldn't

I'm afraid I can't come to the meeting.
(저는 회의에 못 갈 것 같습니다.)

It can't be wrong.
(그것이 잘못 되었을 리가 없습니다.)

They couldn't find the receipt.
(그들은 영수증을 찾을 수 없었습니다.)

(3) can/could 대신 be able to를 쓰는 경우

① will, may, should 등의 다른 조동사와 같이 사용하는 경우

We'll be able to go abroad next summer.
(우리는 내년 여름에 해외로 갈 수 있을 겁니다.)

I might be able to help you.
(당신을 도울 수 있을 겁니다.)

② 과거에 특정한 일을 할 수 있었다는 뜻으로 사용될 때

They were able to save enough money to buy a house.
(그들은 집을 살 충분한 돈을 저축할 수 있었습니다.)

Were you able to meet him?
(당신은 그를 만날 수 있었습니까?)

cf My grandmother could speak four languages. (일반적 능력)
(나의 할머니는 네 개의 언어를 구사할 수 있었습니다.)

2 may/might

(1) 허락(permission)과 추측(guess)을 나타내고 목적의 부사절 등에서 쓰인다.

May I use your computer?
(당신의 컴퓨터를 좀 써도 될까요?)

We may meet some interesting people at the party.
(우리는 파티에서 재미있는 사람들을 만날 것입니다.)

You might enjoy the movie.
(당신은 그 영화를 즐길 수 있을 겁니다.)

We send them a report so that they may have some information about the project.
(우리는 그들에게 그 프로젝트에 관한 정보를 알려주기 위해 보고서를 보냅니다.)

cf May나 might는 의미의 구별이 없이 쓰이나, 비현실적인 가정에서는 might가 쓰인다.

If I knew her better, I might invite her to the party.
(내가 그녀를 더 잘 안다면, 그녀를 파티에 초대할 겁니다.)

(2) may/might not

Sarah may not want to see me.
(Sarah는 나를 보고 싶어하지 않을 것입니다.)

They might not be home today.
(그들은 오늘 집에 없을 지도 모릅니다.)

③ will/would

(1) 단순미래, 주어의 강한 의지, 요청(request), 습관, 고집 등을 나타낸다.

It will rain this weekend.
(이번 주말에 비가 올 것입니다.)

I thought she would go to the concert. (과거시제에서 단순미래)
(나는 그녀가 콘서트에 갈 거라고 생각했습니다.)

Yes, I will do my best.
(네, 최선을 다하겠습니다.)

Would you tell the teacher she's sick?
(선생님께 그녀가 아프다고 말해주시겠습니까?)

Would you like to have lunch with us?
(우리와 함께 점심을 드시겠습니까?)

When we were children, we would go fishing.
(우리는 어렸을 때 낚시를 하곤 했습니다.)

I asked him many times, but he wouldn't tell me. (주어의 고집)
(그에게 여러 번 부탁했으나 그는 내게 말해주지 않습니다.)

(2) won't, wouldn't

I won't tell anyone what I saw.
(나는 내가 본 것을 누구에게도 말하지 않을 것입니다.)

The car won't start.
(차가 도무지 시동이 걸리지 않습니다.)

I wish she wouldn't take things so seriously.
(나는 그녀가 너무 심각하게 생각하지 않길 바랍니다.)

④ shall

제안이나 주어에 대한 화자의 의지를 나타낸다.

Shall we go out for dinner?
(저녁에 외식할까요?)

You shall have my answer tomorrow.
(내일 대답해 드리겠습니다.)

Let's go for a walk, shall we?
(산책하러 갈까요?)

5 should

(1) 의무(obligation), 추측(deduction)을 나타내거나, 특정한 동사(insist, suggest, demand, recommend, require, request, propose, etc.)와 형용사(natural, important, necessary, essential, anxious, etc.) 뒤의 종속절에서 쓰인다.

We should invite Sue to the party.
(우리는 파티에 Sue를 초대해야 합니다.)

Dan should get here soon - he left his office at five.
(Dan은 5시에 사무실에서 출발했으니 분명히 곧 여기에 도착할 것입니다.)

The doctor suggested that she (should) take a walk every day.
(의사는 그녀에게 매일 산책할 것을 제의했습니다.)

It is natural that they (should) miss their siblings.
(그들이 형제, 자매를 보고 싶어하는 것은 당연합니다.)

(2) should not:'~하지 않는 것이 좋겠다'는 충고

You shouldn't drink and drive.
(음주 운전해서는 안 됩니다.)

You shouldn't believe what he said.
(그의 말을 믿지 마세요)

6 must

(1) 강한 의무, 추측을 나타낸다. 의무를 나타낼 때 have to를 쓰기도 한다.

We must boil the drinking water because of germs.
(세균 때문에 식수를 반드시 끓여야 합니다.)

Ann must have a problem - she cries a lot.
(Ann이 계속 우는 걸로 보아 무슨 문제가 있는 것이 틀림없습니다.)

Max can't meet us this evening. He has to work late.
(Max는 오늘 저녁 우리를 만날 수 없습니다. 그는 늦게까지 일해야 합니다.)

(2) must not: 금지, don't have to (need not): 불필요

You must not drink too much.
(당신은 과음해서는 안 됩니다.)

He doesn't have to leave early.
(그는 일찍 출발할 필요 없습니다.)

cf cannot: 강한 부정적 추측

The rumor can't be true.
(소문이 진실일 리 없습니다.)

It can't be my sister. She is in Paris now.
(내 여동생일 리 없습니다. 그녀는 지금 프랑스에 있습니다.)

Task 3

Fill in the blanks with proper auxiliary verbs.

1. If you want to be a pilot, you ________ (have to, may) have good eyesight.
2. I'm sorry I haven't ________ (been able to, could) come and see you earlier.
3. Everyone's asleep. We ________ (must not, could not) make any noise.
4. ________ (Shall, Could) you give me a ride home?
5. Would you like (visit, to visit) the museum this afternoon?
6. There ________ (may not, can't) be enough room for us on the bus - we'll have to wait and see.

Task 4

Choose the best word to complete each sentence.

1. A: Where's Laura?
   B: I'm not sure. She ________ in the kitchen.
   1) is 2) might be 3) must be
2. A: I wonder why Ellen always wears gloves.
   B: I don't know. She ________ some kind of allergy.
   1) may have had 2) has 3) may have
3. A: My son just got a scholarship to Yale!
   B: You ________ be very proud of him.
   1) could 2) must 3) might

4. A: Is that number right?
   B: Well, it _________ be wrong. The computer doesn't make mistakes!

   1) cannot　　2) isn't　　3) is not able to

5. A: Are you in a hurry?
   B: No, I've got plenty of time. I ________ wait.

   1) can　　2) could　　3) must

6. A: What are you going to do this weekend?
   B: My brother has tickets to the baseball game, so I ________ go with him. My favorite team is playing.

   1) could　　2) will　　3) must

Task 5

Fill in the blanks with the proper words from the box.

was able to	may	don't have to	must	would

1. The drugstore was open, so luckily I ________ buy some Tylenol.
2. Nancy ________ not come to school tomorrow. She's a bit ill now.
3. ________ you mind sitting in the back?
4. Mark is not a child. He _________ think about his future.
5. We _________ finish the report today. We can do it tomorrow.

3 Focus

May/could/must/should + have + p.p.

1 may/might have done

과거에 대한 추측을 나타낸다.

Peter didn't answer the phone. He may have been in the bath at the time.
(Peter가 전화를 받지 않았습니다. 그는 그 때 목욕하고 있었을 것입니다.)

She may have gone shopping last night.
(그녀는 어젯밤 쇼핑 갔을 겁니다.)

He might not have been feeling well.
(그는 몸이 좋지 않았을 것입니다.)

2 could have done

(1) 과거에 하지 않은 일에 대한 아쉬움이나 안도감을 나타낸다.

Dennis could have married her.
(Dennis는 그녀와 결혼할 수도 있었습니다.)

You could have stayed with Ann in Boston.
(당신은 보스톤에서 Ann과 함께 머물 수도 있었습니다.)

(2) may/might have done과 마찬가지로 과거에 대한 추측을 나타낸다.

She could have left the key in the restaurant.
(그녀는 열쇠를 레스토랑에 두고 왔을 것입니다.)

Someone could have stolen the box.
(누군가 그 상자를 훔쳤을 것입니다.)

3 must have done

과거에 대한 강한 추측을 나타내는 표현으로, '~이었음에 틀림없다' 라는 뜻이다.

They used to live close to the highway. It must have been noisy.
(그들은 고속도로 근처에 살았습니다. 소음이 심했을 것이 틀림없습니다.)

I can't find one of my gloves. I must have dropped it in the subway.
(장갑 한 짝을 찾을 수가 없습니다. 분명 지하철에 떨어뜨렸을 것입니다.)

The driver did not stop at the intersection. He must not have seen the red light.
(운전자는 교차로에서 멈추지 않았습니다. 빨간 신호를 못 본 게 틀림없습니다.)

4 should have done

'~했어야 하는 데' 라는 아쉬움이나 후회를 나타낸다.

We had a great time last night. You should have come.
(어젯밤 정말 재미있었습니다. 당신도 왔으면 좋았을 텐데요.)

They should have listened to his speech.
(그들은 그의 연설을 들었어야 했습니다.)

Shouldn't have done은 '~하지 말았어야 하는데 (했다)' 라는 뜻으로 역시 후회나 유감을 나타낸다.

She shouldn't have eaten so much.
(그녀는 너무 많이 먹지 말았어야 했습니다.)

Task 6

Choose the best words in the blanks.

1. A: I wonder why Mike is wearing that bandage around his leg.
   B: I don't know. He ___________ it.
   1) would hurt 2) would have hurt
   3) must hurt 4) must have hurt

2. A: Do you think he saw you?
   B: No, he was too far away. He __________ seen me.
   1) could have 2) couldn't have
   3) should have 4) shouldn't have

3. A: I was surprised that Olivia wasn't at the meeting.
   B: She ________ about it.
   1) may not know
   2) may know
   3) might as well know
   4) might not have known

4. A: Where is my cell phone?
   B: You ________ it in the office.
   1) should have left
   2) should not leave
   3) might have left
   4) might not leave

5. A: Ken walked past me without saying hello.
   B: He ________ you.
   1) must not have seen
   2) must see
   3) should not have seen
   4) should not see

6. A: When we went to the restaurant, there were no free tables.
   B: You ________ one.
   1) should not reserve
   2) should have reserved
   3) might not reserve
   4) might have reserved

Culture Corner

Super Bowl

프로 미식축구리그(NFL: National Football League)의 결승전을 Super Bowl이라고 부른다. 이 경기는 1967년부터 시작되었는데, bowl이라는 이름은 경기장의 모습이 움푹 들어간 bowl(사발) 같다고 해서 붙여졌다고 한다. Super Bowl의 인기는 대단한 것이어서 4년마다 있는 대통령의 취임일(1월 20일)이 Super Bowl과 겹치면 취임식을 연기할 정도다. 또한 30초 광고가 무려 26억원을 호가한다. Super Bowl 우승팀은 Vince Lombardi 트로피를 받게 된다. 여기에서 Vince Lombardi는 미식축구 역사상 가장 위대한 감독(head coach)의 이름이다. 그는 Super Bowl이 처음 열렸던 1967년부터 2년 연속 우승을 차지했던 Green Bay Packers의 감독이었다.

2006년 제 40회 Super Bowl에서는 Pittsburgh Steelers가 Seattle Seahawks를 물리치고 우승을 차지했는데, 한국계 선수인 Hines Ward (29, Pittsburgh Steelers)가 MVP(most valuable player)를 차지하는 영예를 얻었다. Hines Ward의 어머니가 역경 속에서 아들을 훌륭히 키워 낸 스토리와 겸손한 생활자세는 선수 자신은 물론 우리에게 굉장한 감동을 준 바 있다.

The Steelers' Hines Ward was voted the most valuable player of Super Bowl XL.

Wrap-up

1. Bob can drive, but he doesn't have a car.
2. May I use your computer?
3. It will rain this weekend.
4. Shall we go out for dinner?
5. We must boil the drinking water because of germs.
6. We had a great time last night. You should have come.

Final Tips

When the sun sets, it gets dark. (O)

When the sun sets, it should get dark. (X)

should는 도덕적 의무를 나타내므로 자연 현상을 기술하는 위 문장에서는 쓸 수 없습니다.

I insisted he eat dinner with us. (O)

I insisted he eats dinner with us. (X)

주장, 명령, 제안 등의 의미가 담긴 동사가 주절에 쓰일 경우 종속절에서 should를 생략하고 동사원형을 씁니다.

You are wrong. / You may be wrong. / You might be wrong.

추측을 나타내는 may와 might는 같은 의미로 쓰입니다.

Translation

해가 지면 어두워집니다.
전 그가 우리와 함께 저녁식사를 해야 한다고 주장했습니다.
당신이 틀렸어요. / 당신이 틀릴 수도 있어요. / 당신이 틀릴 수도 있어요.

Review Test

Choose the correct words.

1. She (will, would) sing whenever she took a bath.

2. The building is now a toy store. It (used to, is used to) be a movie theater.

3. I feel sick. I (wouldn't, shouldn't) have eaten so much food.

4. (Would, Should) you please check this term paper by tomorrow?

5. He proposed that we (raise, raised) money for charity.

6. I don't have time now. Sarah (could, might) be able to help you.

7. It (must, would) have rained yesterday because the ground is wet.

8. I would (rather, like to) take the bus than spend an hour looking for a parking space.

9. If Mozart hadn't died young, he (could finish, could have finished) his great piece "The Requiem".

10. When we got to the restaurant, there were no empty tables. We (should have reserved, have to reserve) a table.

ocus1-Focus3

Chapter 5

SUBJUNCTIVE MOOD

Introduction

Lesson objectives

1. **Subjunctive past** 가정법 과거
2. **Subjunctive past perfect** 가정법 과거완료
3. **Other expressions for subjunctive mood** 가정법의 다른 표현

Check-up

Ben & Olivia's everyday

Olivia : You look tired.

Ben : Well, if you __________ (haven't, hadn't) woken me up in the middle of the night, I __________ (wouldn't, won't) be so tired now.

Olivia : Well, I'm sorry about that, Ben. I wish we __________ (can, could) make some plans for my birthday.

Ben : Of course you do. If you like, I __________ (would, will) book a table for Friday at a fancy restaurant.

Olivia : But, my birthday is on Thursday.

Ben : Like I told you yesterday, I am meeting my friends on Thursday. If we __________ (go, went) out on Friday, it'll be just as good.

Olivia : Well, if you __________ (think, thought) more of your friends than you do of me, you can forget the whole thing.

Ben : I just don't understand you sometimes, Olivia.

Olivia : If you __________ (think, thought) about it again, you'd understand. Anyway, it __________ (will, would) be better if we forgot all about my birthday.

Ben : Calm down, Olivia. If you get into one of your bad moods, it __________ (won't, wouldn't) do any good.

Check-up

Answers

Olivia : You look tired.

Ben : Well, if you (**hadn't**) woken me up in the middle of the night, I (**wouldn't**) be so tired now.

Olivia : Well, I'm sorry about that, Ben. I wish we (**could**) make some plans for my birthday.

Ben : Of course you do. If you like, I (**will**) book a table for Friday at a fancy restaurant.

Olivia : But, my birthday is on Thursday.

Ben : Like I told you yesterday, I am meeting my friends on Thursday. If we (**go**) out on Friday, it'll be just as good.

Olivia : Well, if you (**think**) more of your friends than you do of me, you can forget the whole thing.

Ben : I just don't understand you sometimes, Olivia.

Olivia : If you (**thought**) about it again, you'd understand. Anyway, it (**would**) be better if we forgot all about my birthday.

Ben : Calm down, Olivia. If you get into one of your bad moods, it (**won't**) do any good.

Translation

Olivia : 피곤해 보이네.

Ben : 당신이 한밤중에 깨우지 않았다면, 지금 이렇게 피곤하지 않을 거야.

Olivia : 그 점은 미안하게 생각해, Ben. 내 생일에 무엇을 할 것 인지 정했으면 좋겠어.

Ben : 물론 할 수 있지. 원하면 금요일에 고급 레스토랑에 자리를 예약할게.

Olivia : 그렇지만 내 생일은 목요일이잖아.

Ben : 어제 내가 얘기한 대로, 목요일엔 친구들과 약속이 있어. 우리가 금요일에 나가도 똑 같을 거야.

Olivia : 글쎄, 만약 당신이 나보다 친구들을 더 생각한다면, 다 잊어버려도 돼.

Ben : 난 때로 당신을 이해할 수가 없어, Olivia.

Olivia : 다시 한 번 생각해보면, 이해가 갈 거야. 어쨌든, 내 생일에 대해선 모두 잊는 게 낫겠어.

Ben : 진정해, Olivia. 만약 당신이 이렇게 기분이 상해하면, 좋을 게 없잖아.

1 Focus

Subjunctive Past
가정법 과거

1 직설법 조건문과 가정법 과거

조건문은 실현 가능성이 있는 조건을 표현하고, if절에서 미래를 나타낼 때 현재형 동사가 쓰인다. 반면 가정법 과거는 실현 가능성이 희박한 순수 가정을 표현하고, if절에서 과거형 동사가 쓰인다.

조건문: If I hear any news, I'll call you.
(내가 무슨 소식을 들으면 당신에게 전화할게요.)

가정법: If they offered me the job, I'd take it.
(그들이 나에게 일자리를 준다면 내가 그 일을 할 텐데요.)

2 가정법 과거

현재 사실과 반대되는 것을 가정할 때 쓴다. 조건절에는 동사의 과거형이 나오고, 주절에는 would/should/could/might + 동사원형이 온다. if절에서 be동사의 경우는 원칙적으로 주어에 관계없이 were을 자주 쓴다. '만약 ~한다면 ~할 텐데' 라는 의미이다.

If I saw her, I would give her the message.
(내가 그녀를 본다면, 그 메시지를 전해 줄 텐데요.)

What would you buy if you had a million dollars?
(당신이 백만 달러가 있다면 무엇을 살 겁니까?)

If you helped me, I could pass the exam.
(당신이 나를 도와 준다면 나는 시험에 통과할 수 있을 텐데요.)

He might change his mind if we met him.
(우리가 그를 만난다면 그가 마음을 바꿀 텐데요.)

Task 1

Choose the right verb forms.

1. I'll scream if you (say, said) that one more time.
2. If Tom (didn't go, won't go) to her party, she (would be, was) hurt.
3. If you (look, looked) in the drawer, you'll find your passport.
4. If I (have, had) children, I'd send them to a private school.
5. I (will miss, miss) you if you (move, would move) to Japan.
6. We (could work, will work) this out quicker if we had a computer.

Task 2

Fill in the blanks with correct verb forms. Use the words in parentheses.

1. If we ________ (stay) in a hotel, it would cost too much.
2. If the rain ________ (stop), we'll go out.
3. If Peggy ________ (be) tall, she wouldn't have to look up at people.
4. I won't go out with you if you ________ (wear) that coat.
5. We wouldn't have these problems if we ________ (speak) Chinese.
6. If they ________ (don't) pay him more, he would quit.

REST AREA

Translation

Max	짧은 시간에 집중하게 만드는 텔레비전은 대단한 것 같아.
Max	내가 보기엔 말이야. 어떤 것이 너무 복잡하다면 그것은 좋지 않아. 너무 복잡해서 20초 내에 설명할 수 없다면 아마 그것은 알만한 가치가 없는 걸거야.
Max	내 시간은 소중해. 나는 긴 시간을 한 주제만 생각하며 보낼 수 없어. 생각할 것이 많거든. 나 진짜 바쁜 사람이야.
Alex	여기 3시간 동안이나 텔레비전 앞에 앉아 있는 사람은 누구지?
Max	음....1분에 다섯 가지 생각을 하면서..

2
Focus

Subjunctive Past Perfect
가정법 과거완료

1 자동사와 타동사(Intransitive verbs and transitive verbs)

과거 사실과 반대되는 것을 가정할 때 쓴다. 조건절에는 had + 동사의 과거분사형(p.p.)이 오고, 주절에는 would/should/could/might + have + p.p.가 온다. '만약 ~했다면 ~했을 텐데' 라는 의미이다.

I would have come to the party if I hadn't had to study.
(내가 공부를 하지 않아도 되었으면 파티에 갔을 겁니다.)

If Mozart hadn't died young, he could have finished his great piece Requiem.
(Mozart가 젊은 나이에 죽지 않았다면 그는 위대한 작품 레퀴엠을 끝낼 수 있었을 텐데요.)

What would have happened if I hadn't followed his advice?
(내가 그의 충고를 따르지 않았다면 무슨 일이 일어났을까요?)

If I hadn't been so tired, I might have gone out with her.
(내가 그렇게 피곤하지 않았다면 나는 그녀와 데이트를 했을 텐데요.)

2 혼합구문

조건절에는 가정법 과거완료형이 오고, 주절에서는 가정법 과거형이 올 때 이를 '혼합 가정'이라고 한다. 즉, 조건절에는 had + p.p.가 오고, 주절에는 would/should/could/might + 동사원형이 온다. '만약 ~했다면 ~할 텐데'라는 의미이다.

If we had had a coherent plan at the start, we wouldn't be in this mess now.
(우리가 처음에 일관된 계획이 있었다면 지금 이렇게 혼란스럽지는 않을 겁니다.)

If you hadn't moved so far away, we'd visit you more often.
(당신이 그렇게 멀리 이사 가지 않았다면 우리가 좀 더 자주 갈수 있을 겁니다.)

I wouldn't be so tired if you hadn't woken me up in the middle of the night.
(당신이 나를 한밤중에 깨우지 않았다면 내가 이렇게 피곤하지는 않을 겁니다.)

Task 3

Fill in the blanks using the words in parentheses.

ex

If you had eaten more vegetables, you would be healthier now.

1. If he had been hungry, he ___________ (eat) something.
2. The door __________ (look) better if you hadn't painted it pink.
3. I __________ (buy) it if the sofa had not been on sale.
4. If it __________ (be) so late, I would have called her.
5. If you had taken his advice, you __________ (be) much better now.

Task 4

Write a sentence with if for each situation.

ex

I ate too much, so I feel sick now.

→ If I hadn't eaten so much, I wouldn't feel sick now.

1. The weather was so cold that we couldn't go out.

→ ______________________________________

2. He wasn't tired last night, so he went to the movie.

→ ______________________________________

3. You couldn't leave earlier because you didn't have your car.

→ ______________________________________

4. I didn't win the lottery then, so I am not rich now.

→ ______________________________________

5. I don't have the key, so I can't go into the room.

→ ______________________________________

3 Focus

Other Expressions for Subjunctive Mood
가정법의 다른 표현

1 I wish I knew/had known

(1) I wish … 동사 과거형

현재 사실에 반대되는 것을 바랄 때 쓰는 표현으로 '~하면 좋을 텐데'의 의미이다.

I wish I didn't have so much work tonight.
(내가 오늘 밤에 일을 너무 많이 하지 않으면 좋을 텐데요.)

David wishes he would live in a big city.
(David는 대도시에서 살기를 바랍니다.)

(2) I wish … had + p.p.

과거 사실에 반대되는 것을 바랄 때 쓰는 표현으로 '~했으면 좋았을 텐데'의 의미이다.

I wish you had taught me how to dance.
(당신이 나에게 춤추는 법을 가르쳐 줬으면 좋았을 텐데요.)

Her parents wish she had accepted the offer.
(그녀의 부모는 그녀가 그 제안을 받아 들였으면 하고 바랍니다.)

2 as if/as though

'마치 ~처럼'의 뜻으로 뒤에 가정법 구문이 올 수 있다.

He talks as if he knew her.
(그는 그가 마치 그녀를 아는 것처럼 말합니다.)

Laura looked at me as if she had never seen me before.
(Laura는 전에 나를 전혀 본적이 없는 것처럼 나를 보았습니다.)

3 But for/Without

'~이 없다면'의 뜻으로 가정법 구문에서 쓰인다. 'but for' 보다는 'without' 또는 'if it were not for'가 더 자연스럽다.

But for your help, I couldn't finish the work in time.
(= If it were not for your help, I couldn't finish the work in time.)
(당신의 도움이 없다면 제시간에 그 일을 끝내지 못할 겁니다.)

Without his advice, we would have failed.
(= If it had not been for his advice, we would have failed.)
(그의 도움이 없었다면 우리는 실패했을 겁니다.)

4 It's time

'~할 시간이다, 이제 ~해야지' 라는 의미로, it's time 다음에 과거 시제를 써서 현재를 표현한다.

It's about time you cleaned the car.
(세차를 해야 할 때가 되었습니다.)

It's high time you stopped smoking.
(금연을 해야 할 때 입니다.)

It's time you started for school.
(학교에 가야 할 때입니다.)

cf unless

'if~not'의 의미로 부정의 조건절에서 쓰인다. 가정법에서는 드물게 쓰인다.

I'll be back tomorrow unless there's a plane strike.
(= I'll be back tomorrow if there is not a plane strike.)
(항공사 동맹 파업이 없으면 나는 내일 돌아올 겁니다.)

She said we couldn't go out unless we finished our homework.
(= She said we couldn't go out if we didn't finish our homework.)
(그녀는 우리가 숙제를 마치지 않으면 나갈 수 없다고 말했습니다.)

Task 5

Fill in the blanks by rewriting the sentences. Use the words in parentheses.

1. My wife will be upset if I don't get home early tonight. (unless)

→ My wife will be upset ______________________.

2. If it had not been for the snow, the woman would have been home before dark. (but for)

→ ________________, the woman would have been home before dark.

3. If it were not for air, no living thing could exist. (without)

→ ________________, no living thing could exist.

4. I am sorry I didn't go to the party yesterday. (wish)

→ ________________ to the party yesterday.

5. Because you saved me, I am alive now. (if)

→ ________________, I wouldn't be alive now.

Task 6

Choose the appropriate words.

1. I wish I ________ the answer.
   (1) know (2) knew (3) knows (4) knowing

2. She talks as if she ________ rich.
   (1) were (2) is (3) has been (4) be

3. If Irene ________ another apartment, she would move.
   (1) finds (2) founded (3) has found (4) found

4. If my car hadn't broken down, I ________ over to your place.
   (1) couldn't come (2) would had come
   (3) could have come (4) would came

5. It's time we ________ the kitchen.
   (1) paint (2) painted (3) will paint (4) would have painted

6. If he ________ late tomorrow, the meeting will be called off.
   (1) arrived (2) arrives (3) will arrive (4) has arrived

Culture Corner

DIY- Do it yourself!

DIY는 Do it yourself의 약자로 세계 2차 대전 직후 영국에서 유래되었습니다. 전쟁으로 파괴된 도시를 재건하면서 주택 수리와 개선에 관한 정보지 'DO IT YOURSELF'가 발간되었습니다. 그 후 이 문화는 서구 각국으로 퍼져나갔습니다.

미국인들도 스스로 뭔가를 만들고 해내는 것을 무척이나 좋아합니다. 취미로 새장(bird cage)이나 찬장(cupboard), 책장(bookcase) 등을 만드는 사람들도 있고, 귀걸이 등의 장신구(accessories)를 손수 만들거나, 옷감을 염색하여(dye) 독특한 디자인의 옷을 만드는 사람들도 많습니다. 가끔씩은 벼룩시장(flea market)등을 통해 자신이 만든 창작 작품들을 팔기도 합니다. 그 외에도 모형 자동차, 비행기, 배 등을 조립하는(put together, assemble) 등 뭔가 창조적이고 자신이 직접 해보는 취미 생활을 즐기는 사람들이 많습니다. 또, 새로 집을 꾸밀 때도 우리는 인테리어 회사에 부탁하여 하는 경우가 대부분이지만, 미국인들은 스스로 장식하는(decorate)것을 좋아해서, 직접 벽지를 바르고(paper the wall) 페인트칠도 직접하며 예쁜 울타리를 치면서(make the fence) 가족들이 직접 하는 경우가 많습니다. 그래서 혼자서도 잘 해낼 수 있도록 요령을 가르쳐 주는 DIY(Do it yourself) 프로그램들이 인기가 있습니다. 또한 가정용 건축 자재 유통 회사(home improvement retailer)인 Home Depot와 같은 곳은 늘 재료와 공구를 사려는 사람들로 북적거립니다.

이렇게 스스로 하려는 경향은 우리나라에 비해 서비스 요금(service charge)이 비싸고 서비스를 받기 위해 기다리는 시간도 길기 때문에 더욱 강해진 것 같습니다. 예를 들어 식탁이나 가구가 필요한 경우라도, 완제품을 사기보다는, 조립품을 사서 조립하여 쓰는 경우가 더 흔합니다. 여기에 익숙하지 않은 우리나라 유학생들 중에는 가구점(IKEA 등)에서 가구를 사온 다음날, 서툰 솜씨로 그것을 조립하느라고 하루 온종일 낑낑거리며 고생(?) 아닌 고생을 하기도 합니다.

It's a do-it-yourself project.

Wrap-up

1. If I hear any news, I'll call you.
2. If they offered me the job, I would take it.
3. If I hadn't been so tired, I might have gone out with her.
4. I wish I didn't have much work tonight.
5. Without his advice, we would have failed.

Final Tips

If I find your wallet, I'll tell you. (O)

If I found a wallet in the street, I'd take it to the police. (O)

조건문은 실현 가능성이 있는 조건을 표현하고, 가정법은 실현 가능성이 적은 순수 가정을 표현합니다.

If I were you, I wouldn't buy that bag. (O)

If I was you, I wouldn't buy that bag. (?)

가정법 과거에서는 주어와 상관없이 be동사를 were로 쓰는 게 원칙이나 회화에서는 was를 쓰기도 합니다.

I wish Cathy were here now. (O)

I wish Cathy was here now. (O)

I wish Cathy is here now. (X)

I wish 뒤에는 가정법 구문이 옵니다. 현재 이루지 못한 일을 가정할 때 과거동사를 씁니다.

Translation

당신 지갑을 발견하면 알려 줄게요.
내가 길에서 지갑을 발견하면 경찰서로 가져갈 텐데요.
Cathy가 지금 여기 있으면 좋을 텐데요.

Review Test

Write the correct forms of the verbs in parentheses to complete the sentences.

1. If I _________ (know) her name, I would tellyou.
   (= As I don't know her name, I can't tell you.)

2. What would have happened if I _________ (not, smell) gas?
   (=Nothing happened as I smelled gas.)

3. If he _________ (take) the doctor's advice, he might still be alive.
   (=As he didn't take the doctor's advice, he is dead now.)

4. If she _________ (find) your keys, she'll tell you.

5. I wish you _________ (leave) that unsaid.

Choose the correct words.

6. If he had not been killed in the road accident, he (should have been, would be) 23 years old today.

7. Caroline would have studied English if she (had known, knew) its importance.

8. (Should, Had) you have any comments or ideas for our web site, please let us know.

9. If I (didn't, wouldn't) go to the meeting, they'd be disappointed.

10. If the sun (rises, were to rise) in the west, I would change my mind.

ocus 1-Focus 3

Chapter 6

THE PASSIVE

Introduction

Lesson objectives

1. Active and passive 능동태와 수동태

2. Passive verb forms 수동태 동사 형태

3. Special passive structure 수동태 특수 구문

Check-up

Ben & Olivia's everyday

Ben : Why aren't you ready?

Olivia : I'm not going.

Ben : Why not? The restaurant ________ (booked, is booked).

Olivia : I don't care. My birthday has ________ (ruined, been ruined).

Ben : Are you still upset about me going out with my friends?

Olivia : That would ________ (upset, be upset) anybody.

Ben : No, only someone as unreasonable as you would ________ (upset, be upset) by that.

Olivia : Unreasonable people ________ (upset, are upset) for no good reason. It was unreasonable of you to think that you could go out with your friends on my birthday and think I would be okay ________ (by, with) that.

Ben : Look, I'm sorry, all right? Just get ready and we can still make the booking.

Check-up

Answers

Ben : Why aren't you ready?

Olivia : I'm not going.

Ben : Why not? The restaurant (**is booked**).

Olivia : I don't care. My birthday has (**been ruined**).

Ben : Are you still upset about me going out with my friends?

Olivia : That would (**upset**) anybody.

Ben : No, only someone as unreasonable as you would (**be upset**) by that.

Olivia : Unreasonable people (**are upset**) for no good reason. It was unreasonable of you to think that you could go out with your friends on my birthday and think I would be okay (**with**) that.

Ben : Look, I'm sorry, all right? Just get ready and we can still make the booking.

Translation

Ben : 왜 준비 안 해?

Olivia : 나 안 갈 거야.

Ben : 왜? 레스토랑 예약되어 있단 말이야.

Olivia : 상관없어. 내 생일 다 망쳤잖아.

Ben : 내가 친구들이랑 놀러 나간 것 때문에 아직도 화났어?

Olivia : 누구라도 화가 날 걸.

Ben : 아니지. 당신처럼 이성적이지 못한 사람만 그런 일로 화내는 거야.

Olivia : 이성적이지 못한 사람들은 특별한 이유 없이도 화가 나. 내 생일에 친구들이랑 놀러 나가 놓고 내가 괜찮을 거라고 생각하는 당신이 이성적이지 못한 거라고.

Ben : 내가 잘못했어. 알았지? 얼른 준비하면 예약 시간 맞출 수 있을 거야.

1 Focus

Active and Passive
능동태와 수동태

1 능동태와 수동태 비교

(1) Edison invented the light bulb. (Edison은 전구를 발명하였습니다.)

(2) The light bulb was invented by Edison. (전구는 Edison에 의해 발명되었습니다.)

이 두 문장의 뜻은 같다. 그러나, 무엇에 관해 얘기하고 있는 가가 다르다. 즉, (1)은 발명가 Edison에 관해서, (2)는 전구에 관해서 말하고 있다. (1)과 같이 주어(subject)가 행위자(agent)인 경우를 능동태(active)라 하고, (2)와 같이 주어(subject)가 행위를 당하는 경우를 수동태(passive)라고 한다.

cf have, possess, reach처럼 상태나 소유를 나타내는 동사는 타동사이지만 수동태로 쓰이지 않는다.

2 문장 형식

능동태는 '주어 + 동사 + 목적어'의 형식을 취하고, 수동태는 '주어 + be + 동사의 과거분사(p.p.) + by행위자'의 형식을 취한다. 수동태 문장의 주어는 능동태 문장의 목적어에 해당한다.

The company employed a hundred people. (능동태)

A hundred people were employed by the company. (수동태)

(그 회사는 백 명의 사람들을 고용했습니다.)

(백 명의 사람들이 그 회사에 의해 고용되었습니다.)

Active	Passive
Martha cooks our meals. (Martha는 우리의 식사를 준비합니다.)	Our meals are cooked by Martha. (우리의 식사는 Martha에 의해 준비됩니다.)
Your little boy broke this window. (당신의 아이가 이 창문을 깼습니다.)	This window was broken by your little boy. (이 창문이 당신의 아이에 의해 깨어졌습니다.)
They have increased the bus fares. (그들은 버스 요금을 인상했습니다.)	The bus fares have been increased. (버스 요금이 인상되었습니다.)

3 행위자 (agent)를 언급하지 않는 경우

무슨 일이 일어났는지 사건 자체에 관심이 있을 때는 행위자를 생략한다.

The man was arrested last week.
(그 남자는 지난 주에 체포되었습니다.)

How much money was stolen?
(얼마나 많은 돈을 도난 당했습니까?)

The streets are cleaned every morning.
(거리는 매일 아침 청소 됩니다.)

English is spoken in Australia.
(영어는 호주에서 쓰여집니다.)

The details should be checked.
(세부적인 부분들이 점검 되어야 합니다.)

All flights were canceled because of fog.
(안개 때문에 모든 비행이 취소되었습니다.)

4 수동태를 주로 쓰는 경우

(1) 구어체 보다는 문어체에서 많이 쓰이며, 보고서나 뉴스 등에서 많이 쓰인다.

Pineapples are exported to Europe.
(파인애플은 유럽으로 수출됩니다.)

Cars parked here will be towed away.
(여기에 주차된 차들은 견인 될 겁니다.)

A number of model prisoners have been released.
(많은 모범 죄수들이 석방되었습니다.)

The conference will be held in Paris next month.
(그 회의는 다음 달에 파리에서 열릴 겁니다.)

(2) 앞에 언급한 것을 연결하여 말할 때 쓰인다.

She lives in an old house. It was built in 1930.
(그녀는 오래된 집에 삽니다. 그것은 1930년에 지어졌습니다.)

This milk tastes bad. I think it was left out of the fridge for a long time.
(이 우유는 맛이 이상합니다. 그것이 오랫동안 냉장고 밖에 있었던 것 같습니다.)

Golf is one of the most popular sports. It is played by people of all ages.
(골프는 가장 인기 있는 스포츠 중 하나입니다. 모든 연령층의 사람들이 골프를 칩니다.)

Task 1

Choose the correct words.

1. Our car (stole, was stolen) near the police station.
2. The storm (swept, was swept) across the north of England.
3. The new road will (be finished, finish) in November.
4. Doctors (use, is used) laser beams in surgery.
5. What (is, does) this flower called in English?
6. Ted (fired, was fired) from his job.

Task 2

Complete the sentences using the words in parentheses.

ex

Spanish ______________ (speak) in Mexico.
→ Spanish is spoken in Mexico.

1. Three swimming pools __________ (build) last year.
2. Butter ___________ (make) from milk.
3. The movie will ____________ (show) on TV soon.

4. His mother ___________ (die) when he was 16 years old.

5. Guernica _________ (paint) by Picasso in 1937.

6. She'll _________ (finish) the job before this weekend.

REST AREA

Translation

Pete(Barber) 오늘 어때?
Max 좋아요.
Max 저는 머리 옆 부분을 자르고 머리 가운데 꼭대기 부분에 뾰족하게 힘을 주고 싶어요. 그리고 초록색으로 염색도 해주세요. 알겠지요?
Pete 어떻게 할까요, 부인?
Mother 늘 하던 대로 자르세요, Pete씨.
Max 흠. 이 이발사는 누구에게서 돈이 나오는지 아는군.

REST AREA

Translation

Pete 어때요? 맘에 들어요?
Max 완벽해요.
Max 지금까지 해본 헤어 스타일 중에 제일 좋네요.
Max 면도칼을 든 사람을 비판하면 절대 안돼....

2

Focus

Passive Verb Forms
수동태 동사 형태

1 Simple present (단순현재)

am/is/are + 동사의 과거분사(p.p.)

More chocolate is eaten in the US than in any other country.
(미국에선 다른 어느 나라보다도 더 많은 초콜릿이 소비됩니다.)

Computer data are stored on disks.
(컴퓨터 자료가 디스크에 저장됩니다.)

Passengers are requested to remain seated.
(승객들은 가만히 앉아있도록 요청 받았습니다.)

2 Simple past (단순과거)

was/were + p.p.

These keys were found in the locker.
(이 열쇠들은 사물함에서 발견되었습니다.)

A serious error was made in this week's assignment.
(심각한 오류가 이번 주 과제에서 만들어졌습니다.)

All the trouble was caused by him.
(모든 문제들이 그로 인해 야기되었습니다.)

3 Simple future (단순미래)

will/be going to + be + p.p.

The shop will be closed for two months.
(그 가게는 두 달 동안 문을 닫게 될 것입니다.)

The mail is going to be delivered this afternoon.
(편지가 오늘 오후에 도착할 것입니다.)

Food production will be affected by the drought.
(음식물의 생산은 가뭄에 의해 영향을 받게 될 것입니다.)

4 The passive with modal auxiliary verbs (법조동사가 있는 수동태)

can/may/must/should etc. + be + p.p.

Seats may not be reserved.
(자리가 예약되지 않을 지도 모릅니다.)

This product should be refrigerated after opening.
(이 상품은 개봉 후 냉장보관 되어야만 합니다.)

All orders must be paid in advance.
(모든 주문을 할 때는 미리 돈이 지불되어야만 합니다.)

5 Progressive (진행형)

am/is/are/was/were + being + p.p.

The carpet is being cleaned.
(그 카펫은 청소되고 있는 중입니다.)

The building where I work is being renovated now.
(내가 일하는 건물이 지금 개조되고 있는 중입니다.)

When I arrived at the party, dinner was being served.
(내가 파티에 도착했을 때 저녁이 제공되고 있는 중이었습니다.)

6 Perfect (완료형)

have/has/had + been + p.p.

The two children have been found alive.
(두 아이가 살아있는 채로 발견되었습니다.)

The exam has been canceled by the teacher.
(그 시험은 선생님에 의해 취소되었습니다.)

A lot of new buildings have been built lately.
(최근에 많은 새 건물들이 지어졌습니다.)

Task 3

Fill in the blanks with correct verb forms in passive sentences.

ex

They didn't invite me to the party.

→ I was not invited to the party.

1. Fast driving causes many accidents.
   → Many accidents ___________ by fast driving.
2. The tornado hit several cities last night.
   → Several cities ___________ by the tornado last night.
3. The teacher is not properly explaining the directions.
   → The directions _______________ by the teacher.
4. The company may hire him again.
   → He may ________ again by the company.
5. The man has just done the task.
   → The task ____________ by the man.
6. We will make many changes to improve our image.
   → Many changes _____________ to improve our image.

Task 4

Choose the best answer for each blank.

1. Please don't come in here. The room ___________.
   (1) is being cleaned (2) is cleaning
   (3) have cleaned (4) cleans
2. George ____________ the letter to the college yesterday.
   (1) was posted (2) posted
   (3) will be posted (4) will post

3. Dinner __________ from 5:00 to 9:00 p.m.

(1) was serving　　(2) is served

(3) serves　　(4) be served

4. Membership cards must __________ at the gate.

(1) be shown　　(2) be showing

(3) have shown　　(4) showed

5. The parcel hasn't __________ yet.

(1) had sent　　(2) being sent

(3) been sent　　(4) sent

6. When are you going to __________ the actor?

(1) be interviewed　　(2) interviewed

(3) has interviewed　　(4) interview

3
Focus

Special Passive Structure
수동태 특수 구문

1 I was given···.

능동태에서 목적어가 두 개인 문장은 두 개의 수동태 문장을 만든다. 주로 give, teach, ask, offer, pay, tell, show 등의 동사가 쓰이는 문장의 경우에 두 개의 수동태 문장이 가능하다.

He gave me the information.
(그는 나에게 그 정보를 주었습니다.)

→ I was given the information by him
(나는 그에 의해 그 정보를 얻었습니다.)

→ The information was given to me by him.
(그 정보가 그에 의해 나에게 주어졌습니다.)

Julie will teach us English.
(Julie는 우리에게 영어를 가르칠 겁니다.)

→ We will be taught English by Julie.
(우리는 Julie에게서 영어를 배울 겁니다.)

→ English will be taught to us by Julie.
(영어는 Julie에 의해 우리에게 가르쳐질 겁니다.)

2 It is said that···

능동태에서 that절이 목적어인 경우, 수동태에서 'it + is/was+ p.p. + that절' 구문을 만든다. 특히 말하는 사람을 밝힐 필요가 없을 경우에 쓰인다. 주로 say, think, expect, hope, suppose, believe, explain, report, suggest 등의 동사가 이러한 수동태 구문에서 쓰인다.

It is said that Michael is in love with Jessica.
(= People say that Michael is in love with Jessica.)
(사람들은 Michael이 Jessica와 사랑에 빠졌다고 말합니다.)

It was expected that he would be promoted.
(그가 승진될 것으로 기대되었습니다.)

It was reported that the Prime Minister had suffered from heart disease.
(그 수상이 심장병으로 고통 받은 것으로 보도되었습니다.)

3 Get

때때로 수동태에서 be동사 대신에 get을 쓰기도 한다. 특히 상태가 아닌 동작을 나타낼 때, 또는 예기치 못한 일이 발생했을 때 쓴다.

Our dog got run over by a truck.
(우리의 개가 트럭에 치였습니다.)

The man got arrested for murder.
(그 남자는 살인죄로 체포되었습니다.)

There was a car accident, but nobody got hurt.
(차 사고가 있었지만, 아무도 다치지 않았습니다.)

get은 상태를 나타내는 동사와는 쓰지 않는다.

cf Nothing is known about the newcomer.
(새로 온 사람에 대해 아무것도 알려진 것이 없습니다.)
Nothing gets known about the newcomer. (X)

Task 5

I. Complete the following passive sentences.

1. They offer most employees company shares.
→ Most employees ___________ company shares.
2. People say that the quiz champion has lost his memory.
→ It ___________ that the quiz champion has lost his memory.
3. They did not give us enough time.
→ We ___________ enough time.

II. Complete the sentences using get/got + the words in parentheses.

4. I used to have a motorcycle, but it ___________ (steal).
5. How much did you ___________ (pay) last week?

6. They ___________ (marry) in 2001.

Task 6

If the underlined parts are incorrect, change them. If the sentence is correct, write "correct".

1. I born in Seoul in 1975.
   → ______________

2. The song has been sang many times by the choir.
   → ______________

3. Sugar is sold at that store.
   → ______________

4. I feel we are being following by somebody.
   → ______________

5. The strange man was disappeared three days ago.
   → ______________

6. The bank was robbed yesterday.
   → ______________

Culture Corner

You want to bet?

우리 말에서와 같이 영어에서도 'You want to bet?(너 내기 할래?)' 라는 말을 곧잘 합니다. 내기를 걸 만큼 확실할 때는 'I bet.' 'You bet.' 이라는 표현을 씁니다. 'I bet he will come.'이라고 하면, 정말 내기를 한다기 보다 그만큼 확신한다는 의미입니다. 'Can you help me tonight?' 라고 물었을 때, 'You bet!'이라고 답하면, '네가 내기를 해도 된다.' 라는 말이니, 분명히 도와주겠다는 뜻이 됩니다. 'Sure. No problem. No sweat.' 등과 비슷합니다.

'He says that he's being promoted.(그가 승진될 거라고 떠들고 다녀.)' 라는 말을 듣고, 'I wouldn't bet on it.' 이라고 하면 '내기를 안 하겠다', 즉, '그럴 리가 없다'는 뜻이 됩니다. '그런 일은 결코 일어나지 않는다' 라는 표현으로 'All bets are off.' 를 쓰기도 합니다. 또한 'I think taking a taxi is a better bet.' 이라고 하면 '택시를 타는 것이 더 낫겠다'는 말입니다. '잘 선택했다.' 라는 뜻으로 'That's a good bet.' 이라는 표현도 흔히 씁니다.

정말 확실하다고 말하고 싶을 때는 입고 있는 신발, 마지막 가진 돈, 심지어 목숨까지 내기 한다고 표현합니다. 즉, 'You bet your boots, You bet your bottom dollar. You bet your life.' 라고 말합니다. 또한 '가지고 있는 농장이라도 내기에 걸 정도로 확실하다.'라는 뜻으로 'I'd bet the farm on it.' 이라고도 합니다. 이렇게까지 믿어 달라고 나온다면, 믿어주어야 옳을 것 같습니다.

I bet he will come.

A: Can you help me tonight? B: You bet.

A: He says that he's being promoted. B: I wouldn't bet on it.

I think taking a taxi is a better bet.

That's a good bet. You bet your life.

I'd bet the farm on it. All bets are off.

Wrap-up

1. Edison invented the light bulb.
2. The light bulb was invented by Edison.
3. English is spoken in Australia.
4. She lives in an old house. It was built in 1930.
5. Seats may not be reserved.
6. The carpet is being cleaned,
7. The two children have been found alive.

Final Tips

The room cleans every day. (X)

The room is cleaned every day. (O)

주어가 동작의 주체가 아니라 대상일 때는 수동태를 씁니다.

The problem was disappeared. (X)

The problem has disappeared. (O)

appear, disappear, happen 등의 자동사는 수동태로 쓸 수 없습니다.

There was a fight last night, but nobody got hurt. (O)

He gets liked by everybody. (X)

수동태 구문에서 be 동사 대신 get을 쓰기도 합니다. get+p.p.는 동작을 나타내거나 예기치 못한 일이 발생하였을 때 씁니다. 그러나 상태를 나타낼 때는 get+p.p.를 쓰지 않습니다.

Translation

매일 방을 청소합니다.
문제가 사라졌습니다.
어젯밤 불이 났지만 아무도 다치지 않았습니다.

Review Test

Choose the correct words.

1. Elephants are perhaps the only animals that (have hunted, have been hunted) for their teeth.

2. This university (was found, was founded) in 1954.

3. Mom (persuaded, was persuaded) me to go to the dentist.

4. The people (elect, are elected) the president in the U.S.

5. Culture must (transmit, be transmitted) from one generation to the next through learning and experience.

Indicate whether the sentences are correct (O) or incorrect (X).

6. She wouldn't have injured if she had been wearing a seat belt. ( )

7. Sorry about the noise. The road is being repaired. ( )

8. My little nephews will be taken care by me until my aunt returns. ( )

9. My glasses got broke in the fight. ( )

10. To become a proverb, a saying has to be taken up and used by the people. ( )

Chapter 7

Review

(Chapter 1～6)

Chapter 1 Words and Sentences

1. Components of sentences (문장 구성 요소)

He bought a small red car.
phrase(구)

When he saw her, he ran away.
clause(절)

2. Parts of speech (품사)

The questions were very simple and easy.

The	questions	were	very	simple	and	easy
Det (한정사)	N (명사)	V (동사)	Adv (부사)	Adj (형용사)	Conj (접속사)	Adj (형용사)

3. Sentence role (문장 안에서의 역할)

We saw the movie last night.

We	saw	the movie	last night
S (주어)	V (동사)	O (목적어)	Adv (부사적 어구)

Task 1

Indicate the class of the underlined words.

ex

N(noun), Pro(pronoun), V(verb), Adj(adjective), Adv(adverb),
Det(determiner), Prep(preposition), Conj(conjunction)

Many Africans believed that you didn't exist until you had a name.
(1) (2) (3) (4) (5)

They held special ceremonies for naming babies.
(6) (7)

Task 2

Identify the underlined part as either a main(independent) clause or a subordinate clause.

ex

Main clause (M), Subordinate clause (S)

1. Before you accept the invitation, you should ask your mother. ( )
2. Although he was better at math, he loved art. ( )
3. We all enjoyed the dinner that Dad cooked last Sunday. ( )
4. I need to mow the lawn before the sun sets. ( )
5. When she pressed the button, the elevator stopped. ( )

Task 3

Identify the underlined part as S(subject), V(verb), O(object), C(complement) or Adv(adverbial).

1. During the industrial revolution, workers began using machines. ( )
2. Robert Fulton's steamboat improved water transportation. ( )
3. Alexander Graham Bell invented the telephone. ( )
4. George Stephenson's Rocket was the world's first railroad train. ( )
5. Many inventions improved people's standard of living. ( )

Chapter 2 Verbs

1. Classification of verb (동사의 분류)

- He just left.
  V (동사) = left

- Do you know his name?
  V (동사) = know, O (목적어) = his name

- Leaves turn red and yellow in the fall.
  V (동사) = turn, C (보어) = red and yellow

- They found me a ticket.
  V (동사) = found, IO (간접목적어) = me, DO (직접목적어) = a ticket

- The long walk made us hungry.
  V (동사) = made, O (목적어) = us, OC (목적보어) = hungry

2. Agreement of subjects and verbs (주어와 동사의 일치)

- Nancy looks tired.

- Nancy and Linda look tired.

Task 4

Choose the correct verb forms.

1. There (isn't, aren't) any cheese in the refrigerator.
2. Economics (is, are) his strong subject.
3. We watched him (get, to get) three gold medals.
4. I felt (nervously, nervous) in front of the interviewers.
5. The poor farmer (married with, married) the princess.

Task 5

Find seven errors in the paragraph and correct them.

Yoon-hee go to a college in Texas. This is her freshman year, and everything seem new and exciting to her. After two months at the college, she have many friends and don't feel lonely. She study hard and get good grades, but she also enjoy life with her friends.

______, ______, ______, ______, ______, ______, ______

Task 6

Correct the verb forms in the sentences. If the sentence is correct, write "correct".

1. A strange thing happens at our shop yesterday.

   ________ → ________

2. The dishes on the shelf looks clean.

   ________ → ________

3. Tom wanted me to walk the dog in the park.

   ________ → ________

4. There was Amy and her son in the doorway.

   ________ → ________

5. Last week the lake freezes hard enough for skating.

   ________ → ________

Chapter 3 Tense

1. Verb forms (동사 형태)

She talks about herself.

She talked about herself.

She is talking about herself.

She has talked about herself.

2. Simple tense (단순 시제)

I know them.

3. Perfect (완료형)

They have just returned.

4. Progressive(진행형)

We're staying at a wonderful place.

Task 7

Fill in the blanks with the correct verb forms. Use the words in parentheses.

1. Ellen has __________ (stay) here for a month.
2. I __________ (buy) the chocolate last Valentine's Day.
3. Let's go out now. It's not __________(rain).
4. When did you __________ (get) lost in the woods?
5. Joe wrote the letter. But he hasn't __________ (mail) it yet.

Task 8

Indicate whether the underlined parts are correct or incorrect. Correct the ones that are incorrect.

correct incorrect

1. The car accident has happened a week ago. ______ ______

→ __________

2. I have been waiting for you for two hours. ______ ______

→ __________

3. Usually many people are learning to swim when they are young.

→ __________ ______ ______

4. The last time I saw her in L.A., she was looking for a job.

→ __________ ______ ______

5. When I got home, it was very quiet. Everybody has gone out.

→ __________ ______ ______

Task 9

Choose the correct answers to complete the sentences.

1. A: Did you see the sports news on TV last night?
   B: No. I ________ to bed early.
   1) has gone 2) went 3) was going

2. A: Do you meet Carol and Matt often?
   B: No. I ________ them for two years.
   1) haven't seen 2) didn't see 3) don't see

3. A: How fast __________ when the accident happened?
   B: 90 km/h.
   1) are you driving 2) do you drive 3) were you driving

4. A: _________ to the radio?

B: No. It's too noisy. Please turn it off.

1) Do you listen   2) Have you ever listened   3) Are you listening

5. A: How often _________ to the movies?

B: Once or twice a month.

1) do you go   2) were you going   3) have you gone

REST AREA

Translation

Max 내 숙제를 도와줄래? pronoun이 뭐야?

Alex Pro(professional)인 noun? 아마추어의 지위를 잃은 noun이야.

Max ??!! 선생님이 나의 독창성에 특별 점수를 줄지 의문이네.

Chapter 4 Auxiliary Verbs

1. Modal auxiliary verbs

You can come if you want.

You might enjoy the movie.

2. may/could/must/should + have + p.p.

I must have dropped my gloves in the subway.

She shouldn't have eaten so much.

Task 10

Use these modal auxiliary verbs to complete the sentences.

can't	must	have to	might	would	shouldn't

1. You've been driving for six hours. You _________ be tired.
2. I'm afraid you will _________ work next weekend.
3. He was upset by your remarks. You _________ have said that.
4. Could you speak a little louder? I _________ hear you well.
5. _________ you mind watching my bag for a few minutes?
6. I can't come, but why don't you ask Ben? He _________ be able to come.

Task 11

Choose the best words to complete the sentences.

1. She insisted that he __________ dinner with them.

   1) has 2) have 3) having

2. Mom, __________ I have spaghetti with cream sauce for lunch?

   1) may 2) am 3) would

3. The cause of the flu __________ have been bacteria.

   1) will 2) might 3) should

4. I __________ leave early because I wasn't feeling well.

   1) shall 2) used to 3) had to

5. The street is wet. It __________ have rained yesterday.

   1) must 2) can 3) should

Task 12

Choose the best words to complete the sentences.

1. A: Where is Tina?
   B: She __________ be upstairs. I saw her go up there ten minutes ago.

   1) will 2) must 3) used to

2. A: Did you go to the opera last night?
   B: No. We __________ have gone, but we decided not to.

   1) could 2) must 3) shouldn't

3. A: I wonder why Christine didn't come to the party.
   B: She __________ not have been invited.

   1) should 2) will 3) might

4. A: Is that guy Greg?
   B: No, he __________ be Greg. Greg is much taller than him.

   1) won't 2) must not 3) can't

5. A: Is Nick here yet?
   B: Not yet, but he __________ be here soon.

   1) can't 2) should 3) won't

Chapter 5 Subjunctive Mood

1.Subjunctive past (가정법 과거)

If I saw her, I would give her the message.

2. Subjunctive past perfect (가정법 과거 완료)

I would have come to the party if I hadn't had to study.

3. Other expressions (다른 표현)

I wish I knew the answer.

She talks as if she were rich.

Task 13

Choose the right verb forms.

1. You could do it if you (try, tried).
2. If I were not so poor, I could (buy, have bought) the computer.
3. If everyone (is, were) ready, we will start the lesson.
4. We will miss you very much if you (leave, will leave) Korea.
5. If the driver had stopped at the red light, the accident would not (happen, have happened).

Task 14

Fill in the blanks with correct verb forms. Use the words in parentheses.

1. I wish Laura __________ (be) here now.
2. I'd have forgotten Sarah's birthday if you ____________ (not remind) me.
3. If I ___________ (know) his email address, I would write to him.
4. If the weather ___________ (be) good, we will eat outdoors.
5. He talks as if he ____________ (be) my teacher.

Task 15

Complete a sentence for each situation.

ex

As I am not a bird, I can't fly to you.

→ If I were a bird, I could fly to you.

1. As the car is very expensive, I can't buy it.
   → If the car ____________, I could buy it.

2. As we didn't take a shortcut, we missed the train.
   → If we ____________ a shortcut, we would not have missed the train.

3. When I were a child, I didn't learn how to play the piano. Now I regret it.
   → I wish I ____________ how to play the piano.

4. I didn't go to the meeting last night, so I am not tired now.
   → If I had gone to the meeting last night, I ____________ tired now.

5. If it were not for your help, I couldn't start the business.
   → Without ____________, I couldn't start the business.

Chapter 6 The Passive

1. Active and passive (능동태와 수동태)

The company employed a hundred people.

A hundred people were employed by the company.

2. Passive verb forms (수동태 동사 형태)

The mail is going to be delivered this afternoon.

A lot of new buildings have been built lately.

Task 16

Fill in the blanks to complete passive sentences. Use the words in parentheses.

1. The Taj Mahal __________ around 1640. (build)
2. His glasses got __________ in the fight. (break)
3. English is worth learning. It __________ in many countries. (speak)
4. It __________ that he is somewhere in France. (say)
5. When I arrived at the restaurant, the food was __________. (serve)

Task 17

Choose the proper words in parentheses.

1. The ticket (costs, is cost) two dollars.
2. His teacher (pleased, was pleased) with the news.
3. Linda (could hire, could be hired) by a new computer company.
4. Her child (disappeared, was disappeared) at about 4:00 in the afternoon.
5. My camera (has, has been) stolen from my office.

Task 18

Find all the grammatical errors and correct them. If the sentence is correct, write "correct".

1. The gate is shut at eight in the evening.

   ________ → ________

2. Have you ever be bitten by a dog?

   ________ → ________

3. The whole family should been invited.

   ________ → ________

4. Smoking doesn't permit in public places.

   ________ → ________

5. Applications must be submitted by December 1.

   ________ → ________

ocus1-Focus3

Chapter 8

INFINITIVE AND GERUNDS

Introduction

Lesson objectives

1. To-infinitives to부정사

2. Gerunds 동명사

3. Verb + to-infinitives/ ~ing 동사 + to부정사/ ~ing

Check-up

Ben & Olivia's everyday

Olivia : Where are we planning _________ (to go, going) for the weekend?

Ben : Didn't we decide _________ (to spend, spending) the weekend at home?

Olivia : Yeah, we did. But I really wanna get away for a bit. Let's go somewhere with a nice beach. I enjoy _________ (to lie, lying) on the beach.

Ben : But I don't want to sit on the beach for the entire weekend.

Olivia : Well, I don't mind _________ (to drive, driving) around somewhere with a nice scenery. Oh, you also promised _________ (to go, going) to the mountains with me.

Imagine _________ (to sit, sitting) on a beautiful mountain resort in front of a warm fire!

Ben : A resort? I'm afraid we can't afford _________ (to spend, spending) too much money at the moment.

Olivia : You still owe me for ruining my birthday, remember? Where _________ (to go, going) and that's that.

Check-up

Answers

Olivia : Where are we planning (to go) for the weekend?

Ben : Didn't we decide (to spend) the weekend at home?

Olivia : Yeah, we did. But I really wanna get away for a bit. Let's go somewhere with a nice beach. I enjoy (lying) on the beach.

Ben : But I don't want to sit on the beach for the entire weekend.

Olivia : Well, I don't mind (driving) around somewhere with a nice scenery. Oh, you also promised (to go) to the mountains with me. Imagine (sitting) on a beautiful mountain resort in front of a warm fire!

Ben : A resort? I'm afraid we can't afford (to spend) too much money at the moment.

Olivia : You still owe me for ruining my birthday, remember? Where (to go) and that's that.

Translation

Olivia : 주말에 어디 갈까?

Ben : 집에 있기로 하지 않았어?

Olivia : 응, 그랬지. 그런데 어디론가 잠시 떠나고 싶어. 멋진 해변이 있는 곳 가자. 해변가에 누워있는 거 좋아.

Ben : 하지만 난 주말 내내 해변가에 앉아 있고 싶지 않아.

Olivia : 풍경이 좋은 곳으로 드라이브 가는 것도 괜찮아. 아, 당신 산에 같이 가기로 약속도 했었잖아. 아름다운 휴양림에서 따뜻한 불 앞에 앉아 있는 거 상상해봐.

Ben : 휴양림? 지금 그렇게 많은 돈을 쓸 형편이 안 돼.

Olivia : 당신 내 생일 망쳐서 나한테 빚지고 있는 거 기억하지? 어디로 갈 지 이것만 정해.

1 Focus

To-infinitives
to부정사

Infinitive(부정사) 라는 것은 인칭, 수, 시제의 영향을 받지 않고 동사의 원형을 그대로 유지하는 것을 말한다. To 없이 동사의 원형이 오는 것을 bare infinitive(원형 부정사)라고 하고, to와 함께 쓰이는 것을 to-infinitive (to부정사)라고 한다.

1 부정사의 용법

(1) 명사의 역할

To get up early in the morning is hard for me. (주어)
(아침에 일찍 일어나는 것이 저에게는 힘듭니다.)

His ambition is to be the CEO of the company. (보어)
(그의 야망은 그 회사의 최고 경영자가 되는 것입니다.)

I don't want to live here anymore. (목적어)
(저는 여기 더 이상 살고 싶지 않습니다.)

It is difficult to convince him. (It–가주어, to부정사–진주어)
(그를 납득시키는 것은 힘듭니다.)

(2) 형용사의 역할

Jessica is not the type of person to lie.
(Jessica는 거짓말을 할 타입의 사람이 아닙니다.)

We don't have time to watch TV.
(우리는 TV를 볼 시간이 없습니다.)

(3) 부사의 역할

They went to Australia to study English.
(그들은 영어를 공부하기 위해 호주에 갔습니다.)

I'm glad to see you again.
(저는 당신을 다시 보게 되어 기쁩니다.)

② V + to – infinitive (동사 + to부정사)

(1) **주로 주어의 말이나 생각을 나타내는 다음 동사 뒤에 to-부정사가 목적어로 온다:** agree, offer, want, choose, refuse, decide, expect, hope, learn, plan, arrange, afford, manage, intend, mean, promise, claim

Matt promised to go shopping with me.
(Matt는 저와 함께 쇼핑을 가기로 약속했습니다.)

We can't afford to send our children to college.
(우리는 우리 아이들을 대학에 보낼 여유가 없습니다.)

She managed to get to the meeting in time.
(그녀는 간신히 시간에 맞춰 회의에 도착했습니다.)

(2) **다음 동사 뒤에도 to부정사가 목적어로 온다:** seem, appear, tend, pretend

Andrew seems to be busy now.
(Andrew는 지금 바빠 보입니다.)

My mother tends to forget things.
(우리 어머니는 무슨 일을 잊어버리는 경향이 있습니다.)

(3) **not을 to부정사 앞에 놓아서 부정문을 만든다.**

He agreed not to play the guitar after midnight.
(그는 자정 이후에 기타 연주하지 않는 것에 동의했습니다.)

It was late so we decided not to visit him.
(시간이 늦어서 우리는 그를 방문하지 않기로 결정했습니다.)

He pretended not to recognize her.
(그는 그녀를 알아보지 못한 척 했습니다.)

③ V + O + to-infinitive (동사 + 목적어 + to부정사)

다음 동사 뒤에는 목적어가 오고 to부정사가 온다: advise, allow, tell, ask, order, expect, want, beg, remind, force, enable, encourage, persuade

My teacher advised me to buy the book.
(나의 선생님은 나에게 책을 사라고 권하셨습니다.)

She didn't allow him to come in.
(그녀는 그가 들어오는 것을 허락하지 않았습니다.)

The officer ordered the soldiers to stand by.
(지휘관은 군인들에게 준비하고 있으라고 명령했습니다.)

cf let, make, have 등의 사역 동사 다음엔 목적어와 원형 부정사가 온다.

He's very funny. He always makes me laugh.
(그는 매우 재미있습니다. 그는 언제나 나를 웃게 만듭니다.)

Let me give you something to drink.
(당신에게 마실 것 좀 드릴께요.)

4 V + wh – word + to – infinitives (동사 + 의문사 + to부정사)

다음 동사 다음에는 의문사와 to부정사가 함께 나온다: ask, explain, learn, understand, decided, forget, know, remember

We can't decide where to stay.
(우리는 어디에 머무를지를 결정할 수가 없습니다.)

When did you learn how to ski?
(언제 스키 타는 법을 배웠습니까?)

I've forgotten when to start.
(나는 언제 출발하는 것인 지 잊어버렸습니다.)

Task 1

Complete the sentences using the verbs in parentheses.

1. They finally decided ________. (divorce)
2. Tom finished ________ his homework. (do)
3. Cold weather made us ________ tired. (feel)
4. Many children refused ________ the spinach soup. (eat)
5. It would be a mistake for her ________ jobs just now. (change)
6. Did you learn how ________ the flute? (play)

Task 2

Correct the errors in the sentences. If the sentence is correct, write "correct".

1. They didn't allow us to look at the house.
   _________ → __________

2. He pretended to not like the girl next door.
   _________ → __________

3. He advised me seeing a doctor.
   _________ → __________

4. I can't afford to buy a new cell phone.
   _________ → __________

5. Sarah studies hard have a better chance of getting a job.
   _________ → __________

2
Focus

Gerunds
동명사

1 동명사의 용법

동명사는 명사 역할을 한다.

Doing yoga is good for your health. (주어)
(요가를 하는 것은 당신의 건강에 좋습니다.)

Could you stop making so much noise? (목적어)
(그렇게 시끄럽게 하는 것을 멈춰 주시겠습니까?)

My favorite exercise is swimming. (보어)
(내가 가장 좋아하는 운동은 수영입니다.)

We can't live without eating. (전치사의 목적어)
(우리는 먹지 않고 살 수 없습니다.)

2 V + ~ing (동사 + ~ing)

다음 동사의 뒤에 목적어로 동명사가 온다: stop, enjoy, finish, mind, suggest, avoid, delay, consider, imagine, admit

Suddenly they stopped talking.
(갑자기 그들은 말하기를 멈췄습니다.)

He avoided correcting the student's errors.
(그는 그 학생의 실수를 바로잡는 것을 피했습니다.)

Have you ever considered moving into a new apartment?
(새 아파트로 이사하는 것을 고려해본 적이 있습니까?)

3 give up + ~ing

다음 표현 뒤에도 목적어로 동명사가 온다: give up (= quit), put off (= postpone), go on (= continue), keep on (= continue), carry on(= continue), can't help(= can't stop myself), feel like (= want)

I gave up trying to persuade Max to accept the offer.
(저는 Max가 그 제안을 받아들이도록 설득하는 것을 포기했습니다.)

Don't keep (on) interrupting her while she's talking.
(그녀가 말하고 있는 동안 그녀를 계속해서 방해하지 마십시오.)

Daniel is very amusing. I can't help laughing at his funny stories.
(Daniel은 매우 재미있는 사람입니다. 나는 그의 재미있는 이야기에 웃지 않을 수 없습니다.)

4 go + ~ing

go는 여러 종류의 운동이나 여가 활동(swimming, skating, skiing, jogging, running, sailing, hiking, fishing, hunting, camping, dancing) 또는 쇼핑(shopping) 등의 단어와 함께 쓰인다. '~하러 가다'라는 의미이다.

Rick and Sally often go swimming.
(Rick과 Sally는 종종 수영을 하러 갑니다.)

They went fishing last weekend.
(그들은 지난 주말에 낚시를 갔습니다.)

John has to go shopping this afternoon.
(John은 오늘 오후에 쇼핑을 가야만 합니다.)

5 완료시제

이미 일어난 일에 대해서 얘기할 때는 목적어로 having + p.p.의 형식을 취한다.

They admitted having stolen the jewelry.
(그들은 보석을 훔쳤다는 것을 시인했습니다.)

I'm sorry for having spent the money.
(그 돈을 써버려서 미안합니다.)

I regret having written the letter.
(저는 그 편지를 썼던 것을 후회합니다.)

Task 3

Fill in the blanks by using the verbs in the box. Put the verbs in the right form: to-infinitive, ~ing, or base form (to do, doing, do)

cry	catch	go	splash	read	arrive	turn

1. When you use the shower, try to avoid __________ water on the floor.
2. If you want __________ the train, you had better hurry up.
3. Would you mind __________ the radio down, please?
4. The story was so sad. It made me __________.
5. This book is too difficult for me ________.
6. Is he already here? We expected him __________ much later.
7. I am tired. I don't feel like __________ out tonight.

Task 4

Choose the proper words in parentheses.

1. Jason managed (to pass, passing) the exam.
2. She admitted (to have done, having done) it herself.
3. We cannot help (to admire, admiring) his courage.
4. I can't afford (to pay, paying) her back now.
5. Birds and bats appear (to be, being) similar during the day, but they look totally different at night.
6. Did you go (to dance, dancing) last Friday?

REST AREA

Translation

Max	냄새가 역겨워요
Father	그래, 아들아? 그럼 지금 당장 방으로 가면 되겠네.
Mother	당신 너무 엄격하다고 생각 안 해요? 배고플 텐데.
Father	Max는 매너를 배워야 돼요. 어쨌든 굶어 죽지 않아요. 이건 그에게 좋은 교훈이 될 거예요.
Max	여분의 고기, 치즈, 그리고 소시지가 있는 큰 피자로 하겠어요.

3 Focus

V + to-infinitives/~ing
동사 + to부정사/ ~ing

1 의미의 차이가 거의 없는 동사

begin, start, continue, bother는 뒤에는 목적어로 to부정사가 오거나 동명사가 와도 큰 의미 차이를 보이지 않는다:

It has started to snow. / It has started snowing.
(눈이 오기 시작했습니다.)

Don't bother to fix lunch for me. / Don't bother fixing lunch for me.
(나를 위해 일부러 점심을 준비할 필요 없습니다.)

2 의미의 차이를 가져오는 동사

(1) remember, regret, forget 뒤에 to부정사가 오면, 일어날 일에 대해 말하는 것이고, 동명사가 오면 이미 일어난 일에 대해 말하는 것이다.

I regret to inform you of his death.
(저는 그의 죽음을 당신에게 알려줘야 해서 유감입니다.)

I regret telling you the story.
(저는 당신에게 그 이야기를 했던 것을 후회합니다.)

He remembered to lock the door, but he forgot to turn off the light.
(그는 문을 잠가야 하는 것을 기억했지만, 불을 끄는 것은 잊어버렸습니다.)

He can remember being in the hospital when he was a child.
(그는 그가 어릴 적에 병원에서 지냈던 것을 기억할 수 있습니다.)

I forgot to set my alarm clock last night.
(저는 지난 밤에 저의 알람 시계를 맞춰놓는 것을 잊어버렸습니다.)

I'll never forget meeting the Pope.
(저는 교황을 만났던 것을 결코 잊지 못할 겁니다.)

(2) like, dislike, hate, prefer 뒤에 to부정사가 오면 특정한 경우를 전제로 하고, 동명사가 오면 일반적인 것을 말한다. 그러나 짧은 문장에서는 의미 차이 없이 쓰이기도 한다.

I like to check my work again before I hand it in.
(저는 저의 숙제를 제출하기 전에 다시 한번 확인하고 싶습니다.)

She likes skiing.
(그녀는 스키 타는 것을 좋아합니다.)

I hate to say it again, but grades are important.
(다시 말하고 싶지는 않지만, 점수는 중요합니다.)

She hates washing the dishes.
(그녀는 설거지하기를 싫어합니다.)

(3) try, stop

try + to do(~하려고 노력하다) / try + doing (시험 삼아 ~해보다)
stop + to do (~하기 위해 멈추다) / stop + doing (~하는 것을 멈추다)

We'll try to address your problem as soon as possible.
(우리는 가능한 빨리 당신의 문제를 처리하도록 노력할 것입니다.)

I tried clicking on the box, but it doesn't work.
(저는 그 박스를 클릭해 보았지만, 그것은 작동하지 않습니다.)

An old lady stopped to talk to me.
(한 나이든 여자분이 저에게 말하려고 멈춰 섰습니다.)

Can you all stop talking for a moment, please?
(여러분 모두 잠시 동안 말하기를 멈춰 주시겠습니까?)

(4) 다음 문장에서 need, deserve뒤에 목적어로 쓰이는 동명사는 수동의 의미가 있다.

My shoes need repairing. (= My shoes need to be repaired.)
(제 신발은 수선이 필요합니다.)

I don't think the book deserves reading.
(저는 그 책이 읽을만한 가치가 있다고 생각하지 않습니다.)

Task 5

Correct the underlined parts that are incorrect. If the sentence is correct, write "correct".

1. They enjoy <u>taking</u> a walk every morning.
   → __________
2. He doesn't allow us <u>making</u> personal phone calls.
   → __________
3. She remembers <u>to cry</u> on her first day at school.
   → __________
4. Thomas refused <u>to come</u> back home.
   → __________
5. I regret <u>having spending</u> too much money.
   → __________
6. I am considering <u>to cancel</u> my trip.
   → __________

Task 6

Fill in the blanks by translating the Korean into English.

1. I will remember __________ to the dentist tomorrow.
   (나는 내일 치과에 가는 것을 기억할 겁니다.)
2. Why do you put off __________ his letter?
   (왜 당신은 그의 편지에 답장하기를 미루십니까?)
3. Tracy tends __________ too fast.
   (Tracy는 말을 너무 빨리 하는 경향이 있습니다.)
4. They warned me __________ everything he says.
   (그들은 나에게 그가 하는 말을 모두 믿어서는 안 된다고 경고했습니다.)
5. The car needs __________.
   (그 차는 세차가 필요합니다.)
6. Can you tell me __________ this machine?
   (이 기계를 어떻게 사용하는 지 말씀해주시겠어요?)

Culture Corner

Horatio Alger

19세기 미국에 Horatio Alger라는 소설가가 있었는데, 그의 소설에는 자수성가(a self-made man)하는 미국인의 꿈(American dream)이 잘 나타나 있는 것으로 유명하다. 즉, 그의 소설의 주인공은 대부분 가난한 집안에서 태어나 정직하고 근면하게 노력한 결과 크게 성공하게 된다.

여기에서 나온 a Horatio Alger story라는 표현은 a rags-to-riches story(가난뱅이에서 부자가 되는 이야기)라는 의미로 쓰인다. 1947년에는 어려움을 이겨내고 성공한 사람들을 기리기 위해 the Horatio Alger Association of Distinguished Americans라는 협회가 발족되기도 하였다. 이 협회에서는 매년 Horatio Alger Heroes를 발굴하여 이들에게 Horatio Alger Award를 수여한다. 물론 이 상은 어려움을 극복하고 사회에서 지도자로서 성공한 이들에게 주어지게 된다. 성공한 career woman으로 우리에게 잘 알려진 Oprah Winfrey, 국무장관이었던 Colin Powell, 대통령이었던 Ronald Reagan 등이 이 상을 수상한 바 있다.

It's a true Horatio Alger Story.
She rose from rags to riches.
It's a real success story.
He is a self-made man.

Wrap-up

1. Matt promised to go shopping with me.
2. She didn't allow him to come in.
3. When did you learn how to ski?
4. Suddenly they stopped talking.
5. I'm sorry for having spent the money.
6. I regret telling you the story.

Final Tips

She suggested going to the movies. (O)

She suggested to go to the movies. (X)

suggest, enjoy, mind 등의 동사는 동명사를 목적어로 취합니다.

I now regret saying what I said. (O)

We regret to inform you that we are unable to accept your offer. (O)

regret 다음에 동명사가 오면 이미 일어난 일에 대해서 말하는 것이고, to 부정사가 오면 '~하게 되어서 유감이다' 라는 뜻입니다. 주로 좋지 않은 소식을 전할 때 씁니다.

They don't allow smoking indoors. (O)

They don't allow anyone to smoke indoors. (O)

They don't allow anyone smoking indoors. (X)

allow 다음에 바로 동명사가 목적어로 올 수 있지만, allow 다음에 사람이 목적어로 오면 그 다음에 to 부정사가 목적보어로 옵니다. (allow+o+to 부정사)

Translation

그녀는 영화 보러 가자고 제안했습니다.
나는 지금 내가 한 말을 후회합니다.
당신의 제안을 받아들이지 못한다는 것을 알려드리게 되어서 유감입니다.
실내에서는 금연입니다.

Review Test

Choose the correct words.

1. I expect (get, to get, getting) an e-mail from you soon.

2. I'll never forget (have, to have, having) a great time with my favorite movie star last week.

3. After he finished (watch, to watch, watching) the video, he went to bed.

4. My father let me (help, to help, helping) him plant trees when I was four.

5. She tells him to stop (shout, to shout, shouting), but he doesn't like being told what to do.

Write the correct forms of the verbs in parentheses to complete the sentences. You can add "to" if necessary.

6. He admitted stealing the car but denied ____________ (drive) it dangerously.

7. I don't feel like ____________ (have) noodles for supper.

8. He decided ____________ (make) an early start.

9. She needs to work without ____________. (be disturbed)

10. It was careless of you ____________ (leave) your cell phone in the taxi.

ocus1-Focus3

Chapter 9

PARTICIPLES

Introduction

Lesson objectives

1. Usage of participles 분사의 용법

2. Adjectives ending in *-ing* and *-ed* -ing와 -ed로 끝나는 형용사

3. Participle construction 분사구문

Check-up

Ben & Olivia's everyday

Olivia : That was an _________ (interesting, interested) film, wasn't it?

Ben : You think? I'm not _________ (surprising, surprised) you liked it. Just the kind of strange foreign film you would like. It was completely _________ (boring, bored) to me. I thought it might be worth _________ (watching, watched), but it definitely wasn't.

Olivia : Well, I was also _________ (puzzling, puzzled) with the plot. There were some _________ (confusing, confused) scenes. But I was _________ (satisfying, satisfied) with how it ended.

Ben : Well, I was _________ (boring, bored) from beginning to end.

Olivia : I'm very bored by you at the moment.

Check-up

Answers

Olivia : That was an (interesting) film, wasn't it?

Ben : You think? I'm not (surprised) you liked it. Just the kind of strange foreign film you would like. It was completely (boring) to me. I thought it might be worth (watching), but it definitely wasn't.

Olivia : Well, I was also (puzzled) with the plot. There were some (confusing) scenes. But I was (satisfied) with how it ended

Ben : Well, I was (bored) from beginning to end.

Olivia : I'm very bored by you at the moment.

Translation

Olivia : 재미있는 영화였어, 안 그래?

Ben : 그랬어? 당신 마음에 들었다니 별로 놀라운 일은 아니군. 이상한 외국영화 좋아하잖아. 난 진짜 지루하던데. 볼 만한 가치가 있을지도 모른다고 생각했지만 전혀 아니었어.

Olivia : 내용이 좀 혼란스럽긴 하더라. 헷갈리는 장면이 몇 개 있었어. 하지만 결말은 만족스럽던걸.

Ben : 글쎄, 난 처음부터 끝까지 다 지루하던데.

Olivia : 난 지금 당신이 정말 지루해.

1 Focus

Usage of participles
분사의 용법

1 현재분사와 과거분사

분사는 명사를 수식하는 역할을 한다. 분사에는 현재분사 (~ing)와 과거분사 (~ed)가 있다. 현재분사는 수식하는 명사와 능동의 관계에 있고, 과거분사는 수식하는 명사와 수동의 관계에 있다.

a **barking** dog (a dog that is barking.)
(짖고 있는 개)

a **broken** chair (a chair that is broken.)
(부서진 의자)

분사는 조동사 be, have와 함께 진행형, 완료형, 수동태 등을 만든다.

He was **working** when I called him.
(내가 그에게 전화했을 때, 그는 일하고 있었습니다.)

I've **forgotten** his name.
(나는 그의 이름을 잊었습니다.)

You'll be **told** about the scandal.
(당신은 그 추문에 관해 듣게 될 것입니다.)

2 분사의 위치

분사는 명사를 뒤에서 수식하기도 하고, 앞에서 수식하기도 한다. 분사가 수식 어구를 동반하는 경우는 대개 명사를 뒤에서 수식하게 된다.

(1) 후치 수식(post-modification)

Who's the girl **dancing** with my brother?
(나의 남동생과 춤추고 있는 소녀는 누구입니까?)

None of the people **invited** to the party came.
(파티에 초대된 사람들이 아무도 오지 않았습니다.)

(2) 전치 수식(pre-modification)

They found the crying boy in the building.
(그들은 빌딩에서 울고 있는 그 소년을 발견했습니다)

Do you know the retired man?
(당신은 은퇴한 그 남자를 아시나요?)

cf 위치에 따른 의미 차이

the people concerned (관련된 사람들) / a concerned air (근심스러운 태도)
the people involved (관련된 사람들) / an involved explanation (복잡한 설명)
the solution adopted (채택된 해결책) / an adopted son (양자)

3 분사의 역할

분사는 형용사의 역할을 하기도 하고, 주격 보어나 목적격 보어로 쓰이기도 한다.

(1) 형용사

Please read the **following** examples.
(아래에 있는 예문들을 읽으세요.)

He tried to comfort the **frightened** child.
(그는 겁먹은 어린이를 위로하려고 노력했습니다.)

(2) 주격 보어

The governor's speech was **disappointing**.
(주지사의 연설은 실망스러웠습니다.)

The mystery remained **unsettled**.
(불가사의는 풀리지 않은 채 남겨졌습니다.)

(3) 목적격 보어

The police caught the thief **climbing** the wall.
(경찰은 벽을 오르는 그 도둑을 붙잡았습니다.)

Why don't you have that coat **cleaned**?
(코트를 세탁하지 그러세요?)

Task 1

Choose the right verb forms in parentheses.

1. She says she's got a (breaking, broken) heart.
2. I caught him (stealing, stolen) my jewelry.
3. The people (attending, attended) the conference expressed concern about it.
4. She got the vacuum cleaner (repairing, repaired).
5. Since this room is air-conditioned, we must keep the windows (closing, closed).
6. We couldn't agree on any of the problems (discussing, discussed).

Task 2

Change the verb forms in parentheses.

1. Who is that boy __________ (wear) a big straw hat?
2. We ate the cake __________ (make) at noon today.
3. The ball __________ (roll) down the hill is mine.
4. I got a letter _________ (offer) me a job two days ago.
5. He stood _________ (lean) against the wall.

2
Focus

Adjectives ending in -*ing* and -*ed*

-*ing*와 -*ed*로 끝나는 형용사

1 분사 형용사

분사 중에는 자주 쓰여서 형용사로 된 것들이 있는 데, 주로 감정과 관련된 형용사이다.

boring speech (지루한 연설: 능동의 의미)

bored audience (지루해진 청중: 수동의 의미)

cf Robert is a very **boring** person.
(Robert는 따분하게 하는 사람입니다.)

The news was **surprising**.
(그 뉴스는 놀라웠습니다.)

He was **surprised** at the news.
(그는 그 뉴스에 놀랐습니다.)

Going to Europe will be an **exciting** experience for her.
(유럽에 가는 것은 그녀에게 신나는 경험이 될 것입니다.)

She is really **excited** about going to Europe.
(그녀는 유럽에 가는 것에 정말 흥분이 됩니다.)

My father always told me **interesting** stories.
(나의 아버지는 항상 나에게 재미있는 이야기를 해주셨습니다.)

I was very **interested** in the tales.
(나는 그 이야기들에 매우 흥미를 느낍니다.)

Going for a jog with Mark is **exhausting**.
(Mark 와 조깅하는 것은 나를 지치게 합니다.)

I'm **exhausted** after jogging all the way.
(나는 조깅을 다 한 후에는 지칩니다.)

2 -ing / -ed

-ing	-ed
amusing (재미나는)	amused (즐거워하는)
annoying (성가신)	annoyed (성가시게 느끼는)
astonishing (놀라운)	astonished (놀란)
confusing (혼란 시키는)	confused (혼란스러운)
disappointing (실망시키는)	disappointed (실망한)
depressing (억압적인)	depressed (의기소침한)
disgusting (메스꺼운)	disgusted (정떨어진)
embarrassing (당황케 하는)	embarrassed (당황한)
fascinating (매혹적인)	fascinated (매혹된)
frightening (깜짝 놀라게 하는)	frightened (깜짝 놀란)
irritating (짜증나는)	irritated (짜증난)
puzzling (곤혹스럽게 하는)	puzzled (곤혹스러운)
relaxing (나른하게 하는)	relaxed (긴장을 푼)
satisfying (만족을 주는)	satisfied (만족한)
shocking (충격적인)	shocked (충격을 받은)
terrifying (겁나게 하는)	terrified (겁나는)
tiring (피곤하게 하는)	tired (피곤한)
thrilling (흥분시키는)	thrilled (흥분된)

Task 3

Choose the correct words in parentheses.

1. She was (annoying, annoyed) at his rude manners.
2. The governor's speech was (disappointing, disappointed).
3. This soccer game was very (exciting, excited).
4. Cathy is (interesting, interested) in studying astronomy.
5. The weather makes me (depressing, depressed).
6. The cook was (astonishing, astonished) at his incredible appetite.

Task 4

Complete the sentences by choosing a word from the box.

embarrassing / embarrassed	amusing / amused
surprising / surprised	relaxing / relaxed
confusing / confused	annoying / annoyed

1. He usually stays up till late. It's not __________ that he always looks so tired.
2. When I am __________, I get a red face.
3. Her explanation is __________. Most of the people didn't understand it.
4. Nick is funny. We often laugh at his __________ stories.
5. The mosquitoes were so __________ that I couldn't sleep.
6. The soft music made me feel __________.

REST AREA

Translation

Max 아빠! 제 말 좀 들어봐요. 제 생각에 새 아빠를 얻을 때가 된 것 같아요. 아빠의 임기 만료 기간은 언제예요?
Dad 미안해, Max야. 나는 평생 동안 아빠를 하기로 임명되었지.
Max 평생 동안? 농담이시죠? 말도 안돼요. 새로운 선거는요? 탄핵은요?
Dad 안돼. 불가능하단다.
Max 누가 아빠를 평생 동안 하라고 명령했어요? 헌법을 아빠 스스로가 썼어요?
Dad 흠.... 너의 엄마도 많이 도왔단다.

3
Focus

Participle Construction
분사구문

분사구문은 분사를 사용하여 절을 구로 만든 것입니다.

1 분사구문 형식

(1) 종속절의 주어와 주절의 주어가 일치하는 경우, 종속절의 접속사와 주어를 생략한다. 주어가 일치하지 않으면 종속절의 주어를 그대로 둔다. 의미를 명확히 하기 위해서 종속절의 접속사를 그대로 두는 경우도 있다.

(2) 종속절 동사를 -ing로 바꾼다. 주절의 시제보다 종속절의 시제가 앞서는 경우는 종속절 동사를 having + p.p.로 바꾼다.

When I arrived at the office, I found him dozing on the sofa.
→ **Arriving** at the office, I found him dozing on the sofa.
(내가 사무실에 도착했을 때 나는 그가 소파에서 잠자고 있는 것을 발견했습니다.)

The weather being fine, we went hiking.
(= Since the weather was fine, we went hiking.)
(날씨가 맑아서 우리는 하이킹을 갔습니다.)

There being no taxi, I had to go home on foot.
(= Since there was no taxi, I had to go home on foot.)
(택시가 없었기 때문에 나는 집에 걸어서 가야 했습니다.)

After having annoyed everybody, she went out.
(= After she had annoyed everybody, she went out.)
(그녀는 모든 사람을 화나게 한 뒤, 나가버렸습니다.)

Having had dinner, I went out for a walk.
(=When I had had dinner, I went out for a walk.)
(저녁을 먹고 나는 산책하러 나갔습니다.)

2 -ed 분사구문

주어와 동사의 관계가 수동이면 동사를 -ed로 바꾼다. 동사 앞에 나오는 being은 자주 생략한다.

Wounded in the legs he could not walk.
(=As he was wounded in the legs, he could not walk.)
(그는 다리를 다쳐서 걸을 수가 없었습니다.)

Seen from a distance, the rock looked like a human face.
(=When it was seen from a distance, the rock looked like a human face.)
(멀리서 보았을 때, 그 바위는 사람 얼굴처럼 보였습니다.)

Composed in only a few minutes, the melody was memorable.
(=Although it was composed in only few minutes, the melody was memorable.)
(비록 몇 분만에 작곡된 것이지만, 그 멜로디는 잊혀지지 않습니다.)

3 위치

분사구문은 주절의 앞과 뒤에 모두 올 수 있다.

Returning to the room, I found the book missing
(= When I returned to the room, I found the book missing)
(방에 돌아왔을 때, 나는 그 책이 없어진 것을 알았습니다.)

He walked out of the room, **slamming** the door behind him.
(= He walked out of the room, and slammed the door behind him
(그는 방을 걸어나가서 문을 쾅 닫았습니다.)

4 부정 분사 구문

부정어는 분사 앞에 온다.

Not being interested in any gossip, she tried to change the subject.
(=As she was not interested in any gossip, she tried to change the topic.)
(그는 남의 뒷말 하는 것에 관심이 없어서 주제를 바꾸려고 노력했습니다.)

Not having enough money, I couldn't buy the car.
(= As I didn't have enough money, I couldn't buy the car.)
(나는 충분한 돈을 가지고 있지 않아서 차를 살 수가 없었습니다.)

5 분사구문의 의미

분사구문은 시간, 이유, 조건, 양보, 동시 상황, 연속 동작 등을 나타낸다.

(1) 시간

Opening the door, they heard the clock strike one.
(= When they opened the door, they heard the clock strike one.)
(문을 열었을 때, 시계가 1시를 치는 것을 들었습니다.)

(2) 이유

Having the highest marks in the class, he was offered a scholarship by the college.
(= Since he had the highest marks in his class, he was offered a scholarship by the college.)
(그의 학급에서 최고의 점수를 맞아서 그는 대학 장학금을 제공 받았습니다.)

(3) 조건

Estimating it roughly, we should arrive by ten.
(= If we estimate it roughly, we should arrive by ten.)
(대충 추정해보면 우리는 10시까지는 도착해야 합니다.)

(4) 양보

Not doing anything, I still feel tired.
(= Although I am not doing anything, I still feel tired.)
(비록 아무것도 하지 않고 있지만, 나는 여전히 피곤합니다.)

(5) 동시 상황

The audience walked out of the theater, **looking** excited.
(= The audience walked out of the theater and they looked excited.)
(그 청중들은 흥분된 모습으로 극장을 걸어 나왔습니다.)

(6) 연속 동작

The bus left Seoul at seven, **arriving** at Busan at one p.m.
(= The bus left Seoul at seven and arrived at Busan at one p.m.)
(그 버스는 서울에서 7시에 출발해 부산에 오후 1시에 도착했습니다.)

6 분사 구문 앞의 with

'with+ 목적어 + 분사' 의 형식을 취해서: 동시 상황이나 이유를 나타낸다.

She sat on the sofa, with her legs crossed.
(그녀는 다리를 꼰 채로 소파에 앉아 있었습니다.)

With one eye bandaged, I couldn't see properly.
(눈 한쪽을 붕대로 감아서 나는 정확하게 볼 수가 없었습니다.)

With night coming on, the wind began to blow.
(밤이 다가오자, 바람이 불기 시작했습니다.)

7 독립 분사 구문

주절 주어와 무관하게 관용적으로 쓰이는 분사구문이다. 분사구문에서는 we, they, you, people 등 일반인 주어가 생략되었다고 보면 된다.

Generally speaking, women live longer than men.
(일반적으로 말해서 여자가 남자보다 오래 삽니다.)

Considering everything, it wasn't a bad holiday.
(모든 것을 고려해 볼 때, 나쁜 휴일은 아니었습니다.)

Strictly speaking (엄밀히 말한다면)
Frankly speaking (솔직히 말한다면)
Roughly speaking (대략 말한다면)
Judging from (~로 판단하건대)
Compared with (~와 비교하면)
Provided (that) / Providing (that) / Supposing (that) (만약 ~라면)
Granting (that) /Admitting (that) (~라고 할지라도)

Task 5

Rewrite the underlined parts using a participle construction.

1. <u>As I did not know Cathy</u>, I didn't speak to her.

   → ____________________, I didn't speak to her.

2. <u>If we judge from his appearance</u>, he must be a Japanese.

   → ____________________, he must be a Japanese.

3. When he had finished the term paper, he went out and played basketball.

→ ______________________, he went out and played basketball.

4. Since it is written in easy French, this book is good for beginners.

→ ______________________, this book is good for beginners.

5. Although he was taken by surprise, he did not lose his composure.

→ ______________________, he did not lose his composure.

Task 6

Choose the correct answers.

1. ___________, leisure promotes health, energy, and happiness.
   (1) Having used it wisely (2) Used wisely
   (3) As using wisely (4) Using it wisely

2. _________, he was quite disappointed.
   (1) Seen the movie (2) Having saw the movie
   (3) Having seen the movie (4) When seen the movie

3. _________, they had to finish the journey on foot.
   (1) The car breaking down (2) The car broke down
   (3) Breaking down (4) Break down

4. Having finished his homework, ______________.
   (1) Jack's mother gave him a cup of tea
   (2) a letter was written
   (3) writing a letter was the next thing to do
   (4) Jack went to bed right away.

5. The dog, ______________, will become a faithful friend.
   (1) trained carefully (2) training carefully
   (3) having training carefully (4) it being trained carefully

6. The sun _________, we tried to find a motel for the night.
   (1) being set (2) having set
   (3) had set (4) been set

Culture Corner

Neck and neck

경마 경기에서 유래한 말로 neck and neck이 있는 데, 이것은 기수(jockey)의 채찍을 받는 두 마리 말이 서로 선두 다툼을 할 때, 두 마리 말의 목(neck)이 거의 겹치듯이 나란히 있는 경우를 가리킨다. 따라서 이 표현은, '막상막하, 치열한 접전'을 설명할 때 흔히 쓰인다. 선거에서도 엎치락 뒤치락 접전을 벌일 때 이런 표현을 쓸 수 있다. George Bush was neck and neck with Al Gore during the presidential election campaign. (George Bush와 Al Gore는 대통령 선거 운동 동안 접전을 벌였습니다.)

해마다 동계 올림픽(Winter Olympics)이나 세계 선수권 대회(World Championships)에서 금메달을 따내어서 우리 국민들을 기쁘게 하는 종목으로 Short track speed skating이 있다. 마지막 순간의 순발력이 승패를 좌우하기 때문에 종종 finish line에서 한 선수가 skate를 쭉 내밀어서 극적으로 gold medal를 차지하기도 한다. 이런 경우처럼 간발의 차이로 이겼다고 할 때는 win by a nose 라는 표현을 쓰는데, 이 표현 역시 경마 경기에서 나온 것이다. 말의 신체 부위 중에서 코가 가장 앞부분에 있기 때문에 한 마리의 말이 다른 말보다 코 끝부분이라고 먼저 finish line를 통과하면 승리하게 된다는 데서 나온 표현이다. The racer thrust his skate forward at the last moment and won by a nose. (그 선수는 마지막 순간에 스케이트를 내밀어서 간발의 차이로 승리했습니다.)

또한 달리기 경기 등에서는 finish line을 누가 먼저 통과했는지 도저히 육안으로는 판별하기 힘든 경우도 있다. 이럴 때는 사진 판독으로 구별하게 되는데, 이것을 photo finish라고 한다. 이것은 꼭 사진을 사용하지 않더라도 win by a nose와 비슷한 의미로 쓰이기도 한다. It was a real photo finish. (그건 정말 대단한 접전이었습니다.)

George Bush was neck and neck with Al Gore during the presidential election campaign.
The racer thrust his skate forward at the last moment and won by a nose.
It was a real photo finish.

Wrap-up

1. Who's the girl dancing with my brother?
2. Do you know the retired man?
3. The news was surprising.
4. He was surprised at the news.
5. Arriving at the office, I found him dozing on the sofa.
6. The weather being fine, we went hiking.

Final Tips

I was very boring this weekend. (X)

I was very bored this weekend. (O)

내가 지루해 진 것이므로 과거분사 bored를 써야 합니다.

She enjoys her job, but it's often exhausted. (X)

She enjoys her job, but it's often exhausting. (O)

그 일이 나를 지치게 하므로 현재분사 exhausting을 써야 합니다.

There's nobody living in the house. (O)

There was nobody injured in the accident. (O)

현재분사는 능동의 의미, 과거분사는 수동의 의미를 갖습니다.

Translation

이번 주말은 정말 지루했습니다.
그녀는 자신의 일을 즐기지만 가끔 지치기도 합니다.
이 집에는 아무도 살지 않습니다.
그 사고로 부상당한 사람은 없습니다.

Review Test

Find the underlined parts that are incorrect and correct them. If the sentence is correct, write "Correct".

1. A fire broke out at Sungnyemun, destroyed the oldest wooden structure in Seoul.

____

2. Having finished my homework, I started to cook dinner.

____

3. Not understood what she said, he remained silent.

____

Choose the correct words.

4. John tried to open the (locking, locked) door, but he couldn't.

5. We found the tour of the city (fascinating, fascinated).

6. The passengers (injuring, injured) in the car accident were taken to the hospital.

7. Generally (speaking, spoken), cats are not as faithful pets as dogs.

8. He's one of the most (boring, bored) people I've ever met.

9. Due to the long recession, even graduates who are highly (motivating, motivated) and qualified cannot find jobs.

10. He received a fax (confirming, confirmed) his hotel reservation.

ocus1-Focus3

Chapter 10

RELATIVES

Introduction

Lesson objectives

1. **Relative pronouns** 관계대명사

2. **Usage of relative pronouns** 관계대명사 용법

3. **Relative adverbs** 관계부사

Check-up

Ben & Olivia's everyday

Ben : I'd like to get something to eat.

Olivia : Let's go to the restaurant over there.

Ben : Not there. It looks like one of those places _________ (who, that, whose) charge you a fortune for half a stick of celery. The only people _________ (that, which, whose) want to eat there are those with more money than sense. Anyway, I don't see a menu. I don't like a restaurant _________ (who, that, whose) menu is not displayed.

Olivia : O.K. How about the café _________ (who, that, whose) we just passed?

Ben : I don't want to eat at a café _________ (who, that, whose) only serves dessert and coffee.

Olivia : You are the most annoying man _________ (who, which, whose) was put on this planet, did you know that? Are there any restaurants at all _________ (who, that, whose) you want to go to around here?

Check-up

Answers

Ben : I'd like to get something to eat.

Olivia : Let's go to the restaurant over there.

Ben : Not there. It looks like one of those places (**that**) charge you a fortune for half a stick of celery. The only people (**that**) want to eat there are those with more money than sense. Anyway, I don't see a menu. I don't like a restaurant (**whose**) menu is not displayed.

Olivia : O.K. How about the café (**that**) we just passed?

Ben : I don't want to eat at a café (**that**) only serves dessert and coffee.

Olivia : You are the most annoying man (**who**) was put on this planet, did you know that? Are there any restaurants at all (**that**) you want to go to around here?

Translation

Ben : 뭔가 먹고 싶어.

Olivia : 저기 있는 식당에 가자.

Ben : 저긴 싫어. 샐러리 반 대를 터무니없는 가격에 파는 곳처럼 생겼어. 저런 데서 식사하고 싶어하는 사람들은 돈을 헤프게 쓰는 사람뿐일걸. 게다가 메뉴판도 안 보여. 메뉴판이 진열되어 있지 않은 식당은 싫어.

Olivia : 알았어. 우리가 방금 지나온 카페는 어때?

Ben : 후식과 커피밖에 없는 카페에서는 먹고 싶지 않아.

Olivia : 당신이 이 지구상에서 가장 짜증나는 사람인 거 알아? 이 근처에 가고 싶은 식당이 있기는 한 거야?

1

Focus

Relative Pronouns

관계대명사

관계사는 명사 뒤에 와서 관계사절(relative clauses)를 이끌며, 관계사절은 앞에 나온 명사를 수식하거나 설명한다. 수식을 받는 명사를 선행사(antecedent)라고 한다. 관계사(relatives)에는 who, whose, whom, that, which와 같은 관계대명사(relative pronouns)와 when, where, why와 같은 관계부사(relative adverbs)가 있다.

1 who

관계대명사 who는 사람이 선행사인 경우에 쓰인다. who는 he/she/they를 대신하여 관계사절에서 쓰인다.

The woman is a lawyer.
(그 여자는 변호사입니다.)

She lives next door.
(그녀는 옆 집에 삽니다.)

→ The woman who lives next door is a lawyer.
선행사 관계사절

(옆집에 사는 그 여자는 변호사입니다.)

I met a man who is a novelist.
(저는 소설가인 남자를 만났습니다.)

The waitress who served us was very rude.
(우리의 시중을 들었던 그 여종업원은 매우 무례했습니다.)

The soccer player who took drugs has been banned from playing again.
(약물을 복용한 그 축구 선수는 다시 뛰는 것이 금지되었습니다.)

2 that, which

(1) 관계대명사 that이나 which는 사물이 선행사인 경우에 쓰인다. 일상체에서는 that이 which 보다 더 많이 쓰인다. that은 사람이 선행사인 경우에도 쓸 수 있다.

I can't find the key.
(저는 열쇠를 찾을 수가 없습니다.)

It opens this door.
(그것은 이 문을 엽니다.)

→ I can't find the key that opens this door.
선행사 관계사절
(저는 이 문을 열 열쇠를 찾을 수가 없습니다.)

Where is the Coke that was in the refrigerator?
(냉장고에 있던 콜라가 어디에 있습니까?)

I know a shop which sells really good meat.
(저는 정말 양질의 고기를 파는 상점을 알고 있습니다.)

The people that work in my office are very friendly.
(저의 사무실에 근무하는 사람들은 매우 친절합니다.)

(2) 선행사에 every, any, no, all, the only, the first, the last, the next, 최상급이 포함된 경우에는 관계대명사 that이 많이 쓰인다.

I won't believe anything (that) he says.
(저는 그가 말하는 것도 믿지 않을 것입니다.)

All (that) I could do was stand and watch.
(제가 할 수 있었던 모든 것은 서서 지켜보는 것이었습니다.)

The shop has nothing (that) I want.
(그 상점에는 내가 원하는 것이 아무것도 없습니다.)

3 what

관계대명사 what은 선행사를 포함하고 있다.
what (= the thing(s) that)

I don't like what you bought yesterday.
(저는 당신이 어제 샀던 것을 좋아하지 않습니다.)
What she said surprised everybody.
(그녀가 말한 것은 모두를 놀라게 했습니다.)

Mark will tell you what you need to know.
(Mark는 당신이 알아야 할 것을 당신에게 말해줄 것입니다.)

4 whose, whom

(1) 소유격 관계대명사 whose는 바로 뒤에 명사가 오게 된다. whose는 his/her/their를 대신하여 관계사절에서 쓰인다.

An orphan is a child.
(고아는 아이입니다.)

His parents are dead.
(그의 부모님이 돌아가셨습니다.)

→ An orphan is a child whose parents are dead.
(고아는 그의 부모님이 돌아가신 아이입니다.)

What's the name of the girl whose mother is a pianist?
(그녀의 엄마가 피아니스트인 그 소녀의 이름은 무엇입니까?)

I met a man whose brother works in a radio station.
(저는 그의 형이 라디오 방송국에서 일하는 한 남자를 만났습니다.)

Vicky was looking after a dog whose leg had been broken in an accident.
(Vicky는 사고로 다리가 부러진 개를 돌보고 있었습니다.)

(2) 목적격 관계대명사 whom은 동사나 전치사의 목적어로 관계사절에서 쓰인다. 목적격 whom 대신에 주격 who를 쓰기도 한다. 사물이 선행사인 경우는 목적격 관계대명사 that이나 which가 온다. 목적격 관계대명사의 경우는 생략이 가능하다.

The professor was away on vacation.
(그 교수님은 휴가로 떠나 계셨습니다.)

I went to see him.
(저는 그 분을 만나러 갔습니다.)

→ The professor (whom/who) I went to see was away on vacation.
(제가 만나러 갔던 그 교수님은 휴가를 떠나셨습니다.)

The woman (whom/who) he loved left him after a few months.
(그가 사랑했던 여자는 몇 달 후 그를 떠났습니다.)

Do you know the name of the girl (whom/who) I talked to at the party?
(당신은 제가 파티에서 이야기를 나누었던 그 소녀의 이름을 아십니까?)

The poems (that) Colin wrote are hard to understand.
(Colin이 쓴 시는 이해하기가 어렵습니다.)

Task 1

Choose the right relative pronoun in parentheses.

1. The doctor (who, whom) examined the sick child was very kind.
2. The term paper (whom, that) David is writing must be finished by Friday.
3. The man (who, whose) opinion I respect most is my father.
4. Have you got anything (that, who) will clean this carpet?
5. I know the boy (who, whose) bicycle was stolen.
6. Angela met the woman (who, whose) worked at the post office.

Task 2

Fill in the blanks with the proper relative pronoun.

1. The music was very good. I listened to it yesterday.

   → The music ________ I listened to yesterday was very good.

2. The woman writes well. I'm reading her novel.

   → The woman ________ novel I'm reading writes well.

3. The man gave her flowers. She is in love with him.

   → The man with ________ she is in love gave her flowers.

4. The students are from Japan. They sit in the first row.

   → The students _______ sit in the first row are from Japan.

5. Jonathan went to the meeting. He didn't understand its purpose.

   → Jonathan went to the meeting ________ purpose he didn't understand.

6. The city was beautiful. We spent our vacation there.

   → The city in ________ we spent our vacation was beautiful.

2
Focus

Usage of Relative Pronouns
관계대명사 용법

1 관계대명사의 격

분류	주격	목적격	소유격
사람	who/that	whom/that	whose
사물	which/that	which/that	

2 관계대명사 생략

동사나 전치사의 목적어가 되는 목적격 관계대명사는 생략할 수 있다. 단, 전치사의 목적어로 쓰여 전치사 바로 뒤에 오는 관계대명사는 생략할 수 없다. 또한 that이나 who는 전치사 바로 뒤에 쓸 수 없다.

The suit (that/which) John bought doesn't fit him very well.
(John이 산 옷은 그에게 썩 잘 어울리지는 않습니다.)

The bus (that/which) I'm waiting for is late.
(내가 기다리고 있는 그 버스는 늦습니다.)

Do you know the woman (whom/who/that) David is dancing with?
(당신은 David가 함께 춤 추고 있는 그 부인을 아십니까?)

Do you know the woman with whom David is dancing?

Do you know the woman with David is dancing? (X)

Economics is a subject about which I know very little.
(경제학은 제가 거의 알지 못하는 과목입니다.)

Economics is a subject about that I know very little? (X)

3 두 가지 관계사절

(1) 한정절(Defining/Restrictive clause)

관계사절이 앞에 있는 선행사를 수식하고 제한하는 역할을 할 때, 이것을 한정절이라고 한다. 이 경우, 관계사절 앞에 콤마를 쓰지 않는다.

We stayed at the hotel (that) Melissa recommended to us.
(우리는 Melissa가 우리에게 추천한 호텔에 묵었습니다.)

I know a man who writes film music.
(저는 영화 음악을 쓰는 한 남자를 알고 있습니다.)

(2) 비한정절(Non-defining/Non-restrictive clause)

관계사절이 앞에 있는 선행사를 수식하는 것이 아니라, 선행사를 보충, 설명하는 역할을 할 때, 이것을 비한정절이라고 한다. 이 경우, 관계사절 앞에 콤마를 쓴다.

i) 선행사가 고유명사이거나 앞 문장 전체일 때, 비한정절을 쓴다.

My brother Daniel, who lives in L.A., got married last year.
(나의 오빠인 Daniel은 L.A.에 사는 데, 작년에 결혼했습니다.)

She quit the job, which surprised everyone.
(그녀는 일을 그만 두었는 데, 그것은 모두를 깜짝 놀라게 했습니다.)

It rained all night, which was good for the plants.
(밤새도록 비가 내렸는데 그것은 식물들에게 좋았습니다.)

ii) 관계대명사 that은 비한정절에서는 쓰지 않는다.

She told us about her new job, which she's enjoying very much.
(그녀는 우리에게 그녀의 새 직업에 대해 이야기했는데 그녀는 그것을 매우 즐기고 있었습니다.)

She told us about her new job, that she's enjoying very much. (X)

iii) 목적격 관계대명사도 비한정절에서는 생략할 수 없다.

My sister, whom you once met, works as a tour guide.
(나의 언니는 당신도 한 번 만난 적이 있는 데, 여행 가이드로 일합니다.)

My sister, you once met, works as a tour guide. (X)

Task 3

In some of the following sentences you don't need the underlined relative pronouns. Indicate whether you need them or not.

	need	don't need
1. The man <u>who</u> was injured in the car accident is in the hospital.	______	______
2. The woman <u>whose</u> purse was stolen called the police.	______	______
3. Have you found the book <u>that</u> you lost?	______	______
4. You must thank the people from <u>whom</u> you received many presents.	______	______
5. I love the woman <u>whom</u> I met at the party last Friday.	______	______
6. He said nothing, <u>which</u> made her angry.	______	______

Task 4

Correct the underlined parts if they are incorrect. If the sentence is correct, write "correct".

1. The man to <u>who</u> I spoke gave me some good advice.
   → __________
2. My office, <u>that</u> is on the fourth floor of this building, is very spacious.
   → __________
3. I returned the money <u>that</u> I had borrowed from my friend.
   → __________
4. This is the film <u>which</u> I am interested.
   → __________
5. I apologized to the teacher <u>whose</u> coffee I spilled.
   → __________

REST AREA

Translation

Max	아빠, 어떻게 전구가 작동을 하는 건지 설명해 주세요.
Father	그래. 그건 마술로 인해서 작동하는 거야.
Max	제가 기억하기로는 청소기도 그렇게 작동한다고 아빠가 그러셨던 거 같은데요.
Father	그래. 맞아. 두 개다 마술로 작동하는 거란다.
Max	아빠는 실제로는 그것들이 어떻게 작동하는지 모르는 것 같아요. 그렇죠?
Father	그러니까, 너는 너의 아빠를, 너보다 훨씬 오래 살아온 이 아빠를 안 믿는구나. 너무 많은 질문을 하는구나, Max야. 나는 일할 수 있는 조용한 장소를 찾아봐야겠다.
Max	엄마 봐요. 마술이예요.
Mother	아니, 마술이 아니야.

3 Focus

Relative Adverbs
관계부사

선행사가 시간, 장소, 이유, 방법 등을 나타낼 때, 관계부사 when, where, why, how 등을 쓸 수 있다. 관계부사는 전치사+which로 바꾸어 쓸 수 있다. The day / the year / the time 등이 선행사로 올 때, 관계부사로 that을 쓰기도 한다. 이 경우, 대개 that은 생략된다.

This is the house where the poet lived.
= This is the house in which the poet lived.
= This is the house (which/that) the poet lived in.
(이것은 그 시인이 살았던 집입니다.)

Do you remember the day when we first met?
= Do you remember the day (that) we first met?
(당신은 우리가 처음 만났던 날을 기억합니까?)

That's the reason why Dick doesn't like her.
= That's the reason (that) Dick doesn't like her.
(그것이 Dick이 그녀를 좋아하지 않는 이유입니다.)

방법을 나타내는 관계부사 how의 경우, 선행사 the way와 how 중 하나를 생략하고 쓰게 되는데 the way that은 가능하다.

Can you show me how I use this machine?
(당신은 저에게 제가 이 기계를 사용하는 방법을 보여주실 수 있습니까?)

Can you show me the way how I use this machine? (X)

where과 when은 비한정절에서 쓰이기도 한다.

We went to Applebee's, where we had dinner with Tim.
(우리는 호수 식당에 갔는데, 거기에서 우리는 Tim과 함께 저녁을 먹었습니다.)

Mark likes to drive at night, when the roads are not busy.
(Mark는 밤에 드라이브 하는 것을 좋아하는데, 그 때 도로는 혼잡하지 않습니다.)

Task 5

Choose the proper expressions.

1. The town ______________ is small.
   (1) which I grew up (2) where I grew up
   (3) in that I grew up (4) where I grew up in

2. 1960 is the year ________________________.
   (1) when the revolution took place (2) where the revolution took place
   (3) the revolution took place then (4) on that the revolution took place

3. Did you read about ____________________?
   (1) that happened to Tom (2) where happened to Tom
   (3) what happened to Tom (4) which happened to Tom

4. This is the way ____________________.
   (1) why they found it (2) that they found it
   (3) which they found in it (4) where they found

5. Do you know the reason _______________?
   (1) because she quarreled with her husband
   (2) she quarreled with her husband
   (3) on that she quarreled with her husband
   (4) she quarreled with her husband because of that

6. Tell me all ________________ about the student.
   (1) which you know (2) you know it
   (3) what you know (4) that you know

Task 6

Choose the proper word.

1. The simplest emotion _______ has been observed in human behavior is curiosity.

   (1) whose (2) that

   (3) who (4) what

2. Do you know the city ________ she was born?

   (1) where (2) that

   (3) which (4) how

3. Cathy, _________ has twins, often needs a babysitter.

   (1) that (2) whom

   (3) which (4) who

4. lost the wallet __________ had bought for me.

   (1) my brother (2) whose my brother

   (3) whom my brother (4) with which my brother

5. A stadium ____________ 100,000 people will be built in the city.

   (1) can hold (2)held

   (3) that can hold it (4) which can hold

6. This is __________ geometry problems in France.

   (1) that Descartes solved (2) what Descartes solved

   (3) how Descartes solved (4) Descartes solved

Culture Corner

Salad days

salad days라는 말을 직역하면 '샐러드 나날들'이라는 말이 된다. 이 말은 아직 무엇인가를 배워가는 미숙한 시기를 뜻한다. 영화에서 보면 어머니가 아들의 결혼을 반대하면서 훈계를 할 때 이 표현을 사용한다. Don't be insane. It's time high time you grew up, my boy. Your salad days are over. (정신 없는 짓 그만해라. 이제 철이 들어야 할 때다. 바로 그때야. 너의 철없는 시절은 끝났다.) (이 뒤에 나온 표현은 생략했습니다. 확인해주세요.)

'미숙한, 아직 덜 익은' 이라는 뜻으로 green이 쓰이기도 한다. She is very green. 이라고 하면 '그녀는 매우 미숙하다.' 라는 의미이다. green fruit는 '풋과일'을 뜻하고, greenhorn는 '경험이 없는 사람'의 의미로 쓰인다. He's done pretty well for a greenhorn. (그는 첫솜씨로는 꽤 잘했다.)

한편 green thumb은 '정원을 가꾸는 소질이 있는 사람'을 가리키는 말로 쓰인다. She has a green thumb. Her flowers look so healthy. (그녀는 정원 가꾸기를 아주 잘해서 그녀의 꽃은 너무 싱싱하게 보인다.) green이 들어간 또 다른 표현으로 green with envy라는 것이 있는 데, 이것은 '다른 사람에게 일어난 행운에 대해서 질투하거나 부러워하는 마음'을 나타낸다. Linda was green with envy when she saw Jessica's fiancé. (Linda는 Jessica의 약혼자를 보았을 때 무척 샘이 났다.)

Don't be insane. It's high time you grew up, my boy. Your salad days are over.
She is very green.
He's done pretty well for a greenhorn.
She has a green thumb. Her flowers look so healthy.
Linda was green with envy when she saw Jessica's fiancé.

Wrap-up

1. The woman who lives next door is a lawyer.
2. Mark will tell you what you need to know.
3. The suit (that) John bought doesn't fit him very well.
4. My brother Daniel, who lives in L.A., got married last year.
5. This is the house where the poet lived.

Final Tips

Everything that happened was my fault. (O)

Everything what happened was my fault. (X)

what은 선행사를 포함한 관계대명사이므로 선행사 everything 다음에 쓸 수 없습니다.

The hotel where we stayed wasn't very clean. (O)

The hotel that we stayed wasn't very clean. (X)

관계사절에서 부사의 역할을 하므로 관계부사 where가 쓰입니다.

The hotel wasn't very clean. + We stayed there.

→ The hotel where we stayed wasn't very clean.

Cathy passed her driving test, which surprised everybody. (O)

Cathy passed her driving test, that surprised everybody. (X)

앞 절 전체를 선행사로 쓸 때는 콤마 다음에 관계대명사 which를 씁니다.

Translation

모든 것이 다 제 탓이었습니다.
우리가 묵었던 호텔은 그리 깨끗하지 않았습니다.
Cathy가 운전면허 시험을 통과했는데 이 사실은 모든 사람을 놀라게 만들었습니다.

Review Test

Choose the correct words.

1. She runs an Internet shopping mall (where, which) sells the latest fashions.

2. I don't believe (that, what) you've just said.

3. This is the place (which, where) he caught the squirrel.

4. Some teens skip breakfast, (which, that) is not good for their health.

5. England has the best tea (that, what) one can buy.

6. Find me the girl (whose, that) foot will fit this shoe.

7. Please tell me the reason (why, how) you majored in English.

Make one sentence from two by using relative pronouns.

8. The scientist won the Nobel Prize. He discovered a new element.
   The scientist ____________ discovered a new element won the Nobel Prize.

9. I read a lot of books. Most of them were very useful.
   I read a lot of books, most of ____________ were very useful.

10. The TV program will be rerun this evening. We missed it.
    The TV program ____________ we missed will be rerun this evening.

ocus 1-Focus 3

Chapter 11

COMPARATIVES

Introduction

Lesson objectives

1. Comparison 비교

2. Comparison of Equality 동등 비교

3. Superlative 최상급

Check-up

Ben & Olivia's everyday

Ben : How does it taste?

Olivia : Good. This is the _________ (delicious, more delicious, most delicious) meal I've ever eaten.

Ben : But you look worried. What's the matter?

Olivia : Well, I can't understand why Cathy was promoted and not me. Am I not as _________ (good, better, best) as her? Is she _________ (smart, smarter, smartest) than me? Did she work _________ (hard, harder, the hardest) than me?

Ben : don't know. She may be a little _________ (lucky, luckier, luckiest) than you are.

Olivia : She is not as _________ (intelligent, more intelligent, most intelligent) as I am, but she has been _________ (successful, more successful, most successful) than me. Do you think good luck is more important _________ (as, than, that) talent alone?

Ben : Well, appearance is important too. And Cathy is…

Olivia : What? The most attractive woman in the office? You are the _________ (stupid, stupider, stupidest) man alive sometimes.

Check-up

Answers

Ben : How does it taste?

Olivia : Good. This is the (**most delicious**) meal I've ever eaten.

Ben : But you look worried. What's the matter?

Olivia : Well, I can't understand why Cathy was promoted and not me. Am I not as (**good**) as her? Is she (**smarter**) than me? Did she work (**harder**) than me?

Ben : I don't know. She may be a little (**luckier**) than you are.

Olivia : She is not as (**intelligent**) as I am, but she has been (**more successful**) than me. Do you think good luck is more important (**than**) talent alone?

Ben : Well, appearance is important too. And Cathy is…

Olivia : What? The most attractive woman in the office? You are the (**stupidest**) man alive sometimes.

Translation

Ben : 맛이 어때?

Olivia : 좋아. 지금까지 내가 먹어 본 음식 중 가장 맛있어.

Ben : 그런데 걱정거리가 있는 표정이네. 무슨 일이야?

Olivia : 음, 왜 Cathy가 승진하고 나는 안 되었는지 이해가 안 돼. 내가 Cathy 보다 못해? Cathy가 나보다 똑똑해? 나보다 더 열심히 일했어?

Ben : 난 잘 모르겠어. 너보다 운이 더 좋은 것일 수도 있지.

Olivia : Cathy는 나만큼 똑똑하지 않은데 나보다 더 성공했어. 운이 실력보다 더 중요하다고 생각해?

Ben : 글쎄, 외모도 중요하긴 하지. Cathy는…

Olivia : 뭐? 사무실에서 가장 매력적인 여자라고? 당신은 가끔 보면 세상에서 제일 멍청해.

1 Focus

Comparison
비교

비교 표현은 형식에 따라 원급, 비교급, 최상급으로 구분된다.

(1) 원급 (as ~ as)

Tom is as clever as Mike.
(Tom은 Mike만큼 영리합니다.)

John does not work as quickly as Frank.
(John은 Frank 만큼 일을 신속하게 하지 않습니다.)

(2) 우등 비교 (~er than)

I am taller than Joe.
(저는 Joe보다 키가 큽니다.)

She is more intelligent than her sister.
(그녀는 그녀의 언니보다 더 총명합니다.)

(3) 최상급 (~est)

What's the largest city in Germany?
(독일에서 가장 큰 도시는 무슨 도시입니까?)

Madonna is one of the most famous pop singers ever.
(Madonna는 지금까지 가장 유명한 팝 가수 중의 한 명입니다.)

2 비교급/최상급 형태

(1) 규칙 변화

단어 길이가 짧으면 원급에 -er, -est를 붙여 비교급과 최상급을 만들며 단어가 긴 경우에는 more, most를 붙여 사용한다.

i) 1음절의 경우, -er, -est를 붙인다.

cheap - cheaper - cheapest　　short - shorter - shortest
slow - slower - slowest　　big - bigger - biggest
thin - thinner - thinnest　　hot - hotter - hottest

ii) 2음절 단어 중 -y로 끝나는 것은 -ier로 쓴다.

lucky - luckier - luckiest
easy - easier - easiest
early - earlier - earliest
pretty - prettier - prettiest
heavy - heavier - heaviest
happy - happier - happiest

iii) 2음절 이상의 단어에는 more, most를 붙인다.

expensive - more expensive - most expensive
careful - more careful - most careful
polite - more polite - most polite

iv) -ly로 끝나는 부사에는 more, most를 붙인다.

slowly - more slowly - most slowly
quietly - more quietly - most quietly
seriously - more seriously - most seriously
cf) early - earlier - earliest

(2) 불규칙 변화

good/well - better - best
many/much- more - most
far - farther - farthest(거리)
old - older - oldest (연령)
bad/ill - worse - worst
little - less - least
far - further - furthest (거리/정도)
old - elder - eldest (손위관계)

3 Comparative(비교급)

(1) 비교급 + than

That box is bigger than this one.
(저 상자는 이 상자보다 더 큽니다.)

The shopping mall is more crowded than usual.
(쇼핑몰은 평소보다 더 붐빕니다.)

Brian did worse on the exam than Chris did.
(Brian은 Chris 보다 시험을 못 봤습니다.)

(2) ~than me

She is five inches taller than me.
(= She is five inches taller than I am)
(그녀는 나보다 5인치 더 큽니다.)

They earn more money than us.
(= They earn more money than we do.)
(그들은 우리보다 돈을 더 법니다.)

(3) 비교급 수식

much, far, even, still, a lot, a little, a bit, slightly 등이 비교급 앞에 올 수 있다.

He is not much happier than before.
(그는 전보다 훨씬 더 행복하진 않습니다.)

The movie was far more interesting than I expected.
(그 영화는 내가 예상한 것보다 더 재미있었습니다.)

I thought she was younger than me, but in fact she's slightly older.
(나는 그녀가 나보다 어릴 거라고 생각했습니다. 그러나 사실 나보다 약간 나이가 많습니다.)

(4) 비교급 + and + 비교급

'점점 더 ~하다' 의 뜻이다.

It's getting hotter and hotter.
(날씨가 점점 더워지고 있습니다.)

Sally became more and more beautiful.
(Sally는 점점 더 예뻐졌습니다.)

As each new problem arose, we felt less and less enthusiastic.
(각각의 새로운 문제점이 제기됨에 따라, 우리는 점점 더 열정을 잃어갔습니다.)

(5) the + 비교급, the + 비교급

'~하면 할수록 더욱 ~하다' 의 뜻이다.

The higher we climb, the colder it becomes.
(=As we climb higher, it becomes colder.)
(우리가 산에 높이 오르면 오를수록 점점 추워집니다.)

The better we know her, the more we admire her.
(우리가 그녀를 더 잘 알면 알수록 그녀를 더 존경하게 됩니다.)

What time should we arrive? The sooner the better.
(우리가 몇 시에 도착할 것 같아요? 빠르면 빠를수록 좋아요.)

(6) older and elder

My elder/older brother is a computer programmer.
(나의 손위 형은 컴퓨터 프로그래머입니다.)

My brother is older than I am.
(나의 남자 형제는 나보다 나이가 많습니다.)

My brother is elder than I am. (X)

(7) 최상급 의미

부정어 + 비교급 + than / 비교급 + than any other + 단수명사

No boy in the class is taller than Sam.
(학급에서 Sam보다 더 큰 남학생은 없습니다.)
=Sam is taller than any other boy in the class.
(Sam은 학급의 다른 어떤 소년들보다도 큽니다.)
=Sam is the tallest boy in the class.
(Sam은 학급에서 가장 키가 큰 소년입니다.)

I have never seen a more polite student than this girl.
(나는 이 소녀보다 보다 공손한 학생을 본적이 없어요.)
= This girl is the most polite student I've ever seen.
(이 소녀는 내가 보아온 가장 공손한 학생입니다.)

Task 1

Complete the sentences using the comparative form of the word in parentheses.

1. The climate of Korea is __________ than that of China. (pleasant)
2. Linda spends __________ on clothes than Emma does. (little)
3. I was __________ than usual today. (busy)
4. If you need any __________ details, please contact us by email. (far)
5. Hurry up! The weather is getting ________. (bad)
6. I need a _________ room. I don't have enough space here. (big)

Task 2

Choose the right expression from the box.

more serious	more easily	the better
even	more and more	more popular

1. The higher the price, _________ the service.
2. We could do this _________ with a computer.
3. It's becoming _________ difficult to get a job.
4. He is _________ than any other doctor in the hospital.
5. Jessica is _________ thinner than you.
6. His illness is _________ than we thought.

2 Focus

Comparison of Equality
동등비교

1 as ~ as

John can run as fast as Bill.
(John은 Bill만큼 빨리 뛸 수 있습니다.)

Gary doesn't have as many friends as Roy.
(Gary는 Roy만큼 친구가 많지 않습니다.)

Your advertising is not as effective as ours.
(당신의 광고는 우리 것만큼 효과적이지 않습니다.)

2 as ~ as possible

as ~ as one can과 **바꾸어 쓸 수 있다.**

She studied as hard as possible.
(=She studied as hard as she could.)
(그녀는 할 수 있는 한 열심히 공부했습니다.)

She goes shopping as often as possible.
(=She goes shopping as often as she can.)
(그녀는 할 수 있는 한 자주 쇼핑을 갑니다.)

3 twice as ~ as

Alex has twice as much money as Eric.
(Alex는 Eric 의 2배의 돈을 가지고 있습니다.)

This is three times as long as that.
(이것은 저것보다 3배 깁니다.)

I'm not going out with a man who's twice as old as I am.
(나는 나보다 두 배나 나이가 많은 남자와 데이트하지 않을 겁니다.)

4 the same as

Ed is the same age as Bill.

(Ed는 Bill과 동갑입니다.)

He's very cheerful - just the same as his brother.

(그는 꼭 그의 형만큼이나 매우 쾌활합니다.)

5 동급 수식

nearly, almost, just, not quite 등이 수식할 수 있다.

It's nearly as hot as yesterday.
(날씨가 거의 어제만큼 덥습니다.)

I thought he was very nice at first, but he's just as bad as everybody else.
(나는 처음에 그가 무척 괜찮은 사람이라고 생각했습니다만, 그는 다른 사람들과 꼭 마찬가지로 나쁜 사람입니다.)

I'm not quite as healthy as I was last year.
(나는 작년만큼 그렇게 건강한 것은 아닙니다.)

6 최상급의 의미

부정어+as~as 는 '~만큼 ~한 것은 아무것도 없다' 의 뜻으로 최상급의 의미를 지닌다.

Nothing is as important as good health.
(아무것도 건강만큼 중요한 것은 없습니다.)

= Good Health is the most important thing.
(건강이 가장 중요한 것입니다.)

No other girl in our class is as small as Mary.
(우리 반에서 어떤 여학생도 Mary처럼 작진 않습니다.)

= Mary is the smallest girl in our class.
(Mary는 우리 반에서 가장 작은 여학생입니다.)

Task 3

Choose the proper word in parentheses.

1. Tom is (older, elder) than my eldest sister.
2. It's not cold, but it isn't as (warm, warmer) as yesterday.
3. Her children got up (late, later) than usual.
4. Your hair is the same color (as, than) hers.
5. This is five times as (large, larger) as that.
6. I didn't spend as (much, more) money as you did.

Task 4

Complete the sentences using as ~ as. Choose the word from the box.

long	bad	little	peaceful	much	loudly	carefully

1. There's enough food. You can have __________ you want.
2. It took three times __________ we expected.
3. He drove __________ he could.
4. There are a lot of conflicts in the Middle East. It is not ____________ Europe.

In the following sentences use the comparative forms of one of the words from the box.

5. I know that my handwriting is bad, but my brother's is _________.
6. I can't hear you. Could you speak ___________?
7. Left-brain people are _________ emotional than right-brain people.

REST AREA

Translation

Wendy 안녕 Max. 너 나랑 소꿉장난 할래? 그것이 장난감 차를 갖고 노는 것보다 훨씬 재미있을 거야.

Max 모르겠어. 어떻게 노는 건데?

Wendy 흠. 우선은 네가 직장에서 집으로 와. 그런 다음에 내가 직장에서 집으로 올께.

Wendy 우리는 직장에서 일어난 일에 대해 불평하는 거야. 그리고 누가 저녁을 지을 차례인지 논쟁을 하는 거지.

3 Focus

Superlatives
최상급

1 the + 최상급 표현

(1) 최상급 + of~

Steve is the tallest boy of all his classmates.
(Steve는 그의 학급 친구들 중에서 가장 키가 큰 남학생입니다.)

February is the shortest month of the year.
(2월은 연중 가장 날 수가 적은 달입니다.)

Claire is the youngest of the four girls.
(Claire는 네 명의 딸 중 가장 어립니다.)

(2) 최상급 + in~

Which is the biggest city in the world?
(세상에서 가장 큰 도시는 어디입니까?)

It's the most expensive room in the hotel.
(그것이 호텔에서 가장 비싼 방입니다.)

He's the most annoying person in the whole office.
(그는 사무실 전체에서 가장 짜증나는 사람입니다.)

(3) 최상급 + 완료형

That is the best movie I've ever seen.
(그것은 제가 봤던 최고의 영화입니다.)

He is the most boring person I've ever met.
(그는 제가 만나본 사람들 중 가장 지루한 사람입니다.)

It was the most horrible feeling I've ever had.
(그것은 제가 겪은 가장 끔찍한 감정입니다.)

That's the most helpful idea so far.
(그것은 지금까지 가장 유용한 아이디어입니다.)

(4) one of + 최상급

Ice hockey is one of the most dangerous sports in the Olympics.
(아이스하키는 올림픽 종목 중 최고로 위험한 스포츠 중 하나입니다.)

The telephone is one of the most useful inventions ever.
(전화는 지금까지 가장 유용한 발명품 중 하나입니다.)

Tourism is one of the most promising industries in Korea.
(관광은 한국에서 가장 유망한 산업 중 하나입니다.)

2 the를 붙이지 않는 최상급

(1) 동일물의 자체 성질을 나타낼 때

This mountain is highest at this point.
(이 산은 이 지점이 가장 높습니다.)

cf This mountain is the highest in Korea.
(이 산은 한국에서 가장 높습니다.)

He's nicest when he's had a few drinks.
(그는 술을 몇 잔 마실 때 가장 멋있습니다.)

Animals are most dangerous when they're hungry.
(동물은 배고플 때 가장 위험합니다.)

(2) 최상급이 소유격과 함께 쓰일 때

She is my best friend.
(그녀는 저의 가장 좋은 친구입니다.)

This is your very last chance.
(이것이 당신의 진짜 마지막 기회입니다.)

Have you read his most recent book?
(당신은 그의 가장 최근의 책을 읽었습니까?)

3 최상급 수식

quite, by far, the very 등이 최상급을 수식할 수 있다.

I'll bring my very best wine.
(저는 저의 진짜 최고의 와인을 가져오겠습니다.)

He was by far the most intelligent man she had ever seen.
(그는 그녀가 여태까지 보아왔던 사람 중에서 뛰어나게 지적인 남자였습니다.)

4 second 최상급

Hyundae Motors is the second largest car maker in India.
(현대 자동차는 인도에서 두 번째로 큰 자동차 회사입니다.)

This is the third longest river in this country.
(이것은 이 나라에서 세 번째로 긴 강입니다.)

5 관용표현

at most = not more than (많아야, 기껏해야)
at least = not less than (적어도, 최소한)
at best (기껏해야)
at first (처음에는)
at last (마침내)

I can lend you only 100 dollars at most.
(저는 기껏해야 100달러만 당신에게 빌려줄 수 있습니다.)

She is at least thirty years old.
(그녀는 적어도 서른 살은 되었습니다.)

He is at best a second-rate poet.
(그는 기껏해야 이류 시인입니다.)

The work was hard at first, but I got used to it.
(처음엔 그 일이 어려웠습니다만, 그것에 익숙해 졌습니다.)

At last after a long search, they found their child.
(마침내 오랜 수색 끝에 그들은 그들의 아이를 찾았습니다.)

Task 5

Fill in the blanks using the word in parentheses.

1. No other dramatist is __________ than Shakespeare. (famous)
2. Soccer is one of the __________ sports in the country. (popular)
3. Melissa is the __________ person I've ever met. (patient)
4. The subway is far _________ than a taxi. (cheap)

5. Compared to the others, they are the two __________ students in the class. (bad)

6. Of all outdoor activities Paul likes fishing __________. (well)

Task 6

Choose the correct answers.

1. The history of war ____________ that of man.
   (1) as old as (2) is as old as
   (3) is as older than (4) that as old as

2. The price is reasonable; I would gladly pay _________ he asked.
   (1) as much twice as (2) twice more than
   (3) twice as many as (4) twice as much as

3. The bigger the apartment, __________ the rent.
   (1) higher (2) highest
   (3) the higher (4) the highest

4. Mark is __________ salesman in the company.
   (1) the most successful (2) more successful
   (3) as successful as (4) one of the most successful

5. They were so poor that they had __________ fifty dollars.
   (1) at least (2) at most
   (3) at last (4) at once

6. Health is __________ any other thing.
   (1) not as valuable as (2) not valuable than
   (3) the most valuable (4) more valuable than

Culture Corner

Sunday best

Sunday best는 '나들이 옷'을 뜻한다. 서양 사람들은 평일은 작업복 차림으로 일하다가 일요일이 되면 목욕도 깨끗이 하고 머리 손질도 곱게 하며 옷 중에서 가장 좋은 옷을 입고 온 가족과 함께 교회에 가는데, 이 말은 여기에서 유래했다. 이러한 전통 때문에 교회에 안 나가는 사람들까지도 나들이 옷을 Sunday best라고 부르게 된 것이다. The whole family went to church dressed in their Sunday best. (모든 가족은 잘 차려 입고 교회로 갔다.)

요일과 관련된 다른 표현으로 Monday morning blues 또는 Monday morning feeling이라고 하는 것이 있다. 우리말에도 '월요병'이라는 말이 있듯이 영어에도 월요일이 되면 온 몸이 나른하고 의욕이 떨어지는 증상을 가리켜 이렇게 말한다. 여기에서 blues는 '깊은 슬픔' 이나 '우울한 감정'을 나타낸다. 크리스마스 후유증도 blues를 써서 after(post) Christmas blues라고 한다. After a wild weekend of drinking and dancing, it's not surprising that Bob had the Monday morning blues. (음주 가무로 광란의 주말을 보낸 다음에 Bob이 월요일에 출근을 하면서 우울한 것은 당연한 일이다.)

Super Tuesday라는 말도 들어본 적이 있을 것이다. 미국에서는 대의원들은 주 별로 실시되는 Presidential primary election(대통령 예비선거)를 통해 선출되는데, 사전에 지지후보를 미리 공표한 대의원들을 과반수 이상 한꺼번에 선출하는 3월 첫째 주 화요일을 Super Tuesday라고 부른다. 이날에는 10여 개 주에서 동시에 예비선거가 실시되어, 후보 지명에 필요한 대의원의 절반 정도가 정해지기 때문에 사실상 민주 · 공화 양당의 후보를 결정짓는 중요한 날이 된다. Candidates have to do well on Super Tuesday if they wish to secure their party's nomination. (후보들은 그들의 당 지명을 확실히 하기를 바란다면 Super Tuesday에 잘해야 한다.)

Ash Wednesday는 Lent (사순절)의 첫 날을 의미하는 데, 참회의 상징으로 머리에 재를 뿌린 관습에서 유래했다. Ash Wednesday marks the beginning of the Lenten season, which lasts until the Easter Vigil. (Ash Wednesday는 사순 절기의 시작을 의미하는 데, 사순절은 부활전야까지 지속된다.)

Good Friday(성금요일)은 East Sunday(부활 주일)의 금요일을 일컫는 말로서, 예수님의 십자가형을 기억하는 종교적인 날이다. 부활 주일 다음날인 Easter Monday도 기념을 한다. Good Friday is a public holiday in most European countries as is Easter Monday. (Good Friday는 Easter Monday와 마찬가지로 대부분의 유럽국가들에서 공식적인 휴일이다.) Friday와 관련된 또 다른 표현으로 유명한 TGIF (Thank God, It's Friday!)가 있다. 주5일제 근무를 예전부터 하고 있는 미국에서는 금요일이 되면 주말이 다가오는 기쁨으로 이런 인사말을 즐겨 쓴다. TGIF! Let's go for a drink. (드디어 금요일입니다. 한 잔 하러 갑시다.) Casual Friday라는 표현도 있는데, 한 주간의 마지막 날에 직장에서 정장 대신 캐주얼을 입도록 해주는 미국의 관습을 일컫는 말이다. Steve usually wears a short-sleeved shirt and chinos on Casual Friday. (Steve는 보통 Casual Friday에 짧은 소매 셔츠에 치노를 입는다.)

The whole family went to church dressed in their Sunday best.
After a wild weekend of drinking and dancing, it's not surprising that Bob had the Monday morning blues.
Candidates have to do well on Super Tuesday if they wish to secure their party's nomination.
Ash Wednesday marks the beginning of the Lenten season, which lasts until the Easter Vigil.
Good Friday is a public holiday in most European countries as is Easter Monday.
TGIF! Let's go for a drink.
Steve usually wears a short-sleeved shirt and chinos on Casual Friday.

Wrap-up

1. That box is bigger than this one.
2. The shopping mall is more crowded than usual.
3. The better we know her, the more we admire her.
4. Gary doesn't have as many friends as Roy.
5. It's the most expensive room in the hotel.

Final Tips

The catalogue is filled with the latest fashion for spring and summer. (O)

The catalogue is filled with the last fashion for spring and summer. (X)

'lastest'는 '최근의'라는 뜻이고, 'last'는 '지난, 마지막'이라는 뜻입니다. '지나간 계절의 패션'이라는 의미로 쓰고 싶으면 'last season's fashion'이라고 해야 합니다.

What is the highest mountain in the world? (O)

What is the highest mountain of the world? (X)

What is the happiest day of your life? (O)

최상급 다음에 '세상에서'라고 할 때는 전치사 in을 써서 in the world 라고 표현합니다. of 다음에는 주로 시간을 나타내는 말이 옵니다.

My eldest daughter is 16 years old. (O)

My oldest daughter is 16 years old. (O)

Budhism is one of the world's oldest religions. (O)

Budhism is one of the world's eldest religions. (X)

가족 구성원에 대해서 말할 때는 eldest 또는 oldest라는 표현을 다 쓸 수 있습니다. 그러나 그 외에는 eldest라는 표현을 쓸 수 없습니다.

Translation

그 카탈로그는 봄과 여름을 위한 최신 패션으로 가득 차있습니다.
세상에서 가장 높은 산은 무엇입니까?
당신의 일생중 가장 행복했던 날은 언제입니까?
나의 맏딸은 16살 입니다.
불교는 세상에서 가장 오래된 종교 중의 하나입니다.

Review Test

Choose the correct words.

1. What is the (popular, more popular, most popular) sport in your country?

2. Nothing is as (valuable, more valuable, most valuable) as health.

3. The more carefully you write, the (few, fewer, fewest) mistakes you will make.

4. DVD players in this shop are (expensive, more expensive, most expensive) than in other shops.

5. Here are all the (last, later, latest) novels.

Fill in the blanks using the words in parentheses. You can have one or two words in the blanks.

6. This is one of the ___________ (bad) grades I have ever gotten in my life.

7. Developing the new program is much ___________ (challenging) than maintaining it.

8. Gas is three times as ___________ (expensive) as it was five years ago.

9. What was the ____________ (happy) day of your life?

10. Time is ___________ (precious) than anything else.

ocus1-Focus3

Chapter 12

CONJUNCTIONS

Introduction

Lesson objectives

1. Coordinate conjunctions 등위접속사

2. Subordinate conjunctions - noun clause 종속접속사 - 명사절

3. Subordinate conjunctions - adverbial clause 종속접속사 - 부사절

Check-up

Ben & Olivia's everyday

Ben : Hi, honey. I'm home early today _________ (so, because) you didn't look well this morning. How are you feeling now?

Olivia : I'm not feeling any better _________ (if, although) I've taken some pills.

Ben : Go to bed _________ (and, but) rest a bit more. Do you think _________ (since, that) you'd be able to cook a special dinner tomorrow?

Olivia : Are you out of your mind? You want me to cook when I am feeling awful like this? There is no way I am going to cook you a special dinner.

Ben : But it's important. I'm up for a big promotion _________ (so, because) I invited the boss and his wife over for dinner.

Olivia : Would you get paid much more?

Ben : A lot more, and I would also get a company car.

Olivia : All right. I am going to take some more pills and get to the supermarket _________ (before, after) it closes. You clean the house _________ (while, during) I am out shopping.

Ben : There's no hurry, Olivia. I thought you said you were feeling awful.

Olivia : Well, I'm feeling much better _________ (before, after) hearing your wonderful news, aren't I.

Check-up

Answers

Ben : Hi, honey. I'm home early today (**because**) you didn't look well this morning. How are you feeling now?

Olivia : I'm not feeling any better (**although**) I've taken some pills.

Ben : Go to bed (**and**) rest a bit more. Do you think (**that**) you'd be able to cook a special dinner tomorrow?

Olivia : Are you out of your mind? You want me to cook when I am feeling awful like this? There is no way I am going to cook you a special dinner.

Ben : But it's important. I'm up for a big promotion (**so**) I invited the boss and his wife over for dinner.

Olivia : Would you get paid much more?

Ben : A lot more, and I would also get a company car.

Olivia : All right. I am going to take some more pills and get to the supermarket (**before**) it closes. You clean the house (**while**) I am out shopping.

Ben : There's no hurry, Olivia. I thought you said you were feeling awful.

Olivia : Well, I'm feeling much better (**after**) hearing your wonderful news, aren't I.

Check-up

Translation

Ben : 나 왔어. 오늘 아침에 보니까 당신 몸 안 좋아 보이길래 일찍 퇴근했지. 지금은 좀 어때?

Olivia : 약 먹었는데도 전혀 나아지질 않네.

Ben : 누워서 좀 쉬어. 내일 저녁식사 신경 써서 해 줄 수 있을까?

Olivia : 당신 제정신이야? 이렇게 상태가 안 좋은데 나보고 요리를 하라고? 특별한 저녁을 대접할 일은 절대 없을 거야.

Ben : 하지만 중요한 일이야. 곧 진급날이라 사장님과 사모님을 저녁 식사에 초대했단 말이야.

Olivia : 급여도 많이 받게 돼?

Ben : 훨씬 많이 받지. 그리고 회사 승용차도 받게 될 거야.

Olivia : 알았어. 약을 더 먹고 마트 문 닫기 전에 가야겠다. 내가 장보는 동안 당신이 집 청소해.

Ben : 서두를 거 없어, Olivia. 몸 안 좋다며.

Olivia : 음, 멋진 소식 듣고 나니까 훨씬 좋아졌어.

1 Focus

Coordinate conjunctions
등위접속사

1 접속사와 절

(1) 접속사 종류

접속사는 단어, 구, 절을 연결하는 역할을 한다.

i) 등위 접속사(coordinate conjunction): 단어와 단어, 구와 구, 절과 절을 대등하게 연결한다. (and, but, or, so, etc.)

ii) 종속 접속사(subordinate conjunction): 주절과 종속절을 연결한다. (because, while, if, although, etc.)

(2) 접속사 위치

종속접속사가 이끄는 종속절은 문장의 앞부분에 올 수도 있고, 뒤에 올 수도 있다. 종속절이 앞에 올 때는 대개 콤마가 뒤따른다.

If you need any help, please let me know.
Please let me know if you need any help.
(만약 당신이 도움이 필요하면 나에게 알려주세요.)

(3) 절 (clause)

'주어 + 동사'로 이루어진 단위이다. 문장은 절 하나로 구성될 수도 있고, 여러 개의 절로 구성될 수도 있다. 여러 개의 절은 접속사에 의해 연결된다.

i) 하나의 절로 구성된 문장

He turned off the light.
(그는 불을 껐습니다.)

ii) 두 개 이상의 절로 구성된 문장

I bought a newspaper, but I didn't read it.
(저는 신문을 샀지만 읽지는 않았습니다.)

Always brush your teeth after you eat.
(무엇을 먹은 후에 늘 이를 닦으세요.)

(4) 접속사와 전치사

접속사 뒤에는 절이 오지만, 전치사 뒤에는 절이 올 수 없다.

We met a lot of interesting people while we were on vacation. (접속사)

We met a lot of interesting people during our vacation. (전치사)
(우리는 방학 동안 많은 재미있는 사람들을 만났습니다.)

I'll call you before I come. (접속사)
(제가 오기 전에 전화 드리겠습니다.)

I'll call you before nine o'clock.(전치사)
(9시 전에 제가 전화 드리겠습니다.)

(5) 두 개의 절을 연결하는 하나의 접속사

두 개의 절을 연결할 때는 한 개의 접속사를 쓴다.

Although she was very tired, she went out with him.
(비록 그녀가 매우 피곤했지만 그와 함께 외출했습니다.)

She was very tired, but she went out with him.
(그녀는 매우 피곤했지만 그와 함께 외출했습니다.)

Although she was very tired, but she went out with him (X)

그러나 두 개의 종속절을 연결할 때는 두 개의 종속접속사와 하나의 등위접속사를 쓸 수 있다.

Ryan came back because he ran out of money, and because his wife got sick.
(Ryan은 돈이 떨어졌기 때문에 그리고 그의 부인이 아팠기 때문에 집에 돌아왔습니다.)

2 등위접속사

(1) and

She can play the piano, violin, and guitar.
(그녀는 피아노, 바이올린 그리고 기타를 연주할 수 있습니다.)

My sister is married and (she) lives in Busan.
(제 여동생은 결혼했고 부산에 살고 있습니다.)

(2) but

She is small but strong.
(그녀는 작지만 힘이 셉니다.)

She was poor, but she was honest.
(그녀는 가난했지만 정직했습니다.)

I liked the coat, but I decided not to buy it.
(저는 그 코트가 맘에 들었지만 사지 않기로 결심했습니다.)

(3) or

He doesn't smoke or drink.
(그는 담배를 피우거나 술을 마시지 않습니다.)

Don't do that again or I'll hit you.
(그와 같은 일을 다시는 하지 마세요. 그렇지 않으면 내가 당신을 때릴 것입니다.)

(4) so

They had some free time, so they went to the movies.
(그들은 여유시간이 약간 있어서 영화 보러 갔습니다.)

I felt sorry for her, so I tried to help her
(저는 그녀가 가여워서 그녀를 도우려고 노력했습니다.)

3 등위상관접속사

(1) either A or B

If you want ice cream, you can have either coffee or vanilla.
(아이스크림을 원하시면 커피나 바닐라 중 하나를 드실 수 있습니다.)

I left the ruler either on the table or in the drawer.
(저는 자를 탁자 위나 서랍 속에 두었습니다.)

(2) neither A nor B

He drinks neither tea nor coffee.
(그는 차도 커피도 마시지 않습니다.)

Neither Mary nor Jane is at home.
(Mary도 Jane도 집에 있지 않습니다.)

(3) both A and B

Tom was both hungry and tired.
(Tom은 배도 고팠고 피곤하기도 했습니다.)

Both men and women can vote.
(남녀가 다 투표할 수 있습니다.)

(4) not only A but also B

He not only plays well, but also writes music.
(그는 연주를 잘 할 뿐만 아니라 곡도 씁니다.)

Sam is not only handsome but also intelligent.
(Sam은 잘생겼을 뿐만 아니라 총명하기도 합니다.)

(5) not A but B

She stole, not because she needed the money, but because she liked stealing.
(그녀는 돈이 필요해서가 아니라, 훔치는 것을 좋아해서 훔쳤습니다.)

It is not an option but a necessity for survival.
(그것은 선택이 아니라 생존을 위해 필연적인 것이다.)

Task 1

Choose the appropriate conjunction from the box. Use each conjunction only once.

while	until	or	even though	so	because

1. We went to the zoo __________ it was very cold.
2. Tim is in good shape physically __________ he gets a lot of exercise.
3. She gave me a map, __________ I wouldn't get lost.
4. __________ Mary was reading a book, her children were playing outside.
5. They will stay in New Orleans __________ the festival ends.
6. Turn the heat down __________ the pancake will burn.

Task 2

Correct the underlined part if it is incorrect. If the sentence is correct, write "correct".

1. These shoes are old <u>but</u> comfortable.
   → __________
2. He went home early <u>although</u> he was feeling sick.
   → __________

3. Electric devieces should be turned off <u>during</u> the plane is preparing for take-off.

→ ________

4. Go down the road <u>till</u> you will reach the traffic light.

→ ________

5. That book is <u>neither</u> interesting <u>nor</u> accurate.

→ ________

6. You must hurry, <u>and</u> you'll be late.

→ ________

2 Focus

Subordinate conjunctions - noun clause
종속접속사 - 명사절

종속접속사는 명사절이나 부사절을 이끈다. 명사절을 이끄는 접속사에는 that, if, whether, 의문사 (who, how, when, where, what, why, which)가 포함된다.

1 that

that절은 문장 안에서 주어, 보어, 목적어의 역할을 한다.

It is disappointing that John can't come.
(John이 올 수 없다는 것이 실망스럽습니다.)

The main thing is that they're happy.
(중요한 것은 그들이 행복하다는 것입니다.)

He told me that he loved me.
(그는 나에게 그가 나를 사랑한다고 말했습니다.)

that절은 the fact 다음에 자주 나온다. 또한 형용사 다음에 오기도 한다.

The fact that she has children made it difficult for her to get a job.
(그녀가 아이들이 있다는 사실은 그녀가 일자리를 얻는 것을 힘들게 만들었습니다.)

I'm afraid (that) I can't finish it till next week.
(나는 그것을 다음주까지 끝낼 수 없을까 봐 걱정입니다.)

Please be aware (that) it is dangerous.
(그것이 위험하다는 것을 의식하고 있어야 합니다.)

2 whether, if

I'm not sure whether/if he will apply for the job.
(그가 그 일에 지원할 지 안 할지 확실치 않습니다.)

She asked whether/if I could help her.
(그녀는 제가 그녀를 도울 수 있는지 없는지 물었습니다.)

전치사 다음이나 or not이 바로 뒤따라 올 때는 whether를 쓴다.

There was a big argument about whether we should accept the offer.
(우리가 그 제안을 수용해야 하는지 하지 말아야 하는지에 대한 큰 논쟁이 있었습니다.)

There was a big argument about if we should accept the offer. (X)

Let me know whether or not you can come.
(당신이 올 수 있는지 없는지를 저에게 알려주세요.)

Let me know if or not you can come. (X)

3 의문사

'의문사 + 주어 + 동사'의 어순에 유의한다.

He asked me where she went.
(그는 저에게 그녀가 어디에 갔는지 물었습니다.)

I don't know why they divorced.
(저는 왜 그들이 이혼했는지를 모릅니다.)

Have you heard how they are getting along?
(당신은 그들이 어떻게 지내는지 들었습니까?)

Task 3

Change the question in parentheses to a noun clause.

ex

(How old is she?) I don't know how old she is.

1. (What did he want?) Could you tell us ____________?
2. (When will they arrive?) Do you know ______________?
3. (How much did it cost?) I can't remember ______________.
4. (Is Ann going out tonight?) I don't know ______________.

5. (Which one does he like?) Let's ask him ______________.

6. (Where are you living?) He asked me ______________.

Task 4

Complete the sentences by matching the two parts.

1. Jim can't decide	a) whether or not she will come
2. That it took only four hours to the island	b) both time and money
3. Do you know	c) although the traffic was bad
4. Eric arrived on time	d) is amazing
5. I'm sure	e) whether to go or stay home
6. The research project will take	f) that he will be a good doctor

REST AREA

Translation

Max	아빠, 목마 태워줘요.
Dad	지금은 안돼. 나 바쁘단다. Max야.
Max	아빠 그거 알아요? 나는 곧 성장할 거예요. 아빠는 언제 시간이 이렇게 금방 지나갔는지 의아해 할 거예요.
Max	그리고 세월을 돌아보면서 말하겠죠. "Max는 너무 커. 내가 그에게 목마를 태울 수 있을 정도로 그가 작을 때가 언제였는지 기억도 안 난다." 그러나 그런 날들은 다시는 돌아오지 않겠죠.
Dad	알았어. 충분해. 난 내가 미래에 저지르게 될 지도 모르는 죄를 보상한 거야.
Max	아빠~ 조금만 더요. 담장 하나만 더 넘어요.

3 Focus

Subordinate conjunction - adverbial clause
종속접속사 - 부사절

부사절을 이끄는 접속사는 그 의미에 따라 다음과 같이 나눌 수 있다.

1 시간

(1) when

동시에 일어나는 일이나 연속 동작을 나타낸다.

When I lived in town, I often went shopping.
(제가 도시에서 살았을 때 저는 종종 쇼핑을 갔습니다.)

Don't drive when you're drunk.
(당신이 술에 취했을 때 운전하지 마세요.)

When we pressed the button, the elevator stopped.
(우리가 버튼을 눌렀을 때 엘리베이터는 멈췄습니다.)

(2) while (= during the time that), as

while과 as는 동시적으로 일어나는 일을 나타낸다. 특히 as는 그 순간에 진행이 되고 있는 일을 나타낸다.

While/As I was waiting for the train, it began to rain.
(내가 기차를 기다리는 동안 비가 내리기 시작했습니다.)

While/As he shaved, he thought about the event.
(그가 면도를 하는 동안 그는 그 행사에 대해 생각했습니다.)

As I left the house, I remembered the file.
(내가 집을 떠날 때 그 파일이 기억났습니다.)

(3) before, after, until

Where did they live before they came here?
(그들이 여기 오기 전에는 어디에 살았습니까?)

After she got home, she turned on the TV.
(그녀는 집에 온 후 TV를 켰습니다.)

They waited outside until the concert was over.
(그들은 콘서트가 끝날 때까지 밖에서 기다렸습니다.)

when, while, before, after, until **등이 이끄는 종속절에서는 미래를 나타낼 때 현재 시제를 쓴다.**

I'll talk to you later when I have more time.
(저는 나중에 시간이 좀 더 있을 때 당신과 이야기하겠습니다.)

Mary will take care of my dogs while I'm away.
(Mary는 내가 없는 동안 나의 개들을 돌봐줄 것입니다.)

She'll visit my parents before she leaves.
(그녀는 떠나기 전에 나의 부모님을 방문할 것입니다.)

We'll wait until you come back.
(우리는 당신이 돌아올 때까지 기다릴 것입니다.)

(4) since

He hasn't eaten anything since she left.
(그는 그녀가 떠난 이후로 아무것도 먹지 않았습니다.)

It has been two years since they married.
(그들이 결혼한지 2년이 되었습니다.)

cf I haven't seen Jessica since Christmas.
(크리스마스 이후로 Jessica를 본 적이 없습니다.)

2 원인과 결과

(1) because

They were late because it snowed.
(그들은 눈이 와서 늦었습니다.)

cf They were late because of the snow.
(그들은 눈 때문에 늦었습니다.)

She came home early because she felt dizzy.
(그녀는 현기증이 나서 일찍 집에 왔습니다.)

(2) as

As I was asleep, I didn't answer the phone.
(제가 잠이 들었기 때문에 저는 전화를 받지 못했습니다.)

As he lives near here, we can visit him often.
(그가 이 근처에 살기 때문에 우리는 그를 종종 방문할 수 있습니다.)

(3) since

Since it was too dark to go on, we camped there.
(계속 더 가기엔 너무 어두웠기 때문에 우리는 거기에서 야영을 했습니다.)

All the stores are closed since it is a national holiday.
(국경일이기 때문에 모든 상점들이 닫혔습니다.)

(4) so ~ that

It was so cold that he couldn't move his fingers.
(너무 추워서 그는 그의 손가락을 움직일 수도 없었습니다.)

He spoke so softly that we could not hear him well.
(그는 너무 조용히 말해서 우리는 그의 말을 잘 들을 수 없었습니다.)

3 조건과 양보

(1) if, unless

Is it OK if I use your computer?
(내가 당신의 컴퓨터를 사용해도 괜찮습니까?)

If you need money, I can lend you some.
(당신이 돈을 원한다면 나는 당신에게 좀 빌려줄 수 있습니다.)

There'll be trouble unless you stop that.
(당신이 그것을 멈추지 않는다면 문제가 생길 것입니다.)

조건 부사절에서도 미래를 나타낼 때 현재 시제를 쓴다.

If I don't feel well tomorrow, I won't go out.
(내일 몸이 좋지 않으면 나는 외출하지 않을 것입니다.)

I'll buy you a car if you pass the driving test.
(만약 당신이 운전시험에 합격한다면 내가 당신에게 차를 사줄 것입니다.)

(2) although, though, even though

She accepted the job although the salary is rather low.
(월급은 좀 낮지만 그녀는 그 일을 하기로 했습니다.)

Though you don't like him, you can still be polite.
(비록 당신이 그를 좋아하지 않지만 당신은 여전히 공손하게 대할 수 있습니다.)

I can't accept it even though I fully understand your point of view.
(저는 당신의 견해를 완전히 이해함에도 불구하고 그것을 받아들일 수가 없습니다.)

cf She wanted to go in spite of/despite the danger.
(그녀는 위험에도 불구하고 가기를 원했습니다.)

(3) as

Tired as he was, he gave her a ride.
(비록 피곤했지만 그는 그녀를 차로 바래다 주었습니다.)

Woman as she was, she was very brave.
(그녀는 여자임에도 불구하고 매우 용감했습니다.)

(4) in case

Here's the key in case you get home before me.
(당신이 저보다 먼저 집에 올 경우에 대비해 여기 열쇠가 있습니다.)

I'll prepare some light snacks in case I get hungry.
(제가 배고플 경우를 대비하여 가벼운 간식을 준비할 것입니다.)

Task 5

Choose the appropriate conjunctions.

1. They had a wonderful holiday, (despite, although) it rained.
2. You probably won't need it, but I'll give you some money (in case, if) you need to buy something.
3. (Although, Because) I left in a hurry, I forgot my passport.
4. She was so angry (as, that) she shouted at him.
5. You're not improving (while, as) you don't practice enough.
6. You'll fail your exams (if, unless) you study harder.

Task 6

Choose the error in each sentence and correct it.

1. The pants were (a) nice, so (b) they were too tight (c) for me (d).

   → ________

2. The hammer has been (a) used as (b) a tool since (c) the New Stone Age, when was (d) invented.

   → ________

3. I'll (a) go to Beijing next month. I hope to see (b) Linda during (c) I am (d) there.

   → ________

4. It (a) is obvious what (b) she doesn't (c) understand (d) spoken Japanese.

   → ________

5. Do (a) you know how far (b) is it (c) to (d) Florida?

   → ________

6. You can either (a) write and (b) call to order (c) a copy (d).

   → ________

Culture Corner

Underdog

underdog은 '패배자, 열세인 쪽'을 뜻하는 속어로 특히 영자신문의 정치면이나 스포츠 기사에 자주 등장하는 표현이다. 반대로 '승리자, 우세한 쪽'은 top dog이라고 한다. 이 표현은 투견장에서 유래된 것이기 때문에 점잖은 자리에서는 사용하지 않는 것이 좋다. Korea was originally the underdog, but it surprised everyone by beating Italy by 2 goals to 1. (한국은 원래 열세였으나 이탈리아를 2대 1로 물리쳐서 모두를 놀라게 했다.)

dog과 관련된 재미있는 표현을 몇 개 더 소개한다. 옛날 뱃사람들은 고양이가 폭풍우와 깊은 관련이 있다고 믿었다. 폭풍우가 몰아 칠 때면 마녀(witch)가 검은 고양이를 타고 나타난다고 생각했다. 그리고 개와 늑대는 바람을 상징했다. 즉, 중세에는 고양이는 비를 오게 하며, 개는 바람과 폭풍을 불게 한다고 생각하였던 것이다. 이런 이유로 특히 비바람이 심할 경우에 사람들은 It's raining cats and dogs. 라는 표현을 썼다.

a hair of the dog 는 '해장술'이라는 뜻이다. 고대 로마인들이 미친 개에게 물렸을 경우에 그 개의 꼬리에서 털을 잘라낸 다음 태워서 물린 부위에 바르면 가장 좋은 치료 방법이라고 생각했던 데서 유래한 것이다. After a night of heavy drinking, he needed the hair of the dog. (밤에 과음을 한 후, 그는 해장술이 필요했다.)

dog and pony show는 19세기 후반과 20세기 미국 내에서 유행했던 서커스 순회공연을 뜻한다. 이들이 주로 개와 조랑말로 관객들에게 묘기를 보여준 데서 유래되었다. 요즘엔 겉만 번지르르한 광고나 프리젠테이션 등을 뜻한다. The debate was such a dog and pony show that nobody took it seriously. (그 토론은 겉으로 보이기 위한 것이라 아무도 심각하게 받아들이지 않았다.)

shaggy-dog story는 '떠드는 사람은 신나지만 듣는 사람에게는 지리하고 따분한 긴 이야기 또는 말하는 동물이 나오는 우화'를 라는 뜻한다. The joke was just another one of his endless shaggy-dog stories. (그 농담은 그의 끝없이 지루한 이야기 중의 또 다른 하나였다.)

a dog in a manger에서 manger는 '여물통'을 뜻하는데 소가 그 안의 건초를 먹으려는 순간 개가 여물통 안으로 뛰어 들어와서 먹는 것을 방해한다는 데서 유래했다. '심술쟁이'라는 뜻이다. Even though John didn't want to play with his new toy, he wouldn't let Jim have it either. He was behaving like a dog in a manger. (John은 그의 새 장난감을 가지고 놀고 싶지도 않았지만 Jim이 그것을 가지고 놀지도 못하게 했다. 그는 심술쟁이처럼 행동하고 있었다.)

go home and kick the dog라는 표현은 '집에 가서 개를 찬다'는 뜻으로 우리나라 속담 중에 '종로에서 뺨 맞고 한강에서 눈 흘긴다.'라는 말과 비슷하다. After getting told off by her boss, Janet went home and shouted at her kids. I think she just needed to go home and kick the dog. (Janet은 상사에게 잔소리를 듣고, 집에 가서 아이들에게 소리를 질렀다. 그녀는 엉뚱한 데라도 화풀이를 해야만 했던 것이다.)

dog walker라는 표현은 '개를 산책 시키는 사람'으로 주로 아르바이트로 남의 개를 산책 시킬 경우 쓰는 표현이다. Ann needed some extra money for college, so she got a part-time job as a dog walker. (Ann은 대학을 가기 위해 여분의 돈이 필요했다. 그래서 그는 개를 산책시키는 아르바이트를 구했다.)

마지막으로 puppy love는 '풋사랑'을 뜻한다. Because they were still so young, everybody called it puppy love, but for Tom and Sally it was the real thing. (그들은 아직 너무 어렸기 때문에 모두가 그것을 풋사랑이라고 여겼다. 그러나 Tom과 Sally에게 그것은 진정한 사랑이었다.)

1. Korea was originally the underdog, but it surprised everyone by beating Italy by 2 goals to 1.
2. It's raining cats and dogs.
3. After a night of heavy drinking, he needed the hair of the dog.
4. The debate was such a dog and pony show that nobody took it seriously.
5. The joke was just another one of his endless shaggy dog stories.
6. Even though John didn't want to play with his new toy, he wouldn't let Jim have it either. He was behaving like a dog in a manger.
7. After getting told off by her boss, Janet went home and shouted at her kids. I think she just needed to go home and kick the dog.
8. Ann needed some extra money for college, so she got a part-time job as a dog walker.
9. Because they were still so young, everybody called it puppy love, but for Tom and Sally it was the real thing.

Wrap-up

1. I liked the coat, but I decided not to buy it.
2. If you want ice cream you can have either coffee or vanilla.
3. It is disappointing that John can't come.
4. I don't know why they divorced.
5. When I lived in town, I often went shopping.
6. If you need money, I can lend you some.

Final Tips

When I got home, I took a bath. (O)

As I got home, I took a bath. (X)

접속사 as는 두 가지 일이 동시에 일어날 때 쓸 수 있습니다. 집에 도착하고 나서 목욕을 한 것이기 때문에 as는 쓸 수 없습니다.

ex) As I walked into the room, the phone started ringing.
Although it rained a lot, we enjoyed our vacation. (O)
Despite it rained a lot, we enjoyed our vacation. (X)
Despite a lot of rain, we enjoyed our vacation. (O)

비록 although와 despite가 우리말로는 비슷한 뜻을 지녔지만, although는 접속사이고, despite는 전치사입니다. 전치사 다음에는 주어+동사 형태가 올 수 없습니다. 참고로, while은 접속사이고, during은 전치사입니다.

We will buy some more food in case Bill comes. (O)

We will buy some more food if Bill comes. (O)

위 두 문장은 뜻이 다릅니다. in case는 '~할 경우에 대비해서'라는 뜻이고, if는 '만약 ~한다면'의 뜻입니다. in case가 쓰인 문장은 'Bill이 오든지 오지 않든지 음식을 더 사겠다'는 뜻이고, 다른 문장은 'Bill이 오면 음식을 더 사겠다'는 뜻입니다.

Translation

나는 집에 도착해서 목욕을 했습니다.
비록 비가 많이 내렸지만 우리는 즐겁게 휴가를 보냈습니다.
Bill이 올 경우에 대비해서 우리는 음식을 좀 더 살 겁니다.
만약 Bill이 오면 우리는 음식을 좀 더 살 겁니다.

Review Test

Choose the correct words.

1. You should have done it (so, as) I showed you.

2. He approved of the introduction of the brand-new plan, (but, because) he is worried about the high cost.

3. He is not satisfied with anything (if, unless) he does it himself.

4. (Although, After) Galileo did not invent the telescope, he was the first person to use it to look at the night sky.

5. He must be at home, (because, though) his car is in the driveway.

6. You probably won't need it, but I'll give you my cell phone number (in case, if) you need to contact me.

7. (Even though, Now that) she caught a bad cold, she had to take the exam.

8. The point is (whether, if) or not people will agree with my idea.

9. We just watched TV (since, though) it was too cold to go outside.

10. Enjoy life (while, during) you can.

ocus 1-Focus 3

Chapter 13

Review

(Chapter 8~12)

Chapter 8 Infinitives and Gerunds

1. To-infinitives (to부정사)

We can't afford to send our children to college.
My teacher advised me to buy the book.

2. Gerunds (동명사)

Have you ever considered moving into a new apartment?
I admit having written the letter.

3. Verb + to infinitives/~ing (동사 + to부정사/~ing)

I regret to inform you of his death.
I regret telling you the story.

Task 1

Fill in the blanks with the verbs in the box. Use either a gerund or an infinitive.

talk	read	have	become	run	mail

1. I enjoy __________ the newspaper every morning.
2. Jane decided __________ a nurse.
3. Sam suggested __________ dinner early.
4. Don't forget __________ the letter I gave you.
5. The police officer told the thief to stop, but he kept __________.
6. When the teacher entered the classroom, the students stopped __________.

Task 2

Correct the underlined part if it is incorrect. If the sentence is correct, write "correct".

1. He promised not to be late.

   → ________

2. We expect Cindy to pass the exam.

   → ________

3. Have you seen him to jog in the park?

   → ________

4. The teacher encouraged the students study hard at school.

   → ________

5. She told such a funny joke. I couldn't stop laughing.

   → ________

6. Where are you considering to go for summer vacation?

   → ________

Task 3

Complete the sentences with the correct form of the verb in parentheses.

1. He found out where ________ (buy) inexpensive fruit.
2. Please remember ________ (lock) the door before you leave.
3. We regret ________ (inform) you that we can't offer you the job.
4. Would you mind ________ (wait) a moment?
5. Jack told us ________ (not wait) for Jane.
6. You shouldn't put off ________ (pay) your bills.

Chapter 9 Participles

1. Present participles and past participles (현재분사와 과거분사)

They found the crying boy in the building.
None of the people invited to the party came.

2. Adjectives ending -ing /-ed (-ing와 -ed로 끝나는 형용사)

Going to Europe will be an exciting experience for her.
She is really excited about going to Europe.

3. Participle construction (분사구문)

Opening the door, they heard the clock strike one.
Not having enough money, I couldn't buy the car.

Task 4

Choose the correct verb form in parentheses.

1. Are you (interesting, interested) in classical music?
2. The (stealing, stolen) jewelry was found in the basement of the building.
3. It is an (amusing, amused) story, isn't it?
4. The (exhausting, exhausted) men sat down to rest under the tree.
5. She found herself in an (embarrassing, embarrassed) situation last night.
6. I bought some (freezing, frozen) fish at the market.

Task 5

Find the incorrect part in each dialogue and correct it.

1. A: You look tired(1).

   B: The bus was so(2) crowding(3) that I had to keep standing(4) the whole way here.

   → ________

2. A: It was annoyed(1) to lose(2) my ticket.

   B: You looked really frustrated(3) when you had to buy(4) another one.

   → ________

3. A: Is Jim funny?

   B: No, he's a really bored(1) person. He never stops talking(2) and he never says anything(3) interesting(4).

   → ________

4. A: I'm not very fit(1). I was exhausting(2) after climbing(3) the mountain.

   B: Yes, but I think everyone felt tired(4).

   → ________

5. A: Was it thrilling(1) meeting(2) Brad Pitt?

   B: You bet. It was just about the most fascinated(3) moment of my life. Everybody there was so excited(4).

   → ________

Task 6

Rewrite the underlined parts using a participle construction.

1. If they are compared with monkeys, dogs are not very intelligent.

→ ________________ with monkeys, dogs are not very intelligent.

2. Because he did not know the language, he found it hard to find work there.

→ ____________________ the language, he found it hard to find work there.

3. Although I sat surrounded by many friends, I wasn't so happy.

→ _____________________ by many friends, I wasn't so happy.

4. He fell and struck his head against the door.

→ He fell, _____________ against the door.

5. After I had used my father's car, I returned it to him.

→ ____________ my father's car, I returned it to him.

6. As the day was sunny, we decided to go swimming.

→ ________________, we decided to go swimming.

REST AREA

Translation

Max 학교 다니기 싫어요.!

Max 매일 학교가 끝날 때까지 시간을 세요. 그리고 주말까지 날짜를 세구요. 그런 다음에 저는 달의 끝까지 주를 센 다음 또 여름까지 달을 세요.

Max 공부, 공부, 공부! 저는 놀 시간이 하나도 없어요.

Dad 나머지 다른 사람들도 그렇다.

Max 아빠, 다음 11년 동안 학교에 나가지 않아도 된다고 이 문서에 싸인 해주실래요?

Chapter 10 Relatives

1. Relative pronouns (관계대명사)

The waitress who served us was very rude.
Mark will tell you what you need to know.
The suit (that) John bought doesn't fit him very well.
She quit the job, which surprised everyone.

2. Relative adverbs (관계부사)

The town where I grew up is small.
Do you remember the day (that) we first met?

Task 7

Choose the right relative pronouns in parentheses.

1. I know a lot of people (who, whom) live in the Philippines.
2. Is this the hotel (that, where) he was staying?
3. I went back to the town in (which, that) I was born.
4. (That, What) the teacher said made the children happy.
5. What's the name of the girl (who, whose) pencil you borrowed?
6. These books, (that, which) you can get at any bookstore, will give you all the information you need.

Task 8

Correct the underlined part if it is incorrect. If the sentence is correct, write "correct".

1. He said he had no money, <u>that</u> was not true.

   → ________

2. The building <u>where</u> she lives is very old.

→ ________

3. The music <u>we</u> listened to last night was not bad.

→ ________

4. Mr. Foster, for <u>who</u> I am working, is not very generous.

→ ________

5. I saw some people <u>their</u> car had broken down.

→ ________

6. I didn't believe him at first, but in fact everything <u>what</u> he said was true.

→ ________

Task 9

Make one sentence from two using the relative pronouns and complete the sentences.

1. I explained my absence to the teacher. I had missed her class.
   → I explained my absence to the teacher ________ class I had missed.

2. This is the book. It caused such a sensation.
   → This is the book ________ caused such a sensation.

3. The girl is proud of herself. She won the race.
   → The girl ________ won the race is proud of herself.

4. The people were very kind. We visited them last week.
   → The people ________ we visited last week were very kind.

5. Is there a restaurant? We can have a really good meal there.
   → Is there a restaurant ________ we can have a really good meal?

6. The apartment is now worth $500,000. He paid $100,000 for it.
   → The apartment, for ________ he paid $100,000, is now worth $500,000.

Chapter 11 Comparatives

1. Comparison (비교)

She is five inches taller than I am.
The movie is far more interesting than I expected.
The higher we climb, the colder it becomes.

2. Comparison of equality (동등비교)

I'm not going out with a man who's twice as old as I am.
Nothing is as important as good health.

3. Superlative (최상급)

He's the most annoying person in the whole office.
Soccer is one of the most popular sports in the country.

Task 10

Fill in the blanks using the word in parentheses.

1. I can't hear you. Could you speak ___________ loudly, please? (much)
2. The test was __________ than we expected. (easy)
3. Yesterday was ___________ day of the year. (cold)
4. Nothing is ___________ than time. (precious)
5. The older he gets, ___________ he becomes. (intelligent)
6. That was ___________ movie I've ever seen. (interesting)

Task 11

Choose the best words to complete the sentences.

1. His illness was ________ more serious than the doctor first said.
   1) far 2) very 3) lot

2. ________ you leave, the sooner you will arrive.
   1) Early 2) The earlier 3) The earliest

3. They didn't pay as ________ as we did.
   1) much tax 2) more tax 3) most tax

4. Lions are ________ of all the animals.
   1) strongest 2) the strongest 3) as strong

5. They normally have a lot of things to do, but they're ________ this week.
   1) busy 2) more busy 3) less busy

Task 12

Choose the right word in parentheses.

1. There were (fewer, less) people at this meeting than at the last one.
2. He is the (worse, worst) person I've ever known.
3. The weather is getting (cold and cold, colder and colder) day by day.
4. His novels are (as popular, more popular) as ever.
5. She doesn't live here (any longer, no more).
6. I like this movie (best, the best).

Chapter 12 Conjunctions

1. Coordinate conjunctions (등위접속사)

My sister is married and (she) lives in Busan.
He drinks neither tea nor coffee.

2. Subordinate conjunctions (종속접속사)

My father told me that he loved me.
Do you know when they will arrive?
Mary will take care of my dogs while I'm away.

Task 13

Complete the sentences by matching the two parts.

1. I don't know where he is from	a) I'll never speak to you again
2. She can't decide	b) how to go to the post office
3. Unless you apologize	c) as he speaks both Japanese and Chinese fluently
4. I wanted John and Jenny to come	d) because it rained
5. We decided not to take a trip	e) which one to choose
6. Can you show me	f) but neither of them wanted to

Task 14

Choose the appropriate conjunctions.

1. (In spite of, Although) I worked hard all day long, I'm not tired.
2. (While, Because) she was out, there was a phone call for her.
3. Let's wait at home (if, till) it stops raining.
4. He might be angry (if, unless) I didn't invite him.
5. (After, While) the boy finished his homework, he played a computer game.
6. I can't see her often (even though, as) she lives quite nearby.

Task 15

Choose the appropriate expression.

because whether although that in case so

1. __________ we've known each other for many years, we're not close friends.
2. She heard the news __________ her grandmother was dead.
3. I'm not sure __________ it will rain tomorrow or not.
4. It's not raining now, but take your umbrella with you __________ it rains later.
5. __________ it was getting dark, we stopped playing and came back home.
6. It was dark, __________ I turned the light on.

Culture Corner

Prom

prom은 promenade의 줄임말로서, 미국에서 고등학교나 대학교에서 학년말에 열리는 공식적인 dancing party를 가리킨다. 특히 고등학생에게는 학창 시절에서 손꼽힐 정도로 중요한 행사 중 하나이다. 남학생들은 tuxedo를 갖춰 입고서, 그리고 여학생들은 꽃 모양의 악세서리 corsage가 달린 dress를 입고서 참가한다. 학교 강당에서 열리는 게 보통인데, 일부 학교에서는 고급 호텔을 빌리거나 cruise ship에서 prom행사를 치르기도 한다. In North America, the prom is the highlight of school life, but this tradition isn't found in other English-speaking countries. (북미에서는 prom이 학교 생활의 가장 주목을 받는 부분이다. 그러나 이 행사는 다른 영어권 나라에는 없다.)

가장 멋진 의상을 선보이거나, 가장 아름답고 모범적인 이들에게 Prom King과 Prom Queen 이라는 타이틀을 주기도 한다. 특히 Prom Queen은 학교 축제가 5월에 열리기 때문에 우리에게 친숙한 May Queen이라는 이름으로 불리기도 한다. 또 prom이 열리기 전에 미리 행사장에 도착하여 기념 사진을 찍거나 지인들을 만나는 것을 pre-prom 이라고 한다. Bran and Julie were voted Prom King and Prom Queen by their classmates. (Bran과 Julie는 그들의 반 친구들에 의해 Prom King과 Prom Queen으로 뽑혔다.)

그러나 prom에 대한 비판 여론도 만만치 않다. 옷, 식사, limousine 대여 비용 등으로 prom에서 쓰는 학생 1인당 평균 비용이 638달러(약 60만원)에 이르며, 이에 따라 전체 prom 시장 규모는 무려 연 40조 달러에 달한다고 한다. 몇몇 고등학교 교장은 학생들의 과도한 지출을 이유로 prom을 폐지하는 결정을 내리기도 했다. 또한 prom을 반대하는 학생들은 prom에 대한 반감을 표현하기 위해서 dress-up 대신 자신이 좋아하는 의상을 입고 격식을 갖추지 않은 파티를 여는데 이것을 anti-prom이라고 부른다. Sid wore dirty jeans and a torn t-shirt to the ball as an anti-prom gesture. (Sid는 anti-prom의 표시로 더러운 청바지와 찢어진 티셔츠를 입고 무도회에 갔다.)

Party와 관련된 표현 중에 wallflower 라는 말이 있는데, 이는 무도회에서 상대가 없이 혼자 있는 사람들, 특히 소극적인 여성을 가리킨다. Sheila was very shy. At every party she was a wallflower, sitting by herself in the corner. (Sheila는 매우 소극적이었다. 모든 파티에서 그녀는 상대가 없이 구석에 혼자 앉아있었다.)

In North America, the prom is the highlight of the school life, but this tradition isn't found in other English-speaking countries.
Bran and Julie were voted Prom King and Prom Queen by their classmates.
Sid wore dirty jeans and a torn t-shirt to the ball as an anti-prom gesture.
Sheila was very shy. At every party she was a wallflower, sitting by herself in the corner.

쉽게 배우는

영문법

- 해설 및 정답

성 은 경

EASY-TO-LEARN
ENGLISH GRAMMAR

한국외국어대학교 출판부

Table of Contents

Chapter 1

Words and Sentences

Task 1

Answers

명사구(noun phrase)는 몇 개의 단어가 모여서 명사의 역할을 하는 어구입니다. '주어+동사' 형태는 들어 있지 않습니다.

1. Hot tea is great on a cold morning.
2. Some customers complained about the service.
3. The apartment on the top floor has a fantastic view.

명사절(noun clause)은 '주어+동사' 형태를 갖추고 명사의 역할을 합니다. 그 자체로 완전한 문장을 이루지는 못합니다.

4. What I want to know is the name of the man.
5. She doesn't care how long it will take.
6. He said that Susan couldn't come to the meeting.

Translation

1. 추운 아침에는 뜨거운 차가 좋습니다.
2. 몇몇 손님들은 서비스에 대해서 불평을 했습니다.
3. 아파트의 제일 꼭대기 층은 전망이 아주 멋집니다.
4. 내가 알고 싶은 것은 그 남자의 이름입니다.
5. 그녀는 얼마나 오래 걸릴지 상관하지 않습니다.
6. 그는 Susan이 모임에 못 온다고 말했습니다.

Task 2

Answers

종속절(subordinate clause)은 '주어+동사' 형태를 갖추고 있으나 그 자체가 독립적으로 쓰일 수 없습니다. 주절이 있어야만 그 뜻이 완전해 집니다.

1. Before he came to Seoul, David had taught English in Busan.
2. The lion roared when the hunters appeared.
3. My cat doesn't eat food that comes from a can.
4. I wonder whether the car was sold.
5. As the plane was landing, a bird flew into one of the jet engines.

Translation

1. 서울로 오기 전에 David는 부산에서 영어를 가르쳤었습니다.
2. 사냥꾼들이 나타났을 때 사자가 으르렁거렸습니다.
3. 내 고양이는 캔에 들어있는 음식은 먹지 않습니다.

4. 그 차가 팔렸는지 궁금합니다.
5. 비행기가 착륙하고 있을 때 새 한 마리가 제트 엔진 중의 하나로 날아들었습니다.

Task 3

Answers

N(명사), V(동사), Adj(형용사), Adv(부사), Pro(대명사), Aux(조동사), Prep(전치사), Art(관사), Det(한정사), Conj(접속사) 등으로 나타냅니다.

1. Alex needed a new pencil so he bought one at the supermarket.
   N V Art Adj N Conj Pro V Pro Prep Art N
2. The insects have attacked every tree on my block.
   Art N Aux V Det N Prep Det N
3. Female lions will defend their cubs from males.
   Adj N Aux V Det N Prep N
4. Gracefully, the ballerina leaped across the stage.
   Adv Art N V Prep Art N
5. Ants and spiders represent different species.
   N Conj N V Adj N

Translation

1. Alex는 새 연필이 필요해서 슈퍼마켓에서 하나를 샀습니다.
2. 곤충들이 내 블록에 있는 모든 나무를 공격했습니다.
3. 암사자들이 숫사자들로부터 그들의 새끼를 보호할 것입니다.
4. 우아하게, 발레리나는 무대를 가로질러 뛰어올랐습니다.
5. 개미와 거미는 다른 종을 대표합니다.

Task 4

Answers

주어는 문장의 주체가 되는 부분입니다.

1. The man who lives next door works for the government.
2. Most of the students learn a foreign language.
3. On the grass sat an enormous toad.
4. In the fall, the leaves on the trees fall to the ground.
5. Helping other people makes me feel alive.
6. The policy of the United States government in regard to nuclear weapons is uncertain at present.

Translation

1. 옆집에 사는 남자는 정부에서 일합니다.
2. 대부분의 학생들은 외국어를 배웁니다.
3. 잔디 위에 거대한 두꺼비가 앉아 있습니다.
4. 가을에는 나뭇잎이 땅으로 떨어집니다.
5. 다른 사람들을 돕는 것은 나를 살아있는 것처럼 느끼게 합니다.
6. 핵무기에 대한 미국 정부의 정책은 현재 불확실합니다.

Task 5

Answers

S(주어), V(동사), O(목적어), SC(주격보어), OC(목적격보어), Adv(부사어구) 등으로 나타냅니다.

1. The hurricane (S) destroyed (V) the city (O) in a few hours (Adv).
2. Phillip (S) is (V) depressed (SC) because of the bad news (Adv).
3. This sandwich (S) tastes (V) good (SC).
4. We (S) invited (V) a lot of people (O) to the party (Adv).
5. She (S) wants (V) him (O) to walk the dog (OC).

Translation

1. 허리케인이 몇 시간 후에 그 도시를 파괴하였습니다.
2. Phillip은 그 나쁜 소식 때문에 우울합니다.
3. 이 샌드위치는 맛이 좋습니다.
4. 우리는 여러 사람들을 파티에 초대했습니다.
5. 그녀는 그가 개를 산책시키기를 원합니다.

Review Test

Answers

1. (2) 2. (3) 3. (4) 4. (3) 5. (1)

Translation

1. 16세 미만의 모든 아이들과 그 어머니들은 도시를 떠날 수 있습니다.
2. 그녀는 30대이지만 내가생각했던 것보다 훨씬 젊어 보입니다.
3. (1) 그녀는 신문에서 광고를 보았습니다.
   (2) 이 프로젝트는 이번 토요일까지 완료될 것입니다.
   (3) 그는 그녀를 배웅하러 공항에 갔습니다.
   (4) 무대에서 춤추고 있는소녀는 제 반 친구입니다.
4. 웹 사이트를 원하는 대로 바꾸기 위한 가장 흥미롭고 중요한 방법은 자신의 독특한 취향에 기초한 이야기들을 실은 페이지를 만드는 것입니다.
5. (1) 음악 소리가 너무 컸기 때문에 우리는 대화를 할 수가 없었습니다.
   (2) 제가 회의에 참석할 수 있을지 잘 모르겠습니다.
   (3) 저는 당신이 하는 말을 전혀 이해할 수 없습니다.
   (4) 자유 민주주의는 모두가 동등하게 대접받는다는 뜻입니다.

Chapter 2

Verbs

Task 1

Answers

1. impatient
   grow는 이 문장에서 불완전 자동사로 반드시 보어를 취해야 합니다. 보어는 주로 명사와 형용사가 오므로 여기서는 형용사 impatient가 답이 됩니다.
2. to cancel
   요청, 바람, 설득, 허용을 나타내는 동사 (ask, beg, require, want, encourage, persuade, force, tell)는 불완전타동사인데 목적어 다음에 목적격보어 자리에 to 부정사 만이 올 수 있습니다. 그래서 정답은 to cancel이 됩니다.
3. delicious
   smell은 불완전자동사로 쓰였습니다. 1번에서 설명했듯이 불완전자동사 다음에는 보어가 옵니다.
4. me
   send는 수여동사로 '~에게 ~를' 이라는 말로 '~에게' 라는 간접목적어가 '~를' 이라는 직접목적어 앞에 올 때는 전치사가 필요 없습니다.
5. resembles
   resemble는 타동사로 뒤에 전치사가 올 수 없습니다.

Translation

1. 그녀는 그가 의무를 다하지 않은 것에 대한 끊임없는 변명에 울화가 치밀었습니다.
2. 그는 병 때문에 방문을 취소할 수밖에 없었습니다.
3. 그 통밀 빵에서 맛있는 냄새가 났습니다.
4. 그는 지난 주에 내게 이 메일을 보냈습니다.
5. Ann은 그녀의 아버지를 닮았습니다.

Task 2

Answers

1. A (address about → address)
   address는 타동사로 뒤에 전치사가 올 수 없습니다.
2. D (successfully → successful)
   successful은 be동사의 보어입니다. be 동사는 불완전자동사로 보어를 취해야 합니다. successfully는 부사이므로 보어가 될 수 없습니다.
3. C (looks like → looks)
   look 은 불완전자동사로 보어를 가져야 합니다. 또 하나 "look like" 도 '~처럼 보이다' 라는 의미로 뒤에 반드시 명사가 와야 합니다. 이 문장에서는 형용사 younger가 왔으므로 like를 빼야 합니다.

4. D (to go → go)
   make는 사역동사로 쓰였습니다. '사역동사(made) + 목적어(me) + 목적격보어(동사원형 go)'이 와야 합니다
5. C (reach at → reach)
   reach는 타동사입니다. 타동사는 목적어 앞에 전치사가 필요 없습니다.
6. B (me → to me)
   explain 다음에 사람이 올때 to를 넣어야 합니다.

Translation

1. 정부는 집이 없는 사람에 대해 어떤 조치도 취하지 않은 것에 대한 비판에 대해서 언급하지 않았습니다.
2. Bill Gates는 왜 그렇게 성공했습니까?
3. 그의 어머니는 70대임에도 불구하고 훨씬 젊어 보이십니다.
4. 나는 그 영화가 보고 싶었지만 부모님은 강제로 자게 하셨습니다.
5. 어떤 일이 발생하면, 당신은 언제든 내게 이메일로 연락할 수 있습니다.
6. 그 남자는 그 기계를 작동하는 방법을 나에게 설명하였습니다.

Task 3

Answers

1. has
   영화, 책제목, 학과명, 병명, 게임명, 국가명은 단수 취급합니다. 조류독감은 병명입니다.
2. Were
   there, here, where같은 부사가 문장 앞에 오면 뒤에 오는 명사가 주어입니다. 이 문장에서 주어(many people)가 복수이므로 were가 정답입니다. were는 are의 과거형입니다.
3. contain
   "some, any, most, none, half of 명사"가 오면 그 명사에 따라 동사의 수를 일치 시켜야합니다. 이 문장에서는 the movies라는 복수명사가 왔으니까 contain이 답이 됩니다.
4. was
   neither A nor B, either A or B, not only A but also B에서는 B에 수를 일치시킵니다. 이 문장에서는 A가 the passengers 에 해당되고 B는 the pilot 입니다. the pilot는 단수이므로 was가 답이 됩니다.
5. get
   주어는 The powerful people in a company 까지 입니다. 하지만 정확히 따지면 in a company는 수식어구이고 이런 수식어구는 동사의 수에 영향을 미치지 않습니다. 결국은 the powerful people가 실제 주어가 되므로 답은 get 입니다.

Translation

1. 조류독감이 유럽의 교외로 퍼졌습니다.
2. 방안에 사람이 많았습니까?
3. 요즘 어떤 영화들은 폭력성이 너무 짙습니다.
4. 승객들도 조종사도 다치지 않았습니다.
5. 회사에서 영향력 있는 사람들은 언제나 존경을 받습니다.

Task 4

Answers

1. correct
   'some, any, most, none, half of 명사'가 오면 그 명사에 따라 수를 일치 시켜줍니다. work 다음에 단수동사 is 가 왔으므로 맞는 문장입니다.
2. is
   with~ classmates는 수식어구로 수 일치에 영향을 줄 수 없습니다. 주어는 Mike로 3인칭 단수이므로 are를 is로 고쳐야 합니다.
3. are
   neither A nor B, either A or B, not only A but also B에서는 B에 수를 일치 시킵니다. B는 his representatives 이므로 is를 are로 고쳐야 합니다.
4. correct
   시간, 거리, 돈 등을 하나의 개념으로 보고 단수 취급합니다. 그래서 provides가 맞습니다.
5. has
   to 부정사나 동명사가 주어이면 단수 취급해야 합니다. listening to very loud music of rock concerts 가 주어이므로 have를 has로 고쳐야 합니다.

Translation

1. 일의 절반은 기계로 합니다.
2. Mike는 학우들의 도움으로 6학년을 위한 독서 클럽을 조직하고 있습니다.
3. 대통령이나 그 대리인들이 그 기자회견에 참석하기도 되어 있습니다.
4. 3시간 동안 스키를 타는 것은 많은 운동이 됩니다.
5. 록 콘서트에서 시끄러운 음악을 들어 청력을 잃는 십대들도 몇 몇 있습니다.

Task 5

Answers

1. are
   several paintings 가 주어이므로 복수 동사 are가 정답입니다. by that artist는 수식어입니다.
2. leads
   to 부정사나 동명사가 주어이면 항상 단수 취급해서 leads가 오게 됩니다.
3. makes
   sensitivity가 주어이므로 단수동사 makes가 오게 됩니다. to other people`s feelings는 수식어구입니다.
4. visit
   both A and B(A, B 둘 다) 는 언제나 복수 취급합니다. 그래서 visit 가 오게 됩니다.
5. is
   시간, 거리 등은 하나의 개념으로 봐서 단수 취급합니다. 정답은 is 입니다.

Translation

1. 저 화가의 여러 작품이 지금 쇼핑몰에 전시되어 있습니다.
2. 외국어 공부를 하게 되면 학생들은 종종 그 언어가 쓰이는 나라의 문화에 대해서 배우게 됩니다.

3. 다른 사람들의 감정에 민감하기 때문에 그녀는 이해심 있는 사람입니다.
4. 나의 아버지와 어머니가 가끔씩 나를 보러 오십니다.
5. 20분은 그 임무를 마치는 데 아주 충분한 시간입니다.

Task 6

Answers

(1), (2), (4), (6), (7)
(1) adults and children는 복수명사로 복수동사를 사용해야 하므로 celebrate로 고쳐야 합니다.
(2) every, each는 항상 단수 취급해야 하므로 knows가 되어야 합니다.
(3) 복수명사 people이 주어이므로 복수동사 look가 되어야 합니다.
(4) girls가 주어이므로 수 일치시키면 enjoy가 와야 합니다.
(5) in the family는 수식어구입니다. 실제주어는 girl로 단수이므로 dresses가 맞습니다.
(6) 은 "촛불로 밝힌 왕관"이라는 의미로 crown이 주어입니다. 단수 주어 다음에 are가 아니라 is입니다.
(7) "each of 복수명사"가 와도 항상 단수동사를 써야 합니다. 그래서 wears가 와야 합니다.
(8) girls가 주어이므로 수 일치시키면 bring가 맞습니다.

Translation

스웨덴에서는 어른들과 아이들이 성 루시아 날을 기념합니다. 그 곳의 모든 사람들은 성 루시아가 빛의 여왕이라는 것을 압니다. 많은 사람들이 12월 13일의 축일을 무척 기다립니다. 소녀들은 특히 이 날을 즐깁니다. 전통적으로 가족들 중 가장 나이가 많은 소녀가 성 루시아처럼 옷을 차려 입습니다. 그녀는 불을 밝힌 촛불로 만든 왕관을 머리에 씁니다. 어린 소녀들도 또한 모두 하얀 겉옷을 입습니다. 이른 아침에 옷을 차려 입은 소녀들이 집안의 어른들에게 아침식사를 가지고 갑니다.

Review Test

Answers

1. raised	2. discussed, reach	3. is	4. to go
5. attend	6. easy	7. to me	8. has
9. perfectly	10. sitting		

Translation

1. 그들은 상품 가격을 올렸습니다.
2. 우리는 그 문제에 대해 토의를 했지만 최종 결정에 이르지는 못했습니다.
3. 역이나 극장은 만나기 좋은 장소입니다.
4. 그녀의 부모님은 그 날 밤 그녀의 외출을 허락하지 않으셨습니다.
5. 모든 직원들은 회의에 참석하도록 요구되었습니다.
6. 그가 내게 준 책은 읽기 쉬워 보입니다.
7. 의사는 내가 휴식을 취해야 한다고 권고했습니다.
8. 여기에서 우리가 만난 모든 이들이 매우 도움되고 있습니다.
9. 당신은 그것을 완벽하게 묘사해 냈습니다.
10. 그들은 그녀가 의자에 앉는 것을 보았습니다.

Chapter 3

Tense

Task 1

Answers

	원형	-ing	과거	과거분사
Ex)	skate	skating	skated	skated
1.	rain	raining	rained	rained
2.	imagine	imagining	imagined	imagined
3.	run	running	ran	run
4.	worry	worrying	worried	worried
5.	rob	robbing	robbed	robbed
6.	sleep	sleeping	slept	slept

Task 2

Answers

1. begun
   현재완료는 have+과거분사(p.p.)로 나타냅니다. 동사 begin의 p.p.는 begun입니다.
2. drove
   과거분사(p.p.)는 수동태 (be+p.p.)나 완료시제(have/has+p.p.)에 사용이 되고 독립적으로 시제를 표현하지 못합니다. 그래서 과거형인 drove가 정답입니다.
3. chose
   과거분사형은 수동태(be+p.p.)나 완료시제(have/has+p.p.)에 사용이 되고 독립적으로 시제를 표현하지 못합니다. 그래서 과거형인 chose가 정답입니다.
4. blown
   완료형(have/has+p.p.)에 대한 문제입니다. 동사 blow 의 p.p.는 blown입니다.
5. did
   that very afternoon (바로 그날 오후)라는 명백환 과거를 나타내는 부사구가 있으므로 did가 정답입니다.
6. hit
   in last night's ballgame 이라는 과거를 나타내는 부사구가 있으므로 과거시제를 써야 합니다. 동사 hit은 AAA형이므로 과거형도 hit 입니다.

Translation

1. 우리는 막 프로젝트를 시작했습니다.
2. Lenny 와 Gina는 국토를 횡단했습니다.
3. 그들 팀은 다른 것을 토의 주제로 선택했습니다.
4. 삼일 동안 바람이 세차게 불었습니다.
5. 그는 바로 그날 오후에 실험을 했습니다.

6. 어젯밤 야구 경기에서 John이 또 다른 홈런을 쳤습니다.

Task 3

Answers

1. freezes
   물이 섭씨 0도에서 언다라는 사실은 불변의 진리입니다. 현재시제를 사용해야 하므로 freezes 가 정답입니다.
2. living
   be동사 다음에 진행을 의미하는 ~ing나 수동태를 의미하는 ~ed 가 와야 하는데 이 문장에서는 "그때 당시 살고 있는 중이었다" 라는 과거 진행으로 봐야 합니다.
3. spent
   과거의 동작, 상태, 습관을 나타낼 때는 과거시제를 씁니다. 동사 spend의 과거형은 spent 입니다.
4. sold
   주절의 동사 needed 가 과거이므로 시제 일치의 원칙에 따라 종속절에도 과거형 sold가 와야 합니다.
5. gets
   시간이나 이유를 나타내는 부사절에서는 현재시제가 미래시제를 표현합니다. 시간을 나타내는 when 이 이끄는 부사절에서 동사는 현재형인 gets를 써야 합니다.

Translation

1. 물은 섭씨 0도에서 업니다.
2. 그는 그 당시 사우디아라비아에서 살고 있었습니다.
3. 나는 어린 시절을 독일에서 보냈습니다.
4. 그들은 좀 더 돈이 필요해서 그 집을 팔았습니다.
5. 그녀가 일자리를 얻으면 빚을 갚을 겁니다.

Task 4

Answers

1. stole
   jumped 가 쓰였으므로 시제 일치 원칙에 따라 뒤에 나오는 절에서도 steal 의 과거형인 stole이 와야 합니다.
2. chat
   시제 일치 원칙에 따라 현재형인 chat 이 와야 합니다.
3. has
   makes가 현재로 사용됐기 때문에 앞 문장에서도 현재형인 has를 쓰게 됩니다. everybody 는 단수로 취급합니다.
4. kept
   종속절에 과거형 was가 쓰였으므로 , 주절에서도 keep의 과거형 kept가 옵니다.
5. lay
   문맥으로 보아 lie의 과거형 lay가 옵니다. lie-lay-lain(눕다), lie-lied-lied(거짓말 하다)

Translation

1. 고양이가 판매대 위에 뛰어올라 샌드위치를 훔쳤습니다.
2. 우리 학교에는 컴퓨터 네트워크가 설치되어 있기 때문에 우리는 다른 학교 학생들과 채

팅합니다.
3. 모든 학생들은 e-mail 주소가 있습니다. e-mail로 인해 과제에 관해 질문을 쉽게 할 수 있습니다.
4. 아버지께서는 어릴 때 Iowa에서 자랐는데 양봉을 했습니다.
5. 나는 누워 잠자기 전에 여행에 필요한 모든 것들을 쌌습니다.

Task 5

Answers

1. (2)
   how long 다음에는 다양한 시제가 올 수 있는데, 주어와 동사가 도치된 의문문 형태가 와야 합니다.
2. (1)
   last night 라는 부사구가 있으므로 단순 과거 시제가 와야 합니다.
3. (4)
   be+~ing는 진행의 의미를 나타내지만 this weekend와 같은 미래표시 부사와 쓰이면 미래 시제를 나타냅니다.
4. (1)
   by 2030 라는 부사구가 있으므로 미래시점에서 완료되는 동작을 나타내는 미래완료가 오게 됩니다.
5. (3)
   since 는 '~이후로' 라는 의미로 부사절을 이끕니다. 주절에는 완료 표현을 사용해야 합니다. 주로 [since 주어+과거동사, 주어+현재완료]구조를 갖게 됩니다. 그러나 since가 이끄는 절에서 현재완료 형태가 오기도 합니다.

Translation

1. 당신은 이 방에 얼마나 있었습니까?
2. 어젯밤 Daniel에게 전화하려 했으나 깜빡 잊었습니다.
3. 이번 주말에 파티를 열 예정인데, 당신도 참석하시겠습니까?
4. 2030년까지 과학자들은 그 질병의 치료법을 개발할 것입니다.
5. 2002년에 그 여행사에 입사한 이후 나는 각국에서 온 여러 부류의 사람들을 만났습니다.

Task 6

Answers

1. were married → had been married
   when they got divorced 는 과거시점을 나타내고, 그 때까지 계속되는 일은 과거완료로 표현합니다.
2. eats → is eating
   now 라는 부사는 현재진행형과 함께 쓰입니다.
3. has handed → handed
   an hour ago는 단순과거 시제를 사용해야 합니다.
4. isn't → wasn't
   앞 절의 went와 시제 일치를 시켜야 합니다.
5. wrote → will have written
   by next year 는 미래시점을 나타내므로 그때까지 완료되는 동작을 나타내기 위해 미래완료형을 씁니다.

Translation

1. 그들은 결혼한 지 3년째에 이혼했습니다.
2. Mary는 지금 아침 식사를 하고 있습니다.
3. Edward는 한 시간 전에 레포트를 제출했습니다.
4. 우리는 Ben의 집에 갔지만 그는 집에 없었습니다.
5. Bob은 내년까지 4번째 소설을 쓸 것입니다.

Task 7

Answers

1. provided
   'since+과거시점' 다음에 오는 주절에서는 현재완료가 많이 옵니다. 현재완료 have+p.p.로 나타냅니다.
2. working
   현재완료 진행은 have been ~ing로 나타냅니다.
3. keeps
   현재 사실을 나타내는 단순현재 시제가 와야 합니다.
4. introducing
   when he arrived는 과거 시점을 나타내고 그 시점에서 진행되는 것은 과거진행(was/were +~ing)으로 표현합니다.
5. was
   so 뒤에 오는 절이 과거이므로, 앞 절도 과거로 표현합니다.
6. tried
   he's (= he has) 다음에 완료형을 나타내기 위해 동사의 과거 분사형(p.p.)이 옵니다.
7. rose
   과거시점을 나타내는 부사 yesterday 가 있으므로 단순 과거 시제가 옵니다.

Translation

1. 1993년 이래 그 우주망원경은 우리에게 우주의 중요한 사진을 제공하고 있습니다.
2. Kathy는 여기서 9년째 일하고 있습니다.
3. 나는 가끔 밤에 잠을 이루지 못함에도 불구하고 커피를 즐겨 마십니다.
4. 그가 도착했을 때, 교장은 초대받은 연설자를 소개하고 있었습니다.
5. 나는 몹시 피곤해서 잠시 동안 침대에 누워 있었습니다.
6. 그는 운전 면허 시험에 4번 도전했습니다.
7. 어제 그가 한 골을 넣었을 때, 모든 사람들은 자리에서 일어났습니다.

Review Test

Answers

1. played	2. buys	3. thinking
4. got	5.learned/learnt/been learning	6. will join
7. been	8. ended	9. have known
10. will have		

Translation

1. Andy는 먼저 5년 전에 국가 대표팀에서 활동했습니다.
2. 그가 내 생일 선물로 귀걸이를 사준다면 기쁠 것입니다.
3. 우리는 오랫동안 부엌을 개조하는 것에 대해 생각해 왔습니다.
4. Sarah는 어제 학교에 지각했습니다. 그녀가 교실에 도착했을 때는 이미 수업이 시작한 후였습니다.
5. 우리는 Catherine에게 2년 동안 영어를 배우고 있습니다.
6. 언제 그녀가 우리와 합류할 지 아십니까?
7. 나는 유럽에 몇 번 가 본적이 있습니다.
8. 선생님은 우리에게 6.25 사변이 1953년에 끝났다고 말씀하셨습니다.
9. Mary와 Jane은 초등학교 시절부터 서로 알고 지냈습니다.
10. 당신이 돌아올 때 쯤이면 모든 것이 좋아질 겁니다.

Chapter 4

Auxiliary Verbs

Task 1

Answers

1 .have to
don't have to는 '~할 필요가 없다'는 뜻입니다. don't 다음에 조동사 must는 올 수 없습니다.
2. be
조동사+ 동사원형입니다.
3. take
조동사+ 동사원형입니다.
4. skate
조동사+ 동사원형입니다.
5. having
지금 현재 먹고 있을지도 모른다는 추측과 진행의 의미를 might be ~ing로 표현합니다.

Translation

1. 당신은 내일 아침에 일찍 일어날 필요는 없습니다.
2. Carol은 오늘 첫 번째 바이올린 연주회를 합니다. 분명 매우 긴장하고 있을 것입니다.
3. 승객들은 각각 두 개의 가방을 기내에 갖고 탑승할 수 있습니다.
4. 나는 어릴 때 스케이트를 더 빠르게 탈 수 있었습니다.
5. 나는 Peter가 어디 있는지 잘 모르겠습니다. 아마 점심을 먹고 있을 겁니다.

Task 2

Answers

1. may not be
조동사 +동사원형에서 부정인 not은 조동사와 동사원형 사이에 옵니다.
2. must not drive
조동사 +동사원형에서 부정인 not은 조동사와 동사원형 사이에 옵니다.
3. may have eaten
may have p.p.는 과거의 불확실한 추측을 나타내며 '~ 했을지도 모른다'라고 해석됩니다.
4. Could you tell
주어+조동사+동사원형 의 순서에서 조동사를 주어 앞으로 보내면 의문문이 됩니다.
5. will stop smoking
stop+~ing 는 '~하는 것을 멈추다' 는 뜻입니다.
6. must have left
must have p.p. 는 '~ 했음에 틀림없다.' 라고 해석됩니다.

Translation

1. 그는 늦지 않을 겁니다.
2. 이 표지판은 시속 70 킬로 이상 속력을 내서는 안 된다는 의미입니다.
3. 내 고양이 아픕니다. 독약을 좀 먹은 것 같습니다.
4. 기차가 언제 도착하는지 말해줄 수 있나요?
5. 금연할 것을 약속합니다.
6. Sarah는 아주 조용히 떠났음이 틀림없습니다. 아무도 그녀가 가는 것을 눈치채지 못했습니다.

Task 3

Answers

1. have to
   좋은 시력을 가져야 한다는 의미로 의무를 나타내는 have to를 사용해야 합니다
2. been able to
   조동사 두개를 연속적으로 쓸 수 없습니다. haven't 에서 have는 조동사입니다. 그런데 조동사 could 가 오면 문법적으로 틀리게 됩니다. 그래서 could 의 의미를 가지고 있는 be able to를 써야 합니다.
3. must not
   떠들면 안 된다는 뜻이므로 must not을 사용해야 합니다.
4. Could
   상대방의 허락, 부탁을 요구할 때는 조동사 could를 사용합니다.
5. to visit
   'would like to 동사원형'은 '~하고 싶다.' 는 뜻입니다.
6. may not
   자리가 없을 지도 모른다는 추측이므로 may not 이 정답입니다

Translation

1. 조종사가 되기를 원한다면 시력이 좋아야 합니다.
2. 좀 더 일찍 당신을 보러 올 수 없어서 미안합니다.
3. 모두 잠이 들었으니, 조용히 해야 합니다.
4. 집에까지 태워다 주실 수 있습니까?
5. 오늘 오후에 박물관에 가시겠습니까?
6. 버스에 우리가 앉을 공간이 없을 지도 모릅니다. 기다려 봅시다

Task 4

Answers

1. (2) 추측을 나타내는 might를 사용해야 합니다. may보다 약한 가능성을 나타낼 때는 '어쩌면 ~일지도 모른다'는 의미로 might를 사용합니다.
2. (3) 추측의 조동사 may를 사용해서 표현해야 합니다. may have p.p.는 과거의 추측을 나타냅니다. 현재의 시제를 사용해서 질문했으므로 may have가 답입니다.
3. (2) 강한 추측을 나타내는 must를 사용해야 합니다.
4. (1) '~일리 없다' 는 의미이므로 cannot 을 사용합니다
5. (1) '~할 수 있다'는 의미로 can이 정답입니다.
6. (2) 단순 미래 시제를 나타내기 위해 will 을 사용해야 합니다.

Translation

1. A: Laura가 어딨습니까?
   B: 글쎄요, 부엌에 있을 것입니다.
2. A: Ellen이 왜 늘 장갑을 끼는지 궁금합니다.
   B: 저도 모릅니다. 아마도 알레르기가 있는 것 같습니다.
3. A: 제 아들이 장학금을 받고 예일대에 갔습니다.
   B: 아주 자랑스러우시겠어요.
4. A: 그 번호가 맞습니까?
   B: 틀릴 리 없습니다. 컴퓨터는 실수하지 않습니다.
5. A: 급하세요?
   B: 아뇨, 시간이 충분하니 기다릴 수 있습니다.
6. A: 이번 주말에 무엇을 할 겁니까?
   B: 내 형이 야구 경기 표를 가지고 있습니다. 그래서 함께 갈 겁니다. 내가 가장 좋아하는 팀의 경기입니다.

Task 5

Answers

1. was able to
   '~할 수 있다'는 능력을 나타내는 can 과 의미가 같은 be able to를 사용해야 합니다. '과거에 실제로 ~할 수 있었다'는 의미로 was/were able to를 씁니다.
2. may
   추측을 나타내는 may를 사용해야 합니다
3. Would
   요청을 나타낼 때는 would를 사용합니다.
4. must
   의무를 표현하는 must 가 정답입니다.
5. don't have to
   '~할 필요가 없다'는 don't have to 가 정답입니다.

Translation

1. 다행히 약국이 열려있어서 타이레놀을 살 수 있었습니다.
2. Nancy는 내일 학교에 가지 않을 지도 모릅니다. 지금 약간 아픕니다.
3. 뒤에 앉아도 되겠습니까?
4. Mark는 어린아이가 아닙니다. 그의 미래에 대해 생각해 보아야 합니다.
5. 우리는 오늘 리포트를 끝낼 필요는 없습니다. 내일 해도 됩니다.

Task 6

Answers

1. (4) '~했었음에 틀림 없다'는 must have p.p.가 과거의 추측이므로 정답입니다.
2. (2) '~하지 못했을 것'이라는 뜻으로 couldn't have p.p.를 사용합니다.
3. (4) 추측을 의미하는 might를 씁니다.
4. (3) 과거의 추측이므로 might have p.p. 입니다.
5. (1) '~하지 않았음에 틀림없다'는 뜻으로 must not have p.p.를 사용합니다.

6. (2) '~했었어야 했는데 하지 못했다'는 과거 사실의 후회를 나타낼 때는 should have p.p.를 사용해야 합니다.

Translation

1. A: Mike가 왜 다리에 붕대를 감았는지 궁금합니다.
   B: 글쎄요, 다친 게 분명합니다.
2. A: 그가 당신을 봤다고 생각하십니까?
   B: 아뇨, 너무 멀리 있어서 볼 수가 없었을 겁니다.
3. A: Olivia가 그 회의에 오지 않아서 놀랐습니다.
   B: 아마 그것에 대해 알지 못했을 겁니다.
4. A: 내 핸드폰이 어디에 있죠?
   B: 사무실에 두고 왔을 겁니다.
5. A: Ken은 인사도 없이 나를 지나쳤습니다.
   B: 당신을 못 본 게 틀림없습니다.
6. A: 우리가 레스토랑에 갔을 때, 빈 자리가 하나도 없었습니다.
   B: 예약을 했어야 했습니다.

Review Test

Answers

1. would	2. used to	3. shouldn't	4. Would
5. raise	6. might	7. must	8. rather
9. could have finished	10. should have reserved		

Translation

1. 그녀는 목욕할 때마다 노래를 부르곤 했습니다.
2. 그 건물은 지금 장난감 가게입니다. 예전에는 영화관이었습니다.
3. 속이 안 좋아요. 너무 많이 먹지 말았어야 했어요.
4. 이 학기말 리포트를 내일까지 검토해 주시겠습니까?
5. 그는 우리가 자선 기금을 더 많이 내도록 제안했습니다.
6. 전 지금 시간이 없어요. Sarah가 당신을 도와줄 수 있을 겁니다.
7. 땅이 젖어 있는 걸로 보아 어제 비가 온 것이 틀림없습니다.
8. 주차장을 찾아 한 시간을 소비하느니 버스를 타겠습니다.
9. 모짜르트가 일찍 죽지 않았다면 대작인 레퀴엠을 완성할 수 있었을 텐데요.
10. 우리가 식당에 도착했을 때는 빈 자리가 없었습니다. 예약을 했어야 했습니다.

Chapter 5

Subjunctive Mood

Task 1

Answers

1. say
   직설법 조건절이므로 if 절에서 동사의 현재형을 씁니다.
2. didn't go, would be
   가정법 과거로, 현재사실에 반대되는 사실을 표현합니다. if절에서 동사의 과거형이 쓰이고, 주절에서는 'would+동사원형'이 쓰입니다.
3. look
   직설법 조건절. 따라서 주절이 미래를 나타내므로 조건절에는 동사의 현재형을 씁니다.
4. had
   가정법 과거. If절에 과거형이 와야 합니다.
5. will miss, move
   직설법 조건절. 주절에서는 미래형이 오고, 조건절에서는 현재형이 쓰입니다.
6. could work
   가정법 과거. If절에 과거형이 나왔으므로 주절에서도 'could+동사원형'을 사용해야 합니다.

Translation

1. 당신이 한번만 더 그것을 말하면 나는 소리를 지를 겁니다.
2. Tom이 그녀의 파티에 가지 않으면 그녀는 상처를 받을 겁니다.
3. 서랍에 보면 당신 여권이 있을 겁니다.
4. 내가 아이가 있다면 사립학교에 보낼 겁니다.
5. 당신이 일본으로 이사가면 그리울 겁니다.
6. 우리에게 컴퓨터가 있다면 이것을 더 빨리 해결할 수 있을 턴데요.

Task 2

Answers

1. stayed
   가정법 과거이므로 if절에서 과거형이 쓰입니다.
2. stops
   주절이 미래형이므로 if절에서 현재형이 쓰입니다.
3. were
   가정법 과거이므로 if절에서 과거형이 쓰입니다.
4. wear
   주절이 미래형이므로 if절에서 현재형이 쓰입니다.
5. spoke
   가정법 과거이므로 if절에서 과거형이 쓰입니다.

6. didn't
   가정법 과거이므로 if절에서 과거형이 쓰입니다.

Translation

1. 우리가 호텔에 머무르면 비용이 너무 많이 들 겁니다.
2. 비가 그치면 우리는 나갈 겁니다.
3. Peggy의 키가 크면 그녀는 사람들을 올려다 보지 않아도 될 겁니다.
4. 당신이 그 코트를 입으면 당신과 같이 나가지 않을 거에요.
5. 우리가 중국어를 하면 이런 문제들은 없을 겁니다.
6. 그들이 그에게 돈을 더 주지 않으면 그는 일을 그만둘 겁니다.

Task 3

Answers

1. would've eaten (would have eaten)
   가정법 과거완료이므로 주절에서 would have p.p.형이 와야 합니다.
2. would look
   종속절이 과거 완료형임에도 불구하고 주절은 현재 사실에 반대되는 것이기 때문에 가정법 과거를 사용한 혼합 가정법 문장입니다.
3. couldn't have bought (could not have bought) / wouldn't have bought (would not have bought)
   가정법 과거완료이므로 주절에서 could/would have p.p.형으로 사용합니다.
4. hadn't been (had not been)
   가정법 과거완료이므로 if 절에서 had(not) p.p. 형태가 옵니다.
5. would be
   종속절은 가정법 과거완료이지만 주절은 현재 사실에 반대되는 것이기 때문에 가정법 과거를 사용한 혼합 가정법 문장입니다.

Translation

Ex) 당신이 좀 더 야채를 먹었더라면, 지금쯤 더 건강해 졌을 겁니다.

1. 그가 배가 고팠다면 무엇이라도 먹었을 겁니다.
2. 당신이 문을 분홍색으로 칠하지 않았다면 좀 더 나아 보일 텐데요.
3. 소파가 세일을 하지 않았다면 나는 그것을 사지 못했을 겁니다.
4. 그렇게 늦지만 않았어도 내가 그녀에게 전화를 했을 겁니다.
5. 당신이 그의 충고를 받아들였다면 지금 당신은 훨씬 나을 겁니다

Task 4

Answers

1. If the weather hadn't been so cold, we could have gone out.
   가정법 과거완료. If 주어+had + p.p., 주어 +would/should/could/might +have p.p.
2. If he had been tired last night, he wouldn't have gone to the movie.
   가정법 과거완료
3. You could have left earlier if you had had your car.
   가정법 과거완료
4. If I had won the lottery then, I would be rich now.
   가정법 혼합 구문. If 주어+had + p.p., 주어+would/should/could/might+동사원형

5. If I had the key, I could go into the room.
   가정법 과거 if 주어+ 동사원형, 주어+would/should/could/might +동사원형

Translation

Ex) 내가 그렇게 많이 먹지 않았더라면, 지금 속이 아프지 않을 겁니다.
1. 날씨가 그렇게 춥지 않았다면 우리가 나갈 수 있었을 겁니다.
2. 그가 지난 밤에 피곤했었다면 영화를 보러 가지 않았을 겁니다..
3. 당신이 차가 있었다면 더 일찍 출발할 수 있었을 겁니다..
4. 그때 내가 복권을 탔었으면 지금 부자가 되어 있을 겁니다..
5. 내가 열쇠가 있다면 방으로 들어갈 수 있을 겁니다

Task 5

Answers

1. unless I get home early tonight
   unless는 'if ~not'의 의미입니다.
2. But for the snow
   but for는 '만약 ~이 없다면' 의 뜻입니다.
3. Without air
   without은 '만약 ~이 없다면'의 뜻입니다.
4. I wish I had gone
   I wish 다음에 가정법 과거완료가 쓰인 것입니다.
5. If you had not saved me
   가정법 혼합구문입니다.

Translation

1. 오늘 밤 내가 일찍 들어가지 않으면 집사람이 화를 낼 겁니다.
2. 눈이 오지 않았다면, 그 여자는 어둡기 전에 집에 도착했을 겁니다.
3. 공기가 없으면 생물은 존재할 수 없을 겁니다.
4. 내가 어제 파티를 갔으면 좋았을 텐데요.
5. 당신이 나를 구해주지 않았다면 나는 지금 살아있지 않을 겁니다.

Task 6

Answers

1. (2) 현재 사실이 아닌 것을 바라고 있기 때문에 가정법 과거로 소망을 나타냅니다.
2. (1) 현재에 부자가 아님에도 부자처럼 이야기 하는 것은 현재사실의 반대입니다. 따라서 가정법 과거가 나옵니다.
3. (4) 가정법 과거이므로 if절에서 동사의 과거형이 나옵니다.
4. (3) 가정법 과거완료이므로 주절에서 would(could) have p.p.가 나옵니다.
5. (2) 'It's time +주어+동사 과거형'으로 표현합니다. 뒤에 to 부정사가 오는 경우도 있습니다. Ex) It's time to work.
6. (2) 직설법 조건절을 나타냅니다. 조건절에서는 현재형으로 미래를 나타냅니다.

Translation

1. 내가 해답을 알고 있으면 좋겠습니다.
2. 그녀는 마치 부자인 것처럼 말합니다.

3. Irene이 다른 아파트를 찾으면 그녀는 이사를 갈 겁니다.
4. 내 차가 고장 나지 않았었으면 당신의 집에 갔었을 텐데요.
5. 부엌을 페인트칠 할 때가 되었습니다.
6. 그가 내일 늦게 도착하면, 그 회의는 취소될 것입니다.

Review Test

Answers

1. knew	2. hadn't smelled	3. had taken	4. finds
5. left / had left	6. would be	7. had known	8. Should
9. didn't	10. were to rise		

Translation

1. 내가 그녀의 이름을 안다면 당신에게 알려줄 겁니다.
2. 내가 가스 냄새를 맡지 못했더라면 무슨 일이 발생했을까요?
3. 그가 의사의 조언을 받아들였더라면 아직 살아있을 겁니다.
4. 만약 그녀가 당신 열쇠를 찾으면 당신에게 말할 겁니다.
5. 당신이 그것을 말하지 않고 놔두면 / 놔두었더라면 좋았을 텐데요.
6. 그가 교통사고로 죽지 않았더라면 오늘 23살이 됩니다.
7. Caroline이 영어의 중요성을 알았더라면 영어 공부를 했을 겁니다.
8. 우리 웹사이트에 대해 지적할 만한 사항이나 제안할 것이 있다면 알려주십시오.
9. 내가 회의에 가지 않으면 그들은 실망할 겁니다.
10. 만약 해가 서쪽에서 뜬다면 마음을 바꾸겠습니다. (절대 마음을 바꾸지 않겠습니다.)

Chapter 6

The Passive

Task 1

Answers

1. was stolen
   우리 차가 남에 의해서 도난을 당한 것이기 때문에 수동태로 써야 합니다. be+p.p. 입니다.
2. swept
   문장의 주체가 일을 행했기 때문에 능동태를 써야 합니다.
3. be finished
   도로는 완성이 될 예정이기 때문에 수동태를 써야 합니다.
4. use
   주체가 행위를 하기 때문에 능동태를 써야 합니다.
5. is
   남에 의해서 불리기 때문에 수동태를 써야 합니다.
6. was fired
   Ted가 해고를 당한 것이기 때문에 수동태를 써야 합니다.

Translation

1. 우리 차는 경찰서 근처에서 도난을 당했습니다.
2. 폭풍이 영국 북부를 휩쓸었습니다.
3. 새로운 도로가 11월에 완성될 것입니다.
4. 의사들은 수술에 레이저 광선을 사용합니다.
5. 이 꽃은 영어로 뭐라고 합니까?
6. Ted는 해고 당했습니다.

Task 2

Answers

1. were built
   수영장이 만들어진 것이기 때문에 수동태를 써야 합니다. last year라는 부사구가 있으므로 과거시제가 와야 합니다.
2. is made
   버터가 만들어지기 때문에 수동태를 써야 합니다.
3. be shown
   미래를 나타내므로 will be p.p.가 옵니다.
4. died
   죽었다는 뜻이므로 능동태를 써야 합니다.
5. was painted
   작품은 예술가에 의해서 그려졌기 때문에 수동태를 써야 합니다.

6. finish
주체인 그녀가 일을 마칠 것이기 때문에 능동태를 써야 합니다.

Translation

Ex) 멕시코에서는 스페인어를 씁니다.
1. 세 개의 수영장이 지난해에 지어졌습니다.
2. 버터는 우유로 만들어집니다.
3. 그 영화는 TV에서 곧 방영될 것입니다.
4. 그의 어머니는 그가 16살 때 돌아가셨습니다.
5. Guernica는 Picasso에 의해 1937년에 그려졌습니다.
6. 그녀는 이번 주말 전에 그 일을 마칠 겁니다.

Task 3

Answers

1. are caused
현재형 수동태 표현합니다.
2. were hit
과거형 수동태로 표현합니다. (hit-hit-hit)
3. are not being properly explained
진행형 수동태는 be+being+p.p. 로 표현합니다.
4. be hired
법조동사가 들어있는 수동태를 조동사+be+p.p. 로 표현합니다.
5. has just been done
수동태를 have/has+been+p.p. 로 표현합니다.
6. will be made
미래 수동태는 will/be going to +be+p.p. 로 표현합니다.

Translation

Ex) 그들은 나를 파티에 초대하지 않았습니다.
→ 나는 파티에 초대되지 않았습니다.
1. 빠른 주행은 많은 사고들을 일으킵니다.
→ 많은 사고들이 빠른 주행에 의해 일어납니다.
2. 강한 폭풍이 지난 밤에 여러 도시를 강타했다.
→ 여러 도시가 지난 밤에 강한 폭풍에 의해 강타당했습니다.
3. 그 선생님은 그 방향을 올바르게 설명하고 있지 않습니다.
→ 그 방향은 그 선생님에 의해 올바르게 설명되고 있지 않습니다.
4. 그 회사는 그를 다시 고용할지도 모릅니다.
→ 그는 그 회사에 다시 고용될지도 모릅니다.
5. 그 남자는 그 일을 막 마쳤습니다.
→ 그 일은 그 남자에 의해 막 마쳐졌습니다.
6. 우리는 우리의 이미지를 개선하기 위해 많은 변화를 이루어 나갈 겁니다.
→ 우리의 이미지를 개선하기 위해 많은 변화가 이루어 질 겁니다

Task 4

Answers

1. (1) 현재진행 수동태는 be+being+p.p.로 표현합니다.
2. (2) 주체가 스스로 하는 행동이기 때문에 능동태를 써야 합니다.
3. (2) 저녁은 준비가 되어지는 것이기 때문에 수동태입니다. 일상적으로 되지는 일이므로 현재를 써야 합니다.
4. (1) membership card가 보여지는 것이기 때문에 수동태를 써야 합니다. 법조동사가 들어 있는 수동태는 조동사+be+p.p.로 나타냅니다.
5. (3) 소포는 누군가에 의해서 보내지는 것입니다. 현재완료 수동태는 have/has (not) +been+p.p.로 표현합니다.
6. (4) 사람을 인터뷰하는 것이므로 능동태입니다. be going to+동사원형이 옵니다.

Translation

1. 제발 여기 들어오지 마세요. 방이 청소되고 있습니다.
2. George는 어제 그 대학에 편지를 보냈습니다.
3. 저녁식사는 5시부터 9시까지 제공됩니다.
4. 회원 카드는 정문에서 보여져야만 합니다.
5. 그 소포는 아직 발송되지 않았습니다.
6. 당신은 언제 그 배우를 인터뷰할 겁니까?

Task 5

Answers

1. are offered
   현재 수동태를 써서 표현합니다.
2. is said
   People say that ~이라는 문장을 It is said that~이라는 수동태 문장으로 쓸 수 있습니다.
3. were not given
   주체인 we는 남에 의해서 충분한 시간이 주어지지 않았기 때문에 수동태입니다.
4. got stolen
   능동태 문장의 간접 목적어(us)를 주어로 해서 쓴 수동태 문장입니다. 부정어 not은 be동사 뒤에 옵니다.
5. get paid
   get + p.p.가 쓰인 수동태 문장입니다.
6. got married
   '결혼하다' 는 get married 나 marry를 씁니다.
   Ex) Susan married Edd.
   Her father married Susan off to Edd. (그녀의 아버지는 그녀를 Edd 에게 시집 보냈습니다.)

Translation

1. 그들은 대부분의 직원에게 회사 지분을 제공합니다.
   → 대부분의 직원은 회사 지분을 제공 받습니다.
2. 사람들이 그 퀴즈대회 우승자가 기억력을 상실했다고 말합니다.
   → 그 퀴즈대회 우승자가 기억력을 상실했다고들 합니다.

3. 그들은 우리에게 충분한 시간을 주지 않았습니다.
   → 우리에게는 충분한 시간이 없었습니다.
4. 나는 예전에 오토바이를 가지고 있었는데, 도난 당했습니다.
5. 지난 주에 얼마나 받았습니까?
6. 그들은 2001년에 결혼했습니다.

Task 6

Answers

1. born → was born
   '~에서 태어나다' 라고 할 때는 'be + born' 입니다. Ex) I was born in 1772.
2. been sang → been sung
   be+p.p. 입니다. (sing-sang-sung)
3. correct
   be sold 는 '팔리다' 라는 뜻으로 수동태 구문으로 쓰입니다.
   Ex) The tickets are all sold out. (그 표는 매진되었습니다.)
4. being following → being followed
   현재진행 수동태는 be+being+p.p.로 표현합니다.
5. was disappeared → disappeared
   주체 스스로가 행동을 한 것이기 때문에 능동태입니다.
6. correct
   은행이 털린 것이기 때문에 수동태를 써야 합니다.

Translation

1. 나는 1975년 서울에서 태어났습니다.
2. 그 노래는 그 합창단에 의해 여러 번 불리었습니다.
3. 설탕은 그 상점에서 팔립니다.
4. 나는 우리가 누군가에게 미행당하는 느낌이 듭니다.
5. 그 낯선 남자는 삼일 전에 사라졌습니다.
6. 그 은행이 어제 털렸습니다.

Review Test

Answers

1. have been hunted
2. was founded
3. persuaded
4. elect
5. be transmitted
6. (X She wouldn't have injured if she had worn a seat belt.)
7. (O)
8. (X My little nephews will be taken care of by me until my aunt returns.)
9. (X My glasses got broken in the fight.)
10. (O)

Translation

1. 코끼리는 아마 이빨 때문에 사냥 당하는 유일한 동물일 겁니다.
2. 이 대학은 1954년에 설립되었습니다.
3. 엄마는 내가 치과에 가도록 설득하였습니다.
4. 국민이 미국 대통령을 선출하였습니다.
5. 문화는 학습과 경험을 통해 한 세대에서 다음 세대로 계승되어야 합니다.
6. 그녀가 안전벨트를 착용하고 있었다면 부상당하지 않았을 겁니다.
7. 시끄럽게 해서 죄송합니다. 도로를 수리하고 있는 중입니다.
8. 이모가 돌아오실 때까지 제가 어린 조카를 보살필 겁니다.
9. 싸우다가 제 안경이 부러졌습니다.
10. 하나의 격언이 되기 위해서는 사람들이 많이 사용해야 합니다.

Chapter 7

Review(Chapter 1~6)

Task 1

Answers

(1) N(명사) (2) Pro(대명사) (3) V(동사) (4) Conj(접속사)
(5) Det(한정사) (6) Adj(형용사) (7) Prep(전치사)

Translation

많은 아프리카인들은 당신이 이름을 갖기 전까지는 당신이 존재하지 않는다고 믿었습니다. 그들은 아기들의 이름을 짓기 위한 특별한 의식을 행했습니다.

Task 2

Answers

1. M(주절) 2. S(종속절) 3. S(종속절)
4. S(종속절) 5. M(주절)

Translation

1. 당신이 그 초대를 수락하기 전에 당신의 어머니에게 물어봐야만 합니다.
2. 비록 그가 수학을 더 잘했지만, 미술을 좋아했습니다.
3. 우리 모두는 아빠가 지난 일요일 요리하셨던 저녁을 맛있게 먹었습니다.
4. 나는 해가 지기 전에 잔디를 깎아야만 합니다.
5. 그녀가 버튼을 눌렀을 때 엘리베이터가 작동을 멈췄습니다.

Task 3

Answers

1. Adv(부사구) 2. S(주어) 3. O(목적어)
4. C(보어) 5. V(동사)

Translation

1. 산업혁명 동안 근로자들은 기계를 사용하기 시작했습니다.
2. Robert Fulton의 증기선은 해상 교통을 발전시켰습니다.
3. Alexander Graham Bell이 전화기를 발명했습니다.
4. George Stephenson의 Rocket 은 세계 최초의 철도 기차였습니다.
5. 많은 발명품들이 사람들의 삶의 수준을 향상시켰습니다.

Task 4

Answers

1. isn't
   단수 any cheese 가 주어이므로 isn't가 정답입니다.
2. is
   학명은 단수 취급합니다.
3. get
   'watch+목적어+동사원형' 의 구문을 갖습니다.
4. nervous
   지각 동사 다음에 형용사가 보어로 옵니다.
5. married
   marry는 타동사이기 때문에 전치사 없이 목적어를 바로 취합니다.

Translation

1. 냉장고 속에는 치즈가 없습니다.
2. 경제학은 그가 잘하는 과목입니다.
3. 우리는 그가 세 개의 금메달을 획득하는 것을 지켜보았습니다.
4. 나는 그 면접관들 앞에서 긴장이 되었습니다.
5. 그 가난한 농부는 그 공주와 결혼했습니다.

Task 5

Answers

Yoon-hee goes to a college in Texas. This is her freshman year, and everything seems new and exciting to her. After two months at the college, she has many friends and doesn't feel lonely. She studies hard and gets good grades, but she also enjoys life with her friends.

(1) 주어가 3인치 단수 현재이므로 go에 -es 를 붙여야 합니다.
(2) everything 는 단수로 취급되므로 -s 를 붙여 seems 가 되어야 합니다.
(3) she 는 3인칭 단수이고 이 문장에서 시제는 현재이므로 단수형인 has 가 옵니다.
(4) 주어는 she 입니다. 그러므로 don't 가 아니라 doesn't를 씁니다.
(5) 주어가 3인칭 단수 현재이므로 study 에 -s를 붙여야 합니다. 동사가 -y로 끝날 때는 y 를 i 로 고치고 접미사 -es 를 붙입니다.
(6) 주어가 3인칭 단수 현재이므로 -s를 붙입니다.
(7) 주어가 3인칭 단수 현재일 때, enjoy는 -y가 i로 변하지 않고 y에 바로 -s를 붙입니다.

Translation

윤희는 Texas에서 대학교에 다닙니다. 그녀는 1학년이고, 모든 것이 그녀에겐 새롭고 흥미롭게 느껴집니다. 대학교에 두 달 다닌 후 그녀는 많은 친구를 갖게 되어 외롭지는 않습니다. 그녀는 열심히 공부해서 좋은 성적을 얻습니다. 하지만 그녀는 그녀의 친구들과 삶을 즐기기도 합니다.

Task 6

Answers

1. happens → happened
   yesterday가 있으므로 동사의 과거형이 옵니다.
2. looks → look
   주어는 복수명사 dishes 이므로 수를 일치시켜 복수동사를 써야 합니다.
3. correct
   want는 목적보어로 to 부정사를 취합니다.
4. was → were
   주어(Amy and her son)가 복수명사이므로 수 일치 시켜 복수동사를 씁니다
5. freeze → froze
   last week가 있으므로 동사의 과거형이 와야 합니다.

Translation

1. 우리 가게에서 이상한 일이 어제 일어났습니다.
2. 선반 위에 있는 그릇들은 깨끗해 보입니다.
3. Tom은 내가 공원에서 개를 산책시키길 원했습니다.
4. 문간에는 Amy와 그녀의 아들이 있었습니다.
5. 지난 주에 호수가 스케이트 타기에 충분할 정도로 단단하게 얼었습니다.

Task 7

Answers

1. stayed
   stay는 현재완료 문장으로 have/has+p.p.를 씁니다. (stay- stayed-stayed)
2. bought
   last Valentine's Day라는 부사구는 단순과거 시제와 써야 합니다.
3. raining
   now라는 부사가 있으므로 진행형이 나옵니다. 진행형은 be(not)+~ing로 표현합니다.
4. get
   did 라는 조동사에 다음에는 동사원형을 써야 합니다.
5. mailed
   현재완료 문장으로 have/has(not)+p.p.를 씁니다. mail은 규칙변화 합니다.

Translation

1. Ellen은 여기에서 한 달 동안 머무르고 있습니다.
2. 나는 지난 발렌타인 데이에 그 초코렛을 샀습니다.
3. 지금 나갑시다. 비가 오지 않습니다.
4. 당신은 언제 숲에서 길을 잃었습니까?
5. Joe는 그 편지를 썼습니다. 그러나 그는 아직 그것을 부치지는 못했습니다.

Task 8

Answers

1. incorrect(→ happened)
   a week ago라는 부사구는 현재완료와 함께 쓰일 수 없으며 반드시 과거시제와 함께 쓰입니다.
2. correct
   과거에 시작해서 지금도 계속되는 일을 현재 완료 진행으로 표현할 수 있습니다.
3. incorrect(→ learn)
   일반적인 사실을 표현할 경우엔 단순현재시제로 표기합니다.
4. correct
   과거특정시점에서 일어나는 일을 과거진행으로 표현할 수 있습니다.
5. incorrect(→ had gone/went)
   모두 가버린 것이 집에 도착한 것보다 먼저 일어났기 때문에 과거보다 한 단계 앞선 시제, 즉 과거완료를 씁니다.

Translation

1. 그 차 사고는 일주일 전에 일어났습니다.
2. 나는 당신을 두 시간 동안 기다리고 있습니다.
3. 대개 많은 사람들은 어릴 때 수영을 배웁니다.
4. 지난 번 내가 L.A.에서 그녀를 보았을 때, 그녀는 일자리를 구하고 있었습니다.
5. 내가 집에 왔을 때, 무척 조용했습니다. 모두가 나가고 없었습니다.

Task 9

Answers

1. 2) 과거시제로 질문했기 때문에 과거 시제로 답변해야 합니다.
2. 1) 기간을 나타내는 부사구는 현재완료와 함께 자주 쓰입니다.
3. 3) when 이하가 명백한 과거시점을 표시하므로 주절에서 과거진행을 쓸 수 있습니다.
4. 3) 지금 라디오를 듣고 있는지를 물어야 하므로 현재진행이 와야 합니다.
5. 1) 영화를 얼마나 자주 보러 가는지를 묻고 있으므로 단순현재 시제를 씁니다.

Translation

1 A: 어젯밤 스포츠 뉴스를 보았습니까?
B: 아니요. 일찍 잠자리에 들었습니다.
2. A: Carol과 Matt를 자주 만납니까?
B: 아니요. 그들을 2년 동안 보지 못했습니다.
3. A: 그 사고가 났을 때 얼마나 빨리 운전을 하고 있었습니까?
B: 90km/h로 가고 있었습니다.
4. A: 라디오를 듣고 있습니까?
B: 아니요. 너무 시끄럽군요. 좀 꺼주세요.
5. A: 얼마나 자주 영화 보러 갑니까?
B: 한 달에 한두 번 정도 갑니다.

Task 10

Answers

1. must
   강한 추측을 나타내는 must를 써야 합니다.
2. have to
   조동사는 중복이 되면 안되므로 의무를 나타내는 have to를 써야 합니다.
3. shouldn't
   '~하지 말았어야 했는데' 하는 과거 사실의 유감은 shouldn't have p.p.로 나타냅니다.
4. can't
   '~할 수 없다'는 의미의 can't를 사용해야 합니다.
5. would
   부탁, 권유를 나타낼 때는 would를 사용합니다.
6. might
   추측을 나타내는 may나 might를 사용해야 합니다.

Translation

1. 당신은 6시간째 운전하고 있습니다. 당신은 피곤할 것임에 틀림없습니다.
2. 당신이 다음 주말에 일을 해야만 할까 봐 걱정입니다.
3. 그는 당신 말에 화가 났습니다. 당신이 그렇게 말하지 말았어야만 했습니다.
4. 좀 더 크게 말씀해 주실 수 있겠습니까? 제가 당신의 말을 잘 들을 수가 없습니다.
5. 제 가방을 몇 분만 맡아주시겠습니까?
6. 저는 올 수 없습니다만 Ben에게 물어 보시는 게 어떨까요? 그는 올 수 있을지도 모릅니다.

Task 11

Answers

1. (2) 주장, 요구, 충고, 제안 등을 나타내는 동사(insist, require, advise, suggest, etc.) 뒤에 오는 that절에서는 should+동사원형이 쓰입니다. 조동사가 생략되더라도 동사원형이 와야 합니다.
2. (1) 허락은 may로 나타냅니다.
3. (2) 감기의 원인이 박테리아 때문일지도 모른다는 추측이므로 might 를 사용합니다.
4. (3) 문맥상 "의무"를 나타내는 had to를 사용합니다.
5. (1) 과거의 추측을 나타내기 위해서는 must have p.p.가 쓰입니다.

Translation

1. 그녀는 그가 그들과 함께 저녁 식사를 해야 한다고 주장했습니다.
2. 엄마, 크림소스 스파게티를 점심으로 먹을 수 있을까요?
3. 그 독감의 원인은 박테리아였을지 모릅니다.
4. 나는 몸이 좋지 않아서 일찍 떠나야만 했습니다.
5. 거리가 젖어있습니다. 어제 비가 내렸음에 틀림없습니다.

Task 12

Answers

1. (2) 강한 추측을 나타낼 때는 must를 씁니다.
2. (1) 갈수도 있었지만 가지 않았다는 의미입니다. could have p.p.는 '~할 수도 있었다'는 의미입니다.
3. (3) 과거의 추측을 나타내기 위해서 may/might have p.p.를 씁니다.
4. (3) '~일리 없다' 는 의미로 cannot을 씁니다.
5. (2) '당연히 ~할 것이다'라는 추측을 나타내기 위해 should를 씁니다.

Translation

1. A: Tina가 어디에 있습니까?
   B: 틀림없이 이층에 있을 겁니다. 그녀가 10분 전에 그곳으로 올라가는 것을 보았습니다.
2. A: 어젯밤에 그 오페라에 갔습니까?
   B: 아니요. 갈 수도 있었지만, 가지 않기로 마음 먹었습니다.
3. A: Christine이 왜 그 파티에 오지 않았는지 궁금합니다.
   B: 그녀는 초대를 받지 않았는 지도 모릅니다.
4. A: 저 사람이 Greg입니까?
   B: 아닙니다. 그가 Greg일리가 없습니다. Greg는 그 사람보다 훨씬 키가 큽니다.
5. A: Nick이 벌써 이곳에 왔습니까?
   B: 아직 오지 않았습니다. 그러나 곧 올 겁니다.

Task 13

Answers

1. tried
   가정법 과거문장으로 if절에서도 동사의 과거형을 씁니다.
2. buy
   가정법 과거 문장으로 주절에서 could+동사원형을 씁니다.
3. is
   직설법 조건절에서는 동사의 현재형을 써야 합니다.
4. leave
   직설법 조건절에서는 동사의 현재형을 써야 합니다.
5. have happened
   가정법 과거완료 문장으로 주절에서 would+have+p.p.를 써야 합니다.

Translation

1. 당신은 노력만 하면 할 수 있을 겁니다.
2. 내가 그렇게 가난하지만 않다면 컴퓨터를 살 수 있을 겁니다.
3. 모두가 준비되면 우리는 수업을 시작할 것입니다.
4. 당신이 한국을 떠나면 우리는 당신을 매우 많이 그리워할 것입니다.
5. 그 운전수가 빨간 신호에 멈추었으면, 그 사고는 일어나지 않았을 겁니다.

Task 14

Answers

1. were
   'I wish+주어+동사 과거형'는 '~한다면 좋을 텐데'라는 의미로 현재사실에 반대되는 바를 소원할 때 쓰입니다. 'I wish+주어+had p.p.'는 '~했다면 좋았을 텐데'라는 의미로 과거사실에 반대되는 바를 소원할 때 라는 의미로 쓰입니다. be동사의 경우 was대신 were를 것에 주의해야 합니다.
2. had not reminded
   가정법 과거완료는 과거사실에 반대되는 것을 가정할 때 사용됩니다. If+주어+had p.p., 주어+would etc.+have p.p. "(과거에) 만약 -했다면, (과거에) -했을 텐데"
3. knew
   가정법 과거는 현재의 사실에 반대되는 것을 가정할 때 사용됩니다. If+주어+were/동사의 과거형, 주어+would etc.+동사원형
4. is
   직설법 조건문 입니다. If절에서 현재형 동사가 쓰입니다.
5. were/had been
   '마치 ~처럼'으로 해석되는 것으로 현실과 반대되는 것을 표현하는 가정법의 한 형태입니다. 'as if+주어+동사 과거형'이 오면 '마치-인 것 처럼'이란 뜻으로 현재사실에 반대되는 바를 가정하게 됩니다. 'as if+주어+had p.p.'가 오면 '마치-였던 것처럼'이란 뜻으로 과거사실에 반대되는 바를 가정하게 됩니다.

Translation

1. Laura가 여기에 지금 있으면 좋겠습니다.
2. 당신이 상기시켜주지 않았으면 나는 Sarah의 생일을 잊었을 겁니다.
3. 내가 그의 이메일 주소를 안다면 그에게 메일을 쓸 겁니다.
4. 날씨가 좋다면 우리는 야외에서 식사할 것입니다.
5. 그는 마치 나의 선생님인 것처럼/선생님이었던 것처럼 말합니다.

Task 15

Answers

1. If the car <u>were not very expensive</u>, I could buy it.
   가정법 과거 문장으로 if절에서 동사의 과거형이 쓰입니다.
2. If we <u>had taken</u> a shortcut, we would not have missed the train.
   가정법 과거완료문장으로 if절에서 had p.p. 가 쓰입니다.
3. I wish I <u>had learned</u> how to play the piano.
   과거사실과 반대되는 것을 가정하는 문장으로 I wish다음에 오는 절에서 had p.p. 가 쓰입니다.
4. If I had gone to the meeting last night, I <u>would be</u> tired now.
   혼합가정법은 과거의 사실에 반대되는 가정을 하고 그 결과 현재사실에 반대되는 상상을 하는 과거와 현재가 혼합된 시제입니다 If+주어+had p.p., 주어+would etc.+동사원형 '(과거에) -했다면, (현재에) -할 텐데' 라는 뜻입니다.
5. Without <u>your help</u>, I couldn't start the business.
   If it were not for-, 주어+조동사 과거형(would etc.)+동사원형. '-이 없다면' 하는 가정법 구문입니다. 줄여 말하기를 좋아하는 영어의 습성상 without으로 바꾸어 쓸 수 있습니다.

Translation

1. 차가 많이 비싸지만 않다면 내가 살 수 있을 겁니다.
2. 우리가 지름길을 택했다면, 그 기차를 놓치지 않았을 겁니다.
3. 내가 피아노를 배웠으면 좋았을 텐데요.
4. 내가 어젯밤에 그 모임에 갔다면 지금 피곤할 겁니다.
5. 당신의 도움이 없다면, 사업을 시작할 수가 없을 겁니다.

Task 16

Answers

1. was built
   Taj Mahal이 지어졌기 때문에 수동태를 써야 합니다.
2. broken
   안경이 부서졌기 때문에 수동태를 써야 합니다. get+p.p.로 수동태를 표현합니다.
3. is spoken
   영어가 쓰여지는 것이므로 수동태를 써야 합니다.
4. is said
   'It is said (that)~'는 '~라고 말하여진다'라는 뜻입니다.
5. being served/ served
   음식이 제공되어지는 것이므로 수동태를 써야 합니다.

Translation

1. Taj Mahal은 1640년 경에 건축되었습니다.
2. 그의 안경은 싸우다가 부서졌습니다.
3. 영어는 배울만한 가치가 있습니다. 그것은 많은 나라에서 쓰입니다.
4. 그가 프랑스 어디엔가 있다고들 합니다.
5. 내가 그 음식점에 도착했을 때 음식이 나오고 있었습니다.

Task 17

Answers

1. costs
   cost는 '~가 들다'라는 뜻으로 수동태로 쓰이지 않습니다.
2. was pleased
   be pleased with는 '~에 기뻐하다'라는 뜻입니다.
3. could be hired
   '~에 고용되다' 라는 뜻으로 수동태 문장으로 써야 합니다.
4. disappeared
   disappear는 목적어가 필요 없는 자동사이므로 수동태로 쓰이지 않습니다.
5. has been
   카메라가 도난을 당한 것이기 때문에 수동태를 써야 합니다.

Translation

1. 이 표는 2달러입니다.
2. 그의 선생님은 그 소식을 듣고 기뻐하셨습니다.
3. Linda는 새로운 컴퓨터 회사에 취직될 수도 있습니다.

4. 그녀의 아이가 오후 4시경에 사라졌습니다.
5. 내 카메라가 내 사무실에서 도난 당했습니다.

Task 18

Answers

1. correct
   '닫힌다'라는 뜻으로 수동태입니다.
2. be → been
   현재완료로 have been p.p.로 쓰입니다.
3. been → be /have been
   조동사 should 다음에 동사원형이나 have been p.p.가 올 수 있습니다.
4. doesn't permit → is not permitted
   '허가된다'는 뜻으로 수동태를 써야 합니다.
5. correct
   '제출된다'라는 뜻으로 수동태입니다.

Translation

1. 문이 저녁 8시에 닫힙니다.
2. 개에게 물려본 적이 있습니까?
3. 가족 모두가 초대 되어야만 합니다/ 했습니다.
4. 흡연은 공공 장소에서 허락되지 않습니다.
5. 지원서가 12월 1일까지 제출되어야만 합니다.

Chapter 8 Infinitives and Gerunds

Task 1

Answers

1. to divorce/to get divorced/to get a divorce
   decide 는 to 부정사를 목적어로 취합니다.
2. doing
   finish 는 -ing를 목적어로 취해야 합니다.
3. feel
   사역동사 make는 목적격 보어로 동사원형이 와야 합니다.
4. to eat
   refuse는 to 부정사를 목적어로 취합니다.
5. to change
   'It ~for~to부정사'구문으로 to부정사가 진주어로 쓰였습니다.
6. to play
   learn 과 같은 동사 다음에 의문사와 부정사가 올 수 있습니다. how to play the flute는'플룻 부는 법'으로 해석됩니다.

Translation

1. 그들은 마침내 이혼하기로 결심했습니다.
2. Tom은 그의 숙제를 끝마쳤습니다.
3. 추운 날씨 때문에 우리는 피곤하였습니다.
4. 많은 아이들이 시금치 스프 먹기를 거부했습니다.
5. 그녀가 지금 직업을 바꾸는 것은 실수하는 것일 겁니다.
6. 당신은 플룻 부는 법을 배웠습니까?

Task 2

Answers

1. correct
   allow는 목적보어로 to부정사를 취합니다.
2. to not → not to
   부정어 not을 to부정사 앞에 옵니다. to부정사의 부정형은 not to V입니다.
3. seeing → to see
   advise는 목적보어로 to부정사를 취합니다.
4. correct
   afford는 to 부정사를 목적어로 취합니다
5. have → to have/ in order to have
   '~하기 위해서'라는 의미를 갖기 위해서 to부정사나 in order to 동사원형이 와야 합니다.

Translation

1. 그들은 우리가 그 집을 보는 것을 허락하지 않았습니다.
2. 그는 옆 집 사는 여자 아이를 좋아하지 않는 척 했습니다.
3. 그는 나에게 의사에게 가보라고 충고하였습니다.
4. 저는 새로운 휴대폰을 살만한 여유가 없습니다.
5. Sarah는 직업을 얻을 수 있는 더 좋은 기회를 갖기 위해 열심히 공부합니다.

Task 3

Answers

1. splashing
   avoid 는 동명사를 목적어로 취합니다.
2. to catch
   want 는 to부정사를 목적어로 취합니다.
3. turning
   mind 는 동명사를 목적어로 취하는 동사입니다.
4. cry
   사역동사 make는 목적 보어 자리에 동사원형이 와야 합니다. make+목적어+동사원형
5. to read
   'too~to부정사'는 '너무 ~해서 ~할 수 없다'라는 의미입니다.
6. to arrive
   expect 는 목적보어 자리에 to 부정사가 옵니다. expect+목적어+to부정사
7. going
   'feel like -ing' 는 거의 숙어처럼 굳어진 표현으로 feel like는 동명사를 목적어로 취합니다.

Translation

1. 샤워를 할 때는 물이 바닥에 튀지 않도록 노력하세요.
2. 당신이 그 기차를 잡고 싶으면, 서두르는 편이 낫습니다.
3. 라디오 소리를 좀 낮춰 주시겠습니까?
4. 그 이야기는 너무 슬펐습니다. 그것을 듣고 저는 울었습니다.
5. 이 책은 내가 읽기에는 너무 어렵습니다.
6. 그가 벌써 여기 있습니까? 우리는 그가 훨씬 늦게 도착할 것으로 기대했었습니다.
7. 나는 피곤합니다. 오늘 밤 나가고 싶지 않습니다.

Task 4

Answers

1. to pass
   manage 는 to 부정사를 목적어로 취합니다.
2. having done
   admit은 목적어 자리에 동명사가 옵니다. 이미 일어난 일에 대해서 이야기 할 때는 목적어로 having+p.p.의 형식을 취하게 됩니다.
3. admiring
   cannot help -ing 는 '도저히 -하지 않을 수 없다'는 표현입니다.
4. to pay
   afford는 to 부정사를 목적어로 취합니다.

5. to be
   appear는 to 부정사를 목적어로 취합니다.
6. dancing
   go -ing 는 여가 활동이나 운동, 쇼핑 등의 단어와 함께 사용되어 '-하러 가다'의 의미를 가집니다.

Translation

1. Jason은 간신히 그 시험에 합격했습니다.
2. 그녀는 자신이 그것을 했다는 것을 인정했습니다.
3. 우리는 그의 용기를 칭찬하지 않을 수 없습니다.
4. 저는 지금 그녀에게 돈을 갚을 능력이 없습니다.
5. 새와 박쥐는 낮에는 비슷해 보이지만 밤에는 완전히 달라 보입니다.
6. 지난 금요일에 춤추러 갔습니까?

Task 5

Answers

1. correct
   enjoy는 동명사를 목적어로 취합니다.
2. making → to make
   allow 는 to부정사를 목적보어로 취합니다.
3. to cry → crying
   과거의 사건을 기억하는 것이므로 동명사가 와야 합니다.
4. correct
   refuse는 to부정사를 목적어로 취합니다.
5. having spending → having spent
   이미 일어난 일에 대해서 이야기 할 때는 목적어로 having+p.p.형태를 취합니다.(spend-spent-spent)
6. to cancel → canceling
   consider 는 동명사를 목적어로 취합니다.

Translation

1. 그들은 매일 아침 산책하기를 즐깁니다.
2. 그는 우리가 개인적인 전화를 하는 것을 허락하지 않았습니다.
3. 그녀는 학교에 처음으로 등교하던 날 울었던 것을 기억합니다.
4. Thomas는 집에 돌아오기를 거부했습니다.
5. 저는 너무 많은 돈을 낭비한 것을 후회합니다.
6. 저는 제 여행을 취소할 것을 고려하고 있습니다.

Task 6

Answers

1. to go
   앞으로 일어날 일을 기억하는 것이므로 to 부정사형태로 써야 합니다.
2. answering / replying to
   put off는 목적어로 동명사가 옵니다.

3. to talk / to speak
   tend는 목적어로 to 부정사가 옵니다.
4. not to believe
   warn은 to 부정사를 목적어로 취합니다. 부정어 not은 to부정사 앞에 씁니다.
5. washing / to be washed
   need는 수동의 뜻을 가진 목적어로 -ing 형이 목적어로 올 수도 있고 to be p.p.형이 올 수도 있습니다.
6. how to use
   '~하는 법'이라는 의미로 'how to 동사원형'이 목적어로 옵니다.

Review Test

Answers

1. to get	2. having	3. watching	4. help	5. shouting
6. driving	7. having	8. to make	9. being disturbed	10.to leave

Translation

1. 곧 답 메일 주시기를 기다리고 있겠습니다.
2. 나는 지난 주에 내가 가장 좋아하는 영화 배우와 함께 한 최고의 시간을 절대 잊지 못할 겁니다.
3. 비디오를 다 본 후 그는 잠자러 갔습니다.
4. 내가 네 살 때 아버지께서는 나무 심는 것을 돕게 하셨습니다.
5. 그녀는 그에게 그만 소리지르라고 말하지만, 그는 지시 받는 것을 좋아하지 않습니다.
6. 그는 차를 훔쳤다고 시인했지만 그 차로 험하게 운전했다는 사실은 부인하였습니다.
7. 저녁식사로 국수 먹고 싶은 생각이 별로 없네요.
8. 그는 일찍 시작하기로 결심했습니다.
9. 그녀는 방해 받지 않고 일해야 합니다.
10. 핸드폰을 택시에 놓고 오다니 당신이 부주의했습니다.

Chapter 9

Participles

Task 1

Answers

1. broken
   과거분사가 수동의 의미를 지닌 명사를 수식하고 있습니다.
2. stealing
   목적어 다음에 나온 현재분사(~ing)는 목적어가 동작을 행하는 능동적인 관계를 나타냅니다.
3. attending
   능동의 의미를 지닌 현재분사가 the people을 수식하고 있습니다.
4. repaired
   목적보어로 쓰인 과거분사(~ed)는 목적어가 동작을 당하는 수동적인 관계를 나타냅니다.
5. closed
   창문이 닫히는 것이므로 수동의 뜻을 지닌 과거분사가 와야 합니다.
6. discussed
   그 문제들이 의논되는 것이므로 수동의 뜻을 지닌 과거분사가 와야 합니다.

Translation

1. 그녀는 마음에 상처를 받았다고 말합니다.
2. 나는 나의 보석을 훔치고 있는 도둑을 잡았습니다.
3. 회의에 참석한 사람들은 그것에 대해 걱정을 표명했습니다.
4. 그녀는 청소기를 수리하게 했습니다.
5. 이 방은 에어컨이 있기 때문에 우리는 창문을 닫아야 합니다.
6. 우리는 논의된 문제 중 어떤 것에 대해서도 합의를 보지 못했습니다.

Task 2

현재진행시제를 만드는 역할을 했던 현재분사(~ing)가 형용사로 사용되는 경우 진행/능동의 의미를 지니며 수동태와 완료시제를 만드는 역할을 했던 과거분사(-ed)가 형용사로 사용되는 경우 수동/완료의 의미를 지닙니다. 단독분사의 경우 앞에서 명사를 수식하지만 분사구의 경우 뒤에서 명사를 수식합니다. 대명사는 무조건 뒤에서 수식합니다.

Answers

1. wearing
   현재분사가 명사를 뒤에서 수식하고 있습니다. 소년이 모자를 쓴 것이므로 능동의 의미를 가지는 현재분사가 쓰입니다.
2. made
   cake는 만들어지는 것이므로 수동의 의미를 가지는 과거분사가 쓰입니다.

3. rolling
   공이 굴러 떨어지고 있으므로 능동의 의미를 지니는 현재분사가 명사 뒤에서 수식을 하고 있습니다.
4. offering
   편지에 제안하는 있는 것이므로 능동의 의미를 지닌 현재분사가 옵니다.
5. leaning
   주어인 he가 벽에 기대어 서 있는 것이므로 능동의 의미를 가지는 현재분사가 쓰입니다.

Translation

1. 커다란 밀짚 모자를 쓴 소년은 누구입니까?
2. 우리는 오늘 정오에 만들어진 케이크를 먹었습니다.
3. 언덕 아래로 구르고 있는 공은 나의 것입니다.
4. 이틀 전에 나는 일자리를 주겠다는 편지를 받았습니다.
5. 그는 벽에 기대어 서있었습니다.

Task 3

Answers

1. annoyed
   주어가 she이므로 과거분사가 보어로 옵니다.
2. disappointing
   주어가 the governer's speech이므로 현재분사가 보어로 옵니다.
3. exciting
   주어가 this soccer game이므로 현재분사가 보어로 옵니다.
4. interested
   주어가 Cathy이므로 과거분사가 보어로 옵니다.
5. depressed
   목적어가 me이므로 과거분사가 보어로 옵니다.
6. astonished
   주어가 cook이므로 과거분사가 보어로 옵니다.

Translation

1. 그녀는 그의 무례한 태도에 화가 났습니다.
2. 주지사의 연설은 실망스러웠습니다.
3. 이 축구 경기는 매우 흥미진진했습니다.
4. Cathy 는 천문학을 공부하는 데 관심이 있습니다.
5. 날씨 때문에 나는 의기소침해집니다
6. 그 요리사는 그의 엄청난 식욕에 놀랐습니다.

Task 4

Answers

1. surprising
   It은 가주어 that절이 진주어입니다. 현재분사가 보어로 옵니다.
2. embarrassed, annoyed
   주어가 I 이므로 과거분사가 보어로 옵니다.

3. confusing
주어가 her explanation이므로 현재 분사가 보어로 옵니다.
4. amusing
stories를 꾸며주는 현재분사가 옵니다.
5. annoying
주어가 mosquitoes이므로 현재분사가 보어로 옵니다.
6. relaxed
목적어인 me가 느끼는 것이므로 과거분사가 옵니다.

Translation

1. 그는 보통 밤 늦게까지 자지 않고 있습니다. 그가 늘 그렇게 피곤해 보이는 것은 놀라운 일이 아닙니다.
2. 나는 당황하면 얼굴이 빨개집니다.
3. 그녀의 설명은 혼란스러웠습니다. 대부분의 사람들은 그것을 이해하지 못했습니다.
4. Nick은 재미있습니다. 우리는 자주 그의 재미나는 이야기에 웃습니다.
5. 모기가 너무 괴롭혀서 나는 잠을 잘 수가 없었습니다.
6. 그 감미로운 음악을 들으니 긴장이 풀어집니다.

Task 5

Answers

1. Not knowing Cathy, I didn't speak to her.
   (1) 접속사 as를 없앱니다.
   (2) 주절의 주어와 종속절의 주어 I가 같으므로 종속절의 주어를 생략합니다.
   (3) 종속절의 시제와 주절의 시제가 같으므로 종속절 동사는 현재분사(~ing)의 형태를 취합니다.
   (4) 부정어 not은 분사구문 앞에 위치시킵니다.
2. Judging from his appearance, he must be a Japanese.
   (1) 접속사 if를 없앱니다.
   (2) 주절의 주어와 종속절의 주어가 달라도 종속절의 주어가 막연한 일반인 we 이므로 생략합니다.
   (3) 종속절의 시제와 주절의 시제가 같으므로 종속절 동사는 현재분사(~ing)의 형태를 취합니다.
3. Having finished the term paper, he went out and played basketball.
   (1) 접속사 when을 없앱니다.
   (2) 주절의 주어와 종속절의 주어가 같으므로 종속절의 주어를 생략합니다.
   (3) 종속절의 시제가 주절의 시제보다 한 시제 앞서므로 종속절 동사는 'having+p.p.'형태를 취합니다.
4. (Being) Written in easy French, this book is good for beginners.
   (1) 접속사 since를 없앱니다.
   (2) 주절의 주어와 종속절의 주어가 같으므로 종속절의 주어를 생략합니다.
   (3) 종속절의 시제와 주절의 시제가 같고 수동태이므로 종속절 동사는 being + p.p. 형태를 취합니다. 이때 being은 생략할 수 있습니다.
5. (Being) Taken by surprise, he did not lose his composure.
   (1) 접속사 although를 없앱니다.
   (2) 주절의 주어와 종속절의 주어가 같으므로 종속절의 주어를 생략합니다.
   (3) 종속절의 시제와 주절의 시제가 같고 수동태이므로 being + p.p. 형태를 취합니다. 이때 being은 생략할 수 있습니다.

Translation

1. 나는 Cathy를 몰랐기 때문에 그녀와 이야기 하지 않았습니다.
2. 그의 생김새로 판단해 보면 그는 일본인임에 틀림없습니다.
3. 그는 학기말 리포트를 마쳤을 때 밖에 나가서 농구를 했습니다.
4. 이 책은 쉬운 프랑스어로 쓰여져서 초보자들에게 좋습니다.
5. 그는 비록 몹시 놀랐지만 마음의 평정을 잃지 않았습니다.

Task 6

Answers

1. (2) 종속절의 주어가 주절의 주어와 동일하고 시제도 같습니다. 의미상 수동태이므로 (Being) Used wisely가 정답입니다.
2. (3) 종속절의 주어가 주절의 주어와 같고 종속절의 시제가 주절의 과거시제보다 한 시제 앞서야 하므로 Having seen the movie가 정답입니다.
3. (1) 주어가 다르고 시제는 같으므로 The car breaking down이 정답입니다.
4. (4) 주절의 주어와 같기 때문에 종속절의 주어가 생략 되어습니다. 주절에서는 주어가 필요하므로 Jack went to bed right away가 정답으로 가장 적절합니다.
5. (1) 수동의 의미를 지닌 과거분사가 the dog를 수식합니다. 정답은 trained carefully입니다. 이 문장은 다음과 같은 관계대명사절이 있어도 뜻이 같습니다. The dog which is trained carefully will become a faithful friend.
6. (2) 종속절의 시제가 주절의 시제보다 한 시제 앞서야 하고 능동태이므로 having set이 정답입니다.

Translation

1. 여가가 지혜롭게 사용되면 건강과 에너지와 행복을 증진시킵니다.
2. 영화를 보고 나서 그는 꽤 실망했습니다.
3. 차가 고장 나서 그들은 걸어서 여행을 마쳐야 했습니다.
4. Jack은 숙제를 마치고 나서 바로 잠자리에 들었습니다.
5. 잘 훈련 받은 개는 충실한 친구가 될 것입니다.
6. 해가 지자 우리는 밤에 묵을 모텔을 찾기 위해 노력했습니다.

Review Test

Answers

1. destroying the oldest wooden structure in Seoul/and destroyed the oldest wooden structure in Seoul
2. Correct
3. Not understanding what she said/ Because he didn't understand what she said
4. locked
5. fascinating
6. injured
7. speaking
8. boring
9. motivated
10. confirming

Translation

1. 화재가 발생하여 서울에서 가장 오래된 목조 건축물인 숭례문이 파괴되었습니다.
2. 숙제를 끝낸 후 저녁식사를 준비하기 시작했습니다.
3. 그녀가 한 말을 이해하지 못했기 때문에 그는 침묵을 지켰습니다.
4. John은 잠겨 있는 문을 열려고 시도했지만 열지 못했습니다.
5. 우리는 도시 구경이 너무 환상적이라는 것을 알았습니다.
6. 교통사고로 부상당한 승객들은 병원으로 이송되었습니다.
7. 일반적으로 고양이는 개만큼 충성스러운 애완동물이 아닙니다.
8. 그는 내가 지금까지 만난 사람 중 가장 지루한 사람입니다.
9. 불경기가 오래 지속되어 매우 의욕적이고 자격이 충분한 졸업생들조차 취직이 안 되고 있습니다.
10. 그는 호텔 예약이 승인된 팩스를 받았습니다.

Chapter 10

Relatives

Task 1

Answers

1. who
   the doctor가 선행사이고 동사 examined의 주어인 주격 관계대명사가 와야합니다.
2. that
   선행사가 the term paper이고 동사 writing의 목적어인 목적격 관계대명사가 와야 합니다.
3. whose
   뒤에 명사가 나오므로 소유격 관계대명사가 와야 합니다.
4. that
   선행사가 anything이고 동사 clean의 주어인 주격 관계대명사가 와야 합니다.
5. whose
   뒤에 명사가 나오므로 소유격 관계대명사가 와야 합니다.
6. who
   선행사가 the women이고 동사 work의 주어인 주격 관계대명사가 와야 합니다.

Translation

1. 아픈 아이를 진찰한 의사는 매우 친절했습니다.
2. David가 쓰고 있는 학기말 리포트는 금요일까지 끝마쳐 져야만 합니다.
3. 그 의견을 내가 가장 존중하는 사람은 나의 아버지입니다.
4. 이 카펫을 청소할 무언가가 있습니까?
5. 저는 자전거를 도난 당한 그 소년을 압니다.
6. Angela는 우체국에서 일하는 그 여자를 만났습니다.

Task 2

Answers

1. which/that
   listen to 의 목적어인 목적격 관계대명사가 필요합니다. 선행사가 사물이니 답은 which 또는 that입니다.
2. whose
   뒤에 명사가 나오므로 소유격 관계대명사가 와야 합니다. 소유격 관계 대명사+명사
3. whom
   목적격이 who로도 쓰이긴 하지만 이 경우에는 앞에 전치사가 있기 때문에 반듯이 목적격인 whom을 써야 합니다.
4. who/that
   동사 sit의 주어인 주격 관계대명사 필요합니다. 선행사가 사람이니 who나 that이 올 수 있습니다.

5. whose
   뒤에 명사가 나오므로 소유격 관계대명사가 와야 합니다.
6. which
   선행사가 사물이고, 전치사 in 다음에 목적격 관계 대명사 which가 와야 합니다. 전치사 다음에 that이 올 수 없습니다.

Translation

1. 제가 어제 들은 음악은 매우 좋았습니다.
2. 내가 그 소설을 읽고 있는 그 여자는 글을 잘 씁니다.
3. 그녀가 사랑하는 그 남자가 그녀에게 꽃을 주었습니다.
4. 첫 줄에 앉아 있는 그 학생들은 일본에서 왔습니다.
5. Jonathan은 그 목적을 이해할 수 없는 그런 회의에 갔습니다.
6. 우리의 방학을 보낸 그 도시는 아름다웠습니다.

Task 3

Answers

1. need
   주격관계 대명사는 생략할 수 없습니다.
2. need
   소유격 관계대명사는 생략할 수 없습니다.
3. don't need
   목적격 관계대명사는 생략할 수 있습니다.
4. need
   목적격 관계대명사는 생략할 수 있으나 전치사 다음에서는 생략할 수 없습니다.
5. don't need
   목적격 관계대명사는 생략할 수 있습니다.
6. need
   앞 문장 전체를 받는 관계대명사 which는 생략할 수 없습니다.

Translation

1. 차 사고로 부상을 당한 그 남자는 병원에 있습니다.
2. 지갑을 도난 당한 부인은 경찰에 신고했습니다.
3. 당신이 잃어버렸던 그 책을 찾았습니까?
4. 당신에게 많은 선물을 한 사람들에게 감사해야 합니다.
5. 지난 밤 파티에서 만난 그 여자를 저는 사랑합니다.
6. 그는 아무 말도 하지 않았는데, 그것이 그녀를 화나게 했습니다.

Task 4

Answers

1. whom
   전치사 뒤에 나오는 관계대명사 목적격은 who 대신 whom을 써야 합니다
2. which
   계속적 용법에서 앞 문장 전체를 받을 때는 which를 써야 합니다.

3. correct
   동사 borrowed의 목적어로 관계 대명사 that이나 which 가 올 수 있으며, 이때 관계대명사는 생략할 수도 있습니다.
4. in which
   '~에 흥미있다' 라고 할 때 'be interested in'이라는 구문을 씁니다. 전치사 in은 관계대명사 which앞에 올 수도 있습니다.
5. correct
   뒤에 명사가 오므로 소유격 관계대명사가 옵니다.

Translation

1. 제가 이야기했던 그 남자는 저에게 좋은 충고를 해주었습니다.
2. 제 사무실은 이 건물 4층에 있는 데, 매우 넓습니다.
3. 저는 친구에게서 빌렸던 돈을 돌려주었습니다.
4. 이것은 제가 흥미 있어하는 영화입니다.
5. 저는 그 커피를 쏟은 선생님에게 사과했습니다.

Task 5

Answers

1. (2) 장소를 나타내는 관계부사인 where가 필요합니다. 관계대명사를 쓰려면 전치사와 함께 써서 in which를 표현할 수 잇습니다.
2. (1) 시간을 나타내는 관계부사인 when을 사용합니다. on which도 가능합니다.
3. (3) 선행사를 포함한 관계대명사인 what을 사용합니다.
4. (2) 선행사가 the way인 경우에 how를 사용하지만 현대영어에서는 the way how를 잘 쓰지 않으므로 the way 혹은 how만을 따로 쓰든지, the way that 을 씁니다.
5. (2) 이유를 받는 관계 부사는 why인데 생략할 수 있습니다. why대신에 that을 쓰기도 합니다.
6. (4) all 다음에는 관계대명사로 that을 주로 씁니다.

Translation

1. 제가 자라난 도시는 작습니다.
2. 1960년은 혁명이 일어난 해입니다.
3. Tom에게 어떤 일이 일어 났는지에 대해 읽었습니까?
4. 이것이 그들이 그것을 발견한 방법입니다.
5. 그녀가 남편과 싸운 이유를 아십니까?
6. 저에게 그 학생에 대해 아는 것을 모두 말해주세요.

Task 6

Answers

1. (2) 주격이면서 사물을 받는 것은 보기 중에서 that입니다. 특히 선행사에 최상급이 올 때는 that을 주로 사용합니다. what은 선행사가 있어서 사용이 불가합니다.
2. (1) 장소를 나타내는 관계부사인 where이 와야 합니다.
3. (4) 선행사 Cathy를 설명하는 주격 관계대명사 who가 와야 합니다. that은 계속적 용법에서는 쓰이지 않습니다.
4. (1) 선행사 the wallet 다음에 목적격 관계대명사가 필요합니다. which 또는 that이 올 수 있는데 생략하기도 합니다.

5. (4) 선행사가 a stadium 다음에 주격 관계대명사인 which를 사용해야 합니다. (3)의 that도 가능하지만 뒤에 목적어 it이 있어 오답입니다.
6. (3) 관계부사는 두 개의 글을 결합시키는 접속사와 부사의 구실을 합니다. 선행사 the way 는 생략되었습니다. 방법을 나타내는 how가 정답입니다.

Translation

1. 인간 행위에서 관찰된 가장 단순한 감정은 호기심입니다.
2. 당신은 그녀가 태어난 도시를 아십니까?
3. Cathy는 쌍둥이를 키우기 때문에 자주 애를 봐주는 사람이 필요합니다.
4. 저는 저의 오빠가 저를 위해 사준 지갑을 잃어버렸습니다.
5. 10만 명을 수용할 수 있는 경기장이 이 도시에 세워질 겁니다.
6. 이것이 데카르트가 프랑스에서 기하학 문제를 풀었던 방법입니다.

Review Test

Answers

1. which	2. what	3. where	4. which	5. that
6. whose	7. why	8. who	9. which	10. which/that/ X

Translation

1. 그녀는 최신 유행 패션을 판매하는 인터넷 쇼핑몰을 운영합니다.
2. 당신이 방금 한 말 믿지 못하겠어요.
3. 이곳은 그가 다람쥐를 잡은 장소입니다.
4. 어떤 10대들은 아침 식사를 거르는데 그것은 건강에 좋지 않습니다.
5. 영국에서 사람들은 가장 좋은 차를 살 수 있습니다.
6. 이 신발에 발이 맞는 소녀를 찾아 주세요.
7. 왜 영어를 전공했는지 말해 주세요.
8. 새로운 원소를 발견한 그 과학자는 노벨상을 탔습니다.
9. 나는 책을 많이 읽었는데 대부분 매우 유용했습니다.
10. 우리가 놓친 TV 프로그램이 오늘 저녁에 재방송 될 겁니다.

Chapter 11

Comparatives

Task 1

Answers

1. more pleasant
   pleasant는 more나 most를 붙여서 비교급이나 최상급을 만듭니다.
2. less
   than이 있으므로 비교급이 옵니다.(little-less-least)
3. busier
   than 이 있으므로 비교급이 옵니다.
4. further
   '더 자세한 사항'이라는 뜻으로 further eatails를 씁니다. (far-further-furthest)
5. worse
   bad/ill - worse - worst
6. bigger
   big - bigger - biggest

Translation

1. 한국의 기후는 중국의 기후보다 더 상쾌합니다.
2. Linda 는 Emma 보다 옷을 사는데 돈을 적게 씁니다.
3. 나는 오늘 보통 때보다 더 바빴습니다.
4. 만약에 더 상세히 알기를 원하시면 우리에게 메일로 연락주세요.
5. 서두르세요. 날씨가 점점 나빠지고 있습니다.
6. 저는 더 큰 방이 필요해요. 여기에는 공간이 충분하지가 않습니다.

Task 2

Answers

1. the better
   'The 비교급 , the 비교급' 은 '~하면 할수록 더욱 ~하다'라는 뜻입니다.
2. more easily
   -ly로 끝나는 부사의 비교급과 최상급은 more, most를 붙여서 만듭니다.
3. more and more
   '점점 더' 라는 뜻입니다.
4. more popular
   2음절 이상의 긴 단어는 more, most를 붙여서 비교급과 최상급을 만듭니다.
5. even
   much, far, even, still, a lot, a bit, slightly 등이 비교급을 수식합니다.
6. more serious
   2음절 이상의 긴 단어는 more, most를 붙여서 비교급과 최상급을 만듭니다.

Translation

1. 가격이 높을수록 서비스는 더 좋아집니다.
2. 컴퓨터가 있으면 우리는 그것을 더 쉽게 할 수 있을 겁니다.
3. 일자리를 구하는 것이 점점 더 어려워집니다.
4. 그는 병원에서 어떤 다른 의사보다도 더 인기가 있습니다.
5. Jessica는 당신보다 훨씬 더 날씬합니다.
6. 그의 병은 우리가 생각했던 거보다 더 심각합니다.

Task 3

Answers

1. older
   '~보다 나이가 많다'라고 할 때는 older than이라는 표현을 씁니다. elder than이라는 표현을 쓰지 않습니다. cf) He's my elder brother.
2. warm
   as + 원급+ as 입니다.
3. later
   than 앞에는 비교급이 와야 합니다.
4. as
   '~과 같은' 이라는 의미로 'the same~ as'라는 표현을 씁니다.
5. large
   as+원급+ as 입니다.
6. much
   as+원급+as 입니다.

Translation

1. Tom은 나의 가장 큰 누나보다 나이가 많습니다.
2. 춥지는 않지만 어제만큼 따뜻하지는 않습니다.
3. 그녀의 아이들은 평소보다 늦게 일어났습니다.
4. 당신의 머리 색깔은 그녀의 머리 색깔과 같습니다.
5. 이것은 저것 보다 다섯 배 큽니다.
6. 나는 당신만큼 돈을 많이 지출하지 않았습니다.

Task 4

Answers

1. as much as
   food 는 셀 수 없으므로 much가 옵니다.
2. as long as
   '시간이 오래 걸리다'라는 표현에는 long을 씁니다.
3. as carefully as
   '조심스럽게 운전하다'는 뜻으로 carefully가 쓰입니다.
4. as peaceful as
   '평화스럽다'는 의미로 peaceful이 쓰입니다.
5. worse
   bad- worse-worst

6. more loudly
   긴 단어는 more, most를 써서 비교급과 최상급을 만듭니다.
7. less
   little - less - least

Translation

1. 충분한 음식이 있습니다. 원하는 만큼 많이 드셔도 됩니다.
2. 우리가 예상했던 거보다 세 배의 시간이 걸렸습니다.
3. 그는 할 수 있는 한 조심해서 운전을 하였습니다.
4. 중동 지역에는 많은 분쟁들이 있습니다. 그 곳은 유럽만큼 평화롭지 못합니다.
5. 제 글씨체가 좋지 않다는 것은 압니다. 그러나 제 동생의 글씨체는 더 형편없습니다.
6. 당신 말을 들을 수가 없군요. 좀 더 크게 말씀해주시겠어요?
7. 좌뇌를 많이 쓰는 사람들은 우뇌를 많이 쓰는 사람보다 덜 감정적입니다.

Task 5

Answers

1. more famous
   긴 단어는 more, most를 써서 비교급 최상급을 만듭니다.
2. most popular
   'one of 최상급' 표현입니다.
3. most patient
   최상급 다음에 완료형이 나오기도 합니다.
4. cheaper
   than앞에 비교급이 나옵니다.
5. worst
   '최상급 + in 장소'가 나오는 표현입니다. (bad-worse-worst)
6. best
   최상급 + of all~ 가 구문입니다. of all 부분이 앞 부분에 올 수도 있습니다.
   (good-better-best)

Translation

1. 어떤 다른 극작가도 Shakespeare보다 유명하지는 않습니다.
2. 축구는 그 나라에서 가장 인기 있는 스포츠 중의 하나입니다.
3. Melissa는 제가 만나본 가장 인내심 있는 사람입니다.
4. 지하철이 택시보다 훨씬 쌉니다.
5. 다른 사람들과 비교할 때 그들은 반에서 가장 나쁜 두 명의 학생입니다.
6. Paul은 모든 실외 활동 중 낚시를 가장 좋아합니다.

Task 6

Answers

1. (2) '~만큼 ~하다'라고 표현할 때 as ~as가 쓰입니다. 이 문장의 빈 칸에는 동사도 필요함에 유의하세요.
2. (4) price는 many가 아닌 much가 쓰여져야 합니다. '~의 두배'라는 의미로 twice as~as라는 표현이 쓰입니다.
3. (3) 'the 비교급 the 비교급' 구문..(~할수록 ~하다)이 사용됩니다.

4. (1) 최상급 표현이 와야 합니다.'one of 최상급' 다음에 복수명사가 와야 함에 유의하세요.
5. (2) at last(마침내), at once(즉시)
6. (4) '비교급+than any other~'은 최상급의 뜻을 지닌 표현입니다.

Translation

1. 전쟁의 역사는 인간의 역사만큼 오래되었습니다.
2. 그 가격이 적당합니다. 그가 요구한 것의 두 배라도 기꺼이 내겠습니다.
3. 아파트가 클수록 집세가 비쌉니다.
4. Mark는 그 회사에서 가장 성공한 세일즈맨입니다.
5. 그들은 너무나 가난해서 기껏해야 50 달러밖에 없습니다.
6. 건강은 다른 어떤 것보다 더 가치가 있습니다.

Review Test

Answers

1. most popular	2. valuable	3. fewer	4. more expensive
5. latest	6. worst	7. more challenging	8. expensive
9. happiest	10. more precious		

Translation

1. 당신 나라에서는 어떤 운동이 가장 인기 있습니까?
2. 건강만큼 소중한 것은 없습니다.
3. 당신이 신중하게 글을 쓸수록 실수를 줄이는 것입니다.
4. 이 가게의 DVD 플레이어는 다른 가게보다 비쌉니다.
5. 여기에 최신 소설이 다 있습니다.
6. 이것은 내 평생 받은 최악의 점수 중 하나입니다.
7. 새로운 프로그램을 개발하는 것은 유지하는 것보다 훨씬 어렵습니다.
8. 가스는 5년 전보다 3배 더 비쌉니다.
9. 살면서 가장 행복했던 날은 언제였습니까?
10. 시간은 다른 어떤 것보다도 소중합니다.

Chapter 12

Conjunctions

Task 1

Answers

1. even though
   even though 는 양보를 나타내는 종속접속사로 '비록~일지라도, ~이지만' 이라는 의미이다.
2. because
   원인, 이유를 나타내는 종속접속사 because를 사용해야 합니다.
3. so
   '그래서, 그러므로' 라는 뜻을 가진 등위접속사 so를 사용해야 합니다.
4. While
   '~하는 동안'이라는 뜻을 가진 종속접속사 while을 사용해야 합니다. 문맥상 because도 가능합니다.
5. until
   '~까지' 라는 뜻을 가진 종속접속사 until을 사용해야 합니다.
6. or
   '명령문+or'는 '~해라. 그렇지 않으면~'이라는 뜻을 갖습니다. 문맥상 because 도 가능합니다.

Translation

1. 매우 추웠지만 우리는 동물원에 갔습니다.
2. Tim은 많은 운동을 하기 때문에 좋은 몸매를 유지합니다.
3. 그녀가 저에게 지도를 주어서 저는 길을 잃지 않을 겁니다.
4. Mary가 책을 읽고 있는 동안 그녀의 아이들은 밖에서 놀고 있었습니다.
5. 그 축제가 끝날 때까지 그들은 New Orleans에 머물 겁니다.
6. 불을 줄이세요. 그렇지 않으면 팬케잌이 탈것입니다.

Task 2

Answers

1. correct
   대조되는 뜻을 가진 형용사 old와 comfortable 사이에 접속사 but이 올 수 있습니다.
2. although → because
   원인, 이유를 나타내는 종속접속사 because가 오는 것이 자연스럽습니다.
3. during → while / when
   during은 전치사이므로 뒤에 주어 + 동사 구문이 올 수 없습니다. 접속사 while 이나 when 이 와야 합니다.
4. will reach → reach
   till (=until)은 시간을 나타내는 종속접속사로, till로 시작하는 문장에서는 현재시제가 미래의 의미를 지닙니다.

5. correct
   neither A nor B는 'A도 B도 아니다'라는 뜻입니다.
6. and → or
   명령문 + or 는 '~해라. 그렇지 않으면~'이라는 뜻입니다.

Translation

1. 이 구두는 오래되었지만 편안합니다.
2. 그는 몸이 안 좋아서 일찍 집에 갔습니다.
3. 비행기가 이륙을 준비하는 동안 전자기기는 꺼져있어야 합니다.
4. 신호등에 이를 때까지 그 길을 따라 내려가세요.
5. 그 책은 재미있지도 않고 정확하지도 않습니다.
6. 서두르세요. 그렇지 않으면 당신은 늦을 것입니다.

Task 3

Answers

1. what he wanted
   간접 의문문은 '의문사 + 주어 + 동사' 어순입니다.
2. when they will arrive
   간접 의문문은 '의문사 + 주어 + 동사' 어순입니다.
3. how much it cost
   cost-cost-cost로 변합니다. 여기서는 과거형을 쓴 것입니다.
4. whether/if Ann is going out tonight
   whether, if는 명사절을 이끄는 종속접속사로 의문사가 없는 명사절을 이끕니다.
5. which one he likes
   which one은 '어떤 것' 이라는 뜻입니다.
6. where I was living/ where we were living
   주절의 동사가 과거이므로 종속절에서 동사 과거형(was)을 씁니다.

Translation

Ex) 저는 그녀의 나이가 몇 살인지 모릅니다.
1. 그가 원했던 것이 무엇인 지 우리에게 말해 주겠습니까?
2. 그들이 언제 도착하는지 당신은 알고 있습니까?
3. 저는 그것이 얼마였는 지 기억할 수 없습니다.
4. Ann이 오늘 밤 나가는 지 저는 모르겠습니다.
5. 그가 어떤 것을 원하는지 물어봅시다.
6. 그는 내가/우리가 어디에 살고 있는 지 물었습니다.

Task 4

Answers

1. e) whether to go or stay home
   whether to부정사는 decide의 목적어로 쓰일 수 있습니다.
2. d) is amazing
   종속접속사 that이 이끄는 명사절이 주어의 역할을 하고 있으므로 다음에 동사가 와야 합니다.

3. a) whether or not she will come
whether or not~은 know의 목적절로 쓰일 수 있습니다.
4. c) although the traffic was bad
종속절로 although가 이끄는 부사절이 올 수 있습니다.
5. f) that he will be a good doctor
sure 다음에 that이 이끄는 명사절이 올 수 있습니다.
6. b) both time and money
both A and B는 'A와 B 둘 다' 라는 뜻입니다.

Translation

1. Jim은 가야 할지 집에 머물러야 할지 결정할 수가 없습니다.
2. 그 섬까지 가는 데 단지 네 시간이 걸렸다는 것은 놀랍습니다.
3. 당신은 그녀가 올지 안 올지 알고 있습니까?
4. 비록 교통이 안 좋았지만, Eric은 제 시간에 도착했습니다.
5. 저는 그가 훌륭한 의사가 될 거라고 확신합니다.
6. 그 연구 프로젝트는 시간도 걸리고 돈도 들 겁니다.

Task 5

Answers

1. although
although와 despite은 유사한 의미를 지니고 있지만 despite은 전치사로서 (동)명사를 목적어로 취합니다. 주어와 동사가 나오는 절을 이끄는 것은 접속사 although입니다.
2. in case
아직 일어나지 않았지만 앞으로 일어날 가능성이 있는 일 또는 현재나 과거의 어떤 상황을 가정하면서 '~할 경우에 (대비해서)'라고 할때 in case를 사용합니다.
3. Because
원인, 이유를 나타내는 종속접속사 because를 사용합니다.
4. that
so~that~은 '너무 ~해서~하다'라는 뜻입니다.
5. as
원인, 이유를 나타내는 종속접속사 as를 사용합니다.
6. unless
unless 는 if ~not 의 뜻입니다. (unless you study hard = if you don't study hard)

Translation

1. 비록 비가 내렸지만 그들은 멋진 휴일을 보냈습니다.
2. 아마도 필요 없겠지만, 혹시 무엇을 사야만 될 경우엔 대비해서 약간의 돈을 주겠습니다.
3. 서둘러 떠나느라고 나는 여권을 잊어버렸습니다.
4. 그녀는 너무 화가 나서 그에게 소리를 쳤습니다.
5. 당신은 충분한 연습을 하지 않기 때문에 실력향상이 안됩니다.
6. 당신은 더 열심히 공부하지 않으면 시험에 떨어질 것입니다

Task 6

Answers

1. (b) so → but
   대조되는 내용을 연결할 때 but을 사용합니다.
2. (d) when was → when it was
   when 다음에는 절이 와야 하므로 주어가 필요합니다.
3. (c) during → while, when
   during, while 모두 '~동안'이라는 의미를 지니고 있지만 during은 전치사로서 다음에 명사 상당어구가 와야 합니다.
4. (a) what → that
   명사절을 이끄는 종속접속사 that이 사용합니다.
5. (c) is it → it is
   간접 의문문은 '의문사 + 주어 + 동사' 순입니다.
6. (b) and → or
   either A or B는 'A나 B 둘 중에 하나' 라는 뜻입니다.

Translation

1. 그 바지는 마음에 들었지만, 나에게는 너무 꽉 끼었습니다.
2. 망치는 신석기 시대에 만들어졌는데, 그 이후로 쭉 연장으로 사용되고 있습니다.
3. 다음 달에 나는 북경에 갑니다. 내가 거기에 있는 동안 Linda를 만날 수 있기를 희망합니다.
4. 그녀가 일어를 알아듣지 못하는 것이 확실합니다.
5. 당신은 Florida까지 얼마나 먼 지 아십니까?
6. 복사 한 부를 주문하시려면 편지를 주시거나 전화를 주시면 됩니다.

Review Test

Answers

1. as	2. but	3. unless	4. Although	5. because
6. in case	7. Even though	8. whether	9. since	10. while

Translation

1. 당신은 제가 보여 준 대로 해야 했습니다.
2. 그는 새로운 계획의 도입을 찬성했지만 높은 가격 때문에 걱정합니다.
3. 그는 스스로 하지 않는 한 어떤 것에도 만족스러워하지 않습니다.
4. 갈릴레오는 망원경을 발명한 것은 아니지만 망원경을 이용해 밤하늘을 관찰한 최초의 사람입니다.
5. 그는 집에 있는 것이 틀림없습니다. 그의 차가 주택 진입로에 있기 때문입니다.
6. 아마 필요 없겠지만 제게 연락해야 할 상황에 대비하여 제 핸드폰 번호를 드리겠습니다.
7. 그녀는 비록 독감에 걸렸지만 시험을 봐야 했습니다.
8. 요점은 사람들이 제 생각에 동의를 하느냐 마느냐 입니다.
9. 외출하기에는 너무 추웠기 때문에 우리는 그냥 TV를 보았습니다.
10. 할 수 있을 때 인생을 즐기세요.

Chapter 13

Review(Chapter 8 ~ 12)

Task 1

Answers

1. reading
   enjoy 다음에는 동명사가 옵니다.
2. to become
   decide 다음에는 to부정사가 옵니다.
3. having
   suggest 다음에는 동명사가 옵니다.
4. to mail
   forget to부정사는 '~할 것을 잊다'라는 뜻입니다.
5. running
   keep+ ~ ing는 '계속 ~하다'라는 뜻입니다.
6. talking
   stop+~ing는 '~하는 것을 멈추다'는 뜻입니다. 참고로 stop+to부정사는 '~하기 위해 멈추다'라는 의미입니다.

Translation

1. 저는 매일 아침 신문을 읽는 것을 즐깁니다.
2. Jane은 간호사가 되기로 결심했습니다.
3. Sam은 일찍 저녁을 먹자고 제안했습니다.
4. 제가 당신에게 준 편지를 부치는 것을 잊지 마세요.
5. 경찰관은 도둑에게 서라고 말했지만 그는 계속해서 달렸습니다.
6. 선생님이 교실에 들어오셨을 때, 학생들은 말하기를 멈췄습니다.

Task 2

Answers

1. correct
   promise 다음에는 to부정사가 목적어로 옵니다. 부정어 not은 to부정사 앞에 둡니다.
2. correct
   expect+목적어+to부정사 구문입니다.
3. to jog → jog / jogging
   see/watch/feel/hear+목적어+동사원형/~ing구문입니다.
4. study → to study
   encourage+목적어+to 부정사구문입니다.
5. correct
   stop+~ ing은 '~ 하는 것을 멈추다' 입니다.

6. to go → going
consider+~ing는 '~할 것을 고려하다' 입니다.

Translation

1. 그는 늦지 않겠다고 약속했습니다.
2. 우리는 Cindy가 시험에 합격하기를 기대합니다.
3. 당신은 그가 공원에서 조깅하는 것을 본 적이 있습니까?
4. 그 선생님은 학생들이 학교에서 열심히 공부하도록 격려해주었습니다.
5. 그녀는 재미있는 농담을 했고 저는 웃지 않을 수가 없었습니다.
6. 당신은 여름 휴가 때 어디에 가려고 생각하고 있습니까?

Task 3

Answers

1. to buy
find out 다음에 where/which/how +to 부정사가 올 수 있습니다.
2. to lock
remember + to 부정사는 ' ~ 할 것을 기억하다'라는 뜻이고, remember + - ing는 '~ 한 것을 기억하다'라는 뜻입니다. 여기서는 미래의 일이므로 to 부정사를 사용합니다.
3. to inform
regret + to 부정사는 '~하게 되어 유감이다'라는 뜻입니다.
4. waiting
mind는 '~할 것을 꺼려하다'는 뜻으로 동명사를 목적어로 취합니다.
5. not to wait
tell+목적어+ to부정사 구문입니다. 부정어 not은 to부정사 앞에 둡니다.
6. paying
put off (=postpone) 다음에 동명사가 목적어로 옵니다.

Translation

1. 그는 과일을 비싸지 않게 사는 곳을 알아냈습니다.
2. 당신이 떠나기 전에 문을 잠그는 것을 꼭 기억하세요.
3. 당신에게 그 일자리를 줄 수 없음을 알리게 되어 유감입니다.
4. 잠깐 기다려주시겠습니까?
5. Jack은 우리에게 Jane를 기다리지 말라고 말했습니다.
6. 당신은 청구서를 지불하는 것을 미루지 말아야 합니다.

Task 4

Answers

1. interested
be interested in '~ 관심이 있다.'라는 뜻입니다.
2. stolen
jewelry는 도난 당한 것이기 때문에 과거분사가 나와야 합니다.
3. amusing
story 자체가 재미있는 것이므로 현재분사가 나와야 합니다.
4. exhausted
사람의 감정은 과거분사로 표시됩니다.

5. embarrassing
situation 자체가 당황스럽기 때문에 현재분사가 나와야 합니다.
6. frozen
물고기는 얼려지는 것이기 때문에 과거분사가 나와야 합니다.

Translation

1. 당신은 고전 음악에 관심이 있습니까?
2. 도난 당한 보석이 그 건물의 지하에서 발견되었습니다.
3. 그것은 재미난 이야기 입니다, 그렇죠?
4. 지친 남자들은 쉬기 위해 나무 아래에 앉았습니다.
5. 그녀는 지난 밤 난처한 상황에 처했습니다.
6. 저는 시장에서 냉동 생선을 샀습니다.

Task 5

Answers

1. (3) → crowded
crowded는 '만원이 붐비는' 이란 의미입니다.
2. (1) → annoying
표를 잃어버리는 것이 화나게 하므로 현재분사를 사용해야 합니다.
3. (1) → boring
사람 자체가 따분하다고 할 때는 현재분사를 사용해야 합니다.
4. (2) → exhausted
사람이 지친 것이므로 과거분사를 사용해야 합니다.
5. (3) → fascinating
순간 자체가 환상적이므로 현재분사를 써야 합니다.

Translation

1. A: 당신은 피곤해 보입니다.
B: 그 버스가 너무나 만원이라서 나는 여기까지 쭉 서서 와야만 했습니다.
2. A: 내 표를 잃어버려서 화가 납니다.
B: 또 한 장을 사야만 했을 때, 당신은 정말 화가 난 것 같더군요.
3. A: Jim은 재미있습니까?
B: 아니요. 그는 정말 지루한 사람입니다. 한 번 말하면 멈추질 않고, 그가 말하는 것 중에 재미있는 것은 아무것도 없습니다.
4. A: 나는 건강하지 않은가 봐요. 그 산을 오른 후에 완전히 녹초가 되었어요.
B: 맞아요. 모두가 피곤했던 것 같아요.
5. A: Brad Pitt을 만나는 것은 감격적이었죠?
B: 물론이죠. 내 일생에서 가장 황홀한 순간이었죠. 거기 있던 모든 사람들이 너무나 흥분했어요.

Task 6

Answers

1. Being compared / Compared
접속사와 주어를 생략하고 동사를 being으로 고칩니다. being은 생략할 수 있습니다.
2. Not knowing
접속사와 주어를 생략하고 동사를 현재분사로 고칩니다. 부정어 not은 현재분사 앞에 둡니다.

3. Sitting surrounded
   접속사와 주어를 생략하고 동사를 현재분사로 고칩니다.
4. Striking his head
   접속사를 생략하고 동사를 현재분사로 고칩니다.
5. Having used
   접속사와 주어를 생략하고 조동사를 현재분사로 고칩니다.
6. The day being sunny
   주어가 we와 동일하지 않기 때문에 주어는 그대로 나두고 접속사만 생략하고 동사를 현재분사로 고칩니다.

Translation

1. 원숭이와 비교하면 개는 아주 영리하지가 않습니다.
2. 그 언어를 몰랐기 때문에, 그는 거기에서 일자리를 찾는 것이 힘들다는 것을 알았습니다.
3. 비록 제가 많은 친구들에게 둘러싸여 앉아있었지만 그리 행복하진않았습니다.
4. 그는 넘어지면서 머리를 문에 부딪혔습니다.
5. 제가 아버지의 차를 사용한 후에 그것을 돌려드렸습니다.
6. 해가 났기 때문에 우리는 수영을 하기로 결정했습니다.

Task 7

Answers

1. who
   선행사가 people 이고, 동사 like의 주어이므로 who를 사용해야 합니다.
2. where
   장소를 나타내는 관계부사 where를 사용해야 합니다.
3. which
   전치사 in 다음에 관계대명사 which가 와야 합니다. in which(=where)
4. What
   선행사를 포함한 관계대명사 what이 와야 합니다.
5. whose
   pencil 이라는 명사 앞에 소유격 관계대명사가 와야 합니다.
6. which
   콤마 뒤에는 관계대명사 which가 와야 합니다.

Translation

1. 저는 필리핀에 사는 많은 사람을 압니다.
2. 이것이 그가 머물렀던 호텔입니까?
3. 저는 제가 태어난 도시로 되돌아갔습니다.
4. 선생님이 말한 것으로 인해 아이들은 행복했습니다.
5. 당신이 연필을 빌렸던 그 소녀의 이름은 무엇입니까?
6. 이 책들은 당신이 어떤 서점에서든 구할 수 있는 데, 당신이 필요로 하는 모든 정보를 줄 것입니다.

Task 8

Answers

1. that → which
   뒤에는 관계대명사 which가 옵니다.
2. correct
   관계부사 where가 오는 것이 맞습니다.
3. correct
   목적격 관계대명사 that이나 which가 생략된 경우입니다.
4. who → whom
   전치사 다음에는 목적격 관계대명사가 와야 합니다.
5. their → whose
   명사car 앞에 소유격 관계대명사가 와야 합니다.
6. what → that
   선행사 everything 다음에 관계대명사 that이 와야 합니다.

Translation

1. 그는 돈이 없다고 했는데, 그것은 사실이 아니었습니다.
2. 그녀가 살고 있는 그 건물은 아주 오래되었습니다.
3. 우리가 지난 밤에 들었던 음악이 나쁘지는 않았습니다.
4. Mr. Foster는 나의 상사인데, 그리 관대하지 않습니다.
5. 나는 자동차가 고장 난 몇몇의 사람들을 보았습니다.
6. 나는 처음에는 그를 믿지 않았습니다. 그러나 사실 그가 말한 모든 것은 진실이었습니다.

Task 9

Answers

1. whose
   명사 class앞에 소유관계대명사인whose가 필요합니다.
2. which / that
   선행사가 the book이므로 which나 that이 필요합니다.
3. who
   선행사가 the girl이므로 주격 관계대명사 who가 필요합니다.
4. who / whom
   동사 visited의 목적어이므로 목적격 관계대명사인 whom이나 who가 필요합니다. 목적격 관계대명사는 생략할 수도 있습니다.
5. where
   장소를 나타내는 관계부사인 where가 필요합니다.
6. which
   전치사 for 다음에 목적격 관계대명사 which가 와야 합니다. which to paid $ 100,000 for와 같이 전치사를 뒤에 둘 수도 있습니다.

Translation

1. 저는 제가 수업을 못들은 그 과목 선생님에게 저의 결석을 설명했습니다.
2. 이것이 큰 물의를 일으켰던 그 책입니다.
3. 경주에서 승리한 그 소녀는 자신을 자랑스러워합니다.

4. 우리가 지난 주에 방문했던 사람들은 매우 친절했습니다.
5. 정말 좋은 식사를 할 수 있는 음식점이 있습니까?
6. 그가 10만 불을 지불했던 그 아파트가 지금은 50만 불이 되었습니다.

Task 10

Answers

1. more
   loudly의 비교급은 more loudly입니다.
2. easier
   than이 있으니 비교급을 사용해야 합니다.
3. the coldest
   of 명사 앞에서 최상급을 사용해야 합니다.
4. more precious
   precious의 비교급은 more precious 입니다.
5. the more intelligent
   the비교급, the비교급 구문입니다.
6. the most interesting
   '내가 지금까지 ~한'이라는 현재완료 구문 앞에서 최상급 표현을 씁니다.

Translation

1. 저는 당신 말을 들을 수가 없습니다. 좀 더 크게 말씀해 주시겠습니까?
2. 그 시험은 우리가 기대했던 것보다 쉬웠습니다.
3. 어제는 올해의 가장 추운 날이었습니다.
4. 시간보다 더 소중한 것은 아무것도 없습니다.
5. 그는 나이가 들수록 더 총명해 집니다.
6. 그것은 제가 지금까지 봤던 영화 중 제일 재미난 영화였습니다.

Task 11

Answers

1. 1) 비교급 수식하는 것은 even, still, far, a lot, much 입니다.
2. 2) the 비교급, the 비교급 구문으로 '~할수록 더~하다'는 뜻입니다.
3. 1) as 원급 as 구문입니다.
4. 2) of all , in the~, 앞에서 최상급이 주로 쓰입니다.
5. 3) 덜 바쁘다는 뜻으로 less busy가 쓰입니다.

Translation

1. 그의 병은 의사선생님이 처음에 말했던 것보다 훨씬 더 심각했습니다.
2. 당신이 좀 더 일찍 떠날수록 더 일찍 도착할 것입니다.
3. 그들은 우리만큼 많은 세금을 지불하지 않았습니다.
4. 사자는 모든 동물들 중 가장 힘이 셉니다.
5. 그들은 대체로 할 일이 많습니다. 그러나 이번 주에는 덜 바쁩니다

Task 12

Answers

1. fewer
   사람은 셀 수 있으므로 few의 비교급을 써야 합니다.
2. worst
   I've ever~등 현재완료 구문 앞에서 최상급을 씁니다.
3. colder and colder
   'get + 비교급 and 비교급'은 '점점 더 ~해 진다' 라는 뜻입니다.
4. as popular
   'as 원급 as ever'는 '변함없이 ~하다'라는 뜻입니다.
5. any longer
   not~any longer 은 '더 이상 ~하지 않는다'는 표현입니다.
6. best
   부사급의 최상급은 the를 쓰지 않습니다.

Translation

1. 이번 모임에는 지난번보다 더 적은 사람들이 있었습니다.
2. 그는 내가 지금껏 알아왔던 사람 중에 가장 나쁜 사람입니다.
3. 날씨가 하루하루 더 추워지고 있습니다.
4. 그의 소설은 변함없이 인기가 있습니다.
5. 그녀는 더 이상 여기 살지 않습니다.
6. 저는 이 영화를 가장 좋아합니다.

Task 13

Answers

1. c) 이유를 나타내는 절이 옵니다.
2. e) decide의 목적어가 되는 명사절이 옵니다.
3. a) unless가 이끄는 종속적 다음에 주절이 와야 합니다.
4. f) 등위 접속사로 두 개의 절이 연결되어 있습니다.
5. d) 이유를 나타내는 절이 옵니다.
6. b) show의 목적어 가 되는 명사절이 옵니다.

Translation

1. 저는 그가 일어와 중국어를 다 유창하게 말하기 때문에 어느 나라 사람인지 모릅니다.
2. 그녀는 어떤 것을 선택할지 결정할 수가 없습니다.
3. 만약 당신이 사과하지 않는다면 저는 당신과 다시는 얘기하지 않을 것입니다.
4. 저는 John과 Jenny가 오기를 원했는데 그들은 둘 다 오고 싶어하지 않았습니다.
5. 비가 왔기 때문에 우리는 여행을 가지 않기로 결정했습니다.
6. 저에게 우체국에 가는 길을 좀 알려주시겠습니까?

Task 14

Answers

1. Although
   접속사인 although가 와야 합니다.
2. While
   이유가 아니라 '~동안'이라고 해석되는 접속사가 오는 것이 자연스럽습니다.
3. till
   '~까지' 라고 till이 해석되는 접속사가 오는 것이 자연스럽습니다.
4. if
   부정어 not을 내포하고 있는 unless가 와야 합니다.
5. After
   시간의 순서를 나타내므로 after가 와야 합니다.
6. even though
   양보절을 이끄는 접속사인 even though가 와야 합니다.

Translation

1. 저는 하루 종일 열심히 일했지만 피곤하지 않습니다.
2. 그녀가 외출해 있는 동안 그녀에게 전화가 걸려 왔었습니다.
3. 비가 그칠 때까지 집에서 기다립시다.
4. 내가 그를 초대하지 않는다면 그는 화가 날지도 모릅니다.
5. 그 소년은 숙제를 마친 후 컴퓨터 게임을 하였습니다.
6. 그녀가 아주 가까이 살지만 저는 그녀를 자주 볼 수 없습니다.

Task 15

Answers

1. Although
   양보절을 이끄는 접속사 although 가 와야 합니다.
2. that
   뉴스가 어떤 내용인지 설명해 주는 that절이 와야 합니다.
3. whether
   sure다음에 명사절이 오는데, 문장 끝이 or not이 있으므로 whether나 if가 이끄는 절이 와야 합니다.
4. in case
   in case는 '~할 경우를 대비해서' 라는 뜻입니다.
5. Because
   이유를 설명하기 때문에 because 가 와야 합니다.
6. so
   결과를 나타내는 so가 와야 합니다.

Translation

1. 우리는 여러 해 동안 알고 지냈지만, 가까운 친구는 아닙니다.
2. 그녀는 그녀의 할머니가 돌아가셨다는 소식을 들었습니다.
3. 내일 비가 올지 안 올지 저는 확실히 모르겠습니다.
4. 지금 비가 오는 것은 아니지만, 나중에 비가 올 경우에 대비해서 우산을 가져가세요.
5. 날이 점점 어두워지고 있었기 때문에 우리는 놀기를 멈추고 집으로 돌아왔습니다.
6. 어두워서 불을 켰습니다.

쉽게 배우는 영문법(개정판)

초 판 발행 2007년 4월 20일
개정판 1쇄 발행 2010년 3월 20일
개정판 2쇄 발행 2013년 3월 20일

발 행 인 ▪ 성 은 경
발 행 인 ▪ 박 철
발 행 처 ▪ 한국외국어대학교 출판부
130-791 서울시 동대문구 이문로 107
전화 (02)2173-2495~7
팩스 (02)2173-3363
홈페이지 http://press.hufs.ac.kr
전자우편 press@hufs.ac.kr
출판등록 ▪ 제6-6호(1969. 4. 30)
디자인 · 편집 ▪ (주)이환디앤비 (02)2254-4301
인쇄 · 제본 ▪ (주)동화인쇄공사 02)719-7181

ISBN 978-89-7464-450-5 18740 정가 15,000원(mp3 CD포함)

* 잘못된 책은 교환하여 드립니다.